DUTCH AFRO BECOMINGS

Before you start to read this book, take this moment to think about making a donation to punctum books, an independent non-profit press,

@ https://punctumbooks.com/support/

If you're reading the e-book, you can click on the image below to go directly to our donations site. Any amount, no matter the size, is appreciated and will help us to keep our ship of fools afloat. Contributions from dedicated readers will also help us to keep our commons open and to cultivate new work that can't find a welcoming port elsewhere. Our adventure is not possible without your support.

Vive la Open Access.

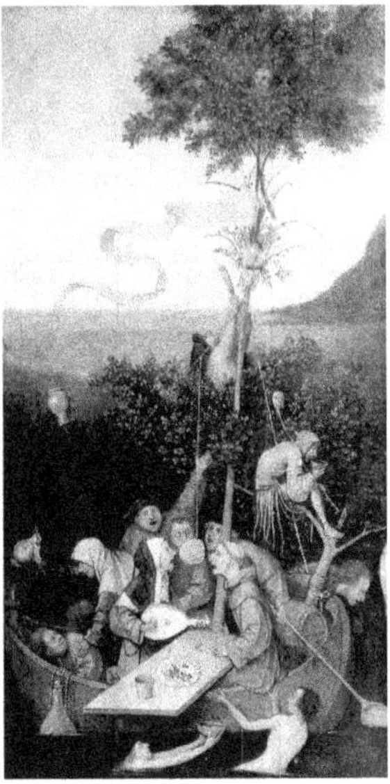

Fig. 1. Detail from Hieronymus Bosch, *Ship of Fools* (1490–1500)

Published in 2026 by punctum books, Earth, Milky Way
https://punctumbooks.com

ISBN-13: 978-1-68571-288-4 (paperbound)
ISBN-13: 978-1-68571-289-1 (PDF)
ISBN-13: 978-1-68571-311-9 (EPUB)

DOI: 10.53288/0537.1.00

LCCN: 2026936019
Library of Congress Cataloging Data is available from the Library of Congress

Editing: Vincent W.J. van Gerven Oei, Jonas Staal, and SAJ
Book design: Vincent W.J. van Gerven Oei
Cover image: Charl Landvreugd, *Atlantic Transformerz — île de Ngor Senegal* (2014)

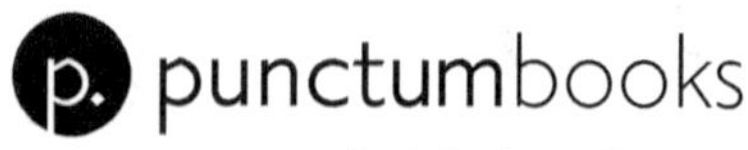

spontaneous acts of scholarly combustion

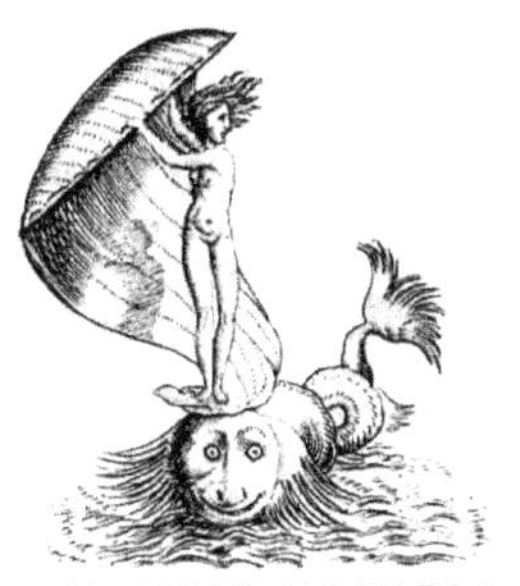

HIC SVNT MONSTRA

Charl Landvreugd

Dutch Afro Becomings
Hybrid Being in Black Art and Culture

p.

Contents

Acknowledgments

This manuscript emerges from a doctoral project completed at the Royal College of Art, where I was fortunate to work under the steady intellectual companionship of Victoria Walsh and the generous support of Grant Watson. Their rigor and trust shaped the trajectory of this research in ways that remain foundational. I owe equal gratitude to my examiners, Paul Goodwin and Gilane Tawadros.

The ideas developed here grew through sustained dialogue with colleagues — artists, curators, and thinkers across the Netherlands, the United Kingdom, and the United States. I owe particular thanks to Simon O'Sullivan (Goldsmiths, University of London), who supported my questioning of the origins of contemporary philosophy; Rosalind Krauss (Columbia University), who supported my questions regarding the very definition of art; and Kellie Jones (Columbia University), who encouraged a more precise reading of the differences — and the imagined similarities — within the Afro-diasporic experience. Their guidance grounded the intellectual arc that carried me from my BA into this PhD and beyond. My thanks also go to all those who challenged and extended the work, offering essential grounds for testing and refining the concept of the imagined normal space — hybridity as degree zero.

Parts of this work were drafted with the support of the Dr. Hendrik Muller Vaderlandsch Fonds, Prins Bernhard Cultuurfonds, and the Royal College of Art. The hospitality of the Van

Abbemuseum and the Remy Jungerman Archive made sustained research possible.

I am grateful to friends and companions whose conversations and care carried this project through its more difficult moments. Thank you to Jonas Staal and Vincent W.J. van Gerven Oei for believing in this publication; and to Dennis van Alphen, for the quiet forms of support that make intellectual life possible.

This book is dedicated to those who continue to imagine — and enact — worlds otherwise.

Introduction

Turning the Gaze Black

Blue.

While migrating from Suriname to the Netherlands in 1974, at the tender age of three, Atlantic blues combined with the slightly different light blue that meets the ocean at the horizon and fills the sky. Shrouded in shades of blue, a conscious record of the environment reveals a classroom in Rotterdam with pre-schoolers, all acquiring skills that prepare them for elementary school. Education in the inner city of Rotterdam meant being immersed in an environment where difference developed into the default. During the 1970s and 1980s, variations in language, fashion, and custom slowly melted into a common standard with the physical being the only notable, albeit unimportant, difference. From my perspective as a teenager, this was what the world looked like.

It was in 1990 when someone yelled "Go back to your own country!" that I first consciously registered this phrase, and I remember thinking, "What does that mean?" I had an idle awareness of my Surinamese background through music, food, language, and customs at home. But home, in turn, was located in Rotterdam. Growing up as Dutch with people whose parents came from Italy, Greece, Spain, Yugoslavia, Turkey, Morocco, India, Suriname, and many other places, it had not occurred to me that "your own country" could mean something other than the Netherlands. Although I'd received comments on my skin color or cultural background before this encounter, these had always been neutralized by the difference of those who made the comment. This difference never questioned the issue of belonging. But the utterance "Go back to your own country!" is intended to displace its target, based on the idea that skin color means something more than (mere) biological variation.

During the 1990s I came to terms with the understanding that, in certain cases, my presence evoked assumptions that had nothing to do with my self-image. Effectively, the processes that formed my Dutch identity were acknowledged as a Surinamese subjectivity.

It is in this period that the question of perceived cultural background signaled by skin color, and the presumed behavior, expected capability, and social prospects that come with it, emerged. As I started to understand that equality [*gelijkheid*] does not mean equivalence [*gelijkwaardigheid*], it would take me well into the 2000s to realize that the biological variation of skin color is actually a thing. Unearthing how racial discrimination hides in a nonracial equivalence meritocracy of cultural difference unsettled my Dutch identity and over the years shifted my subjectivity and my gaze. Black.

During the 1990s my life took place at night. I started out as a vogue dancer in nightclubs, and by 1993, at the age of 22, my imagination materialized through the first nightclub I opened and managed in Rotterdam. Over the years more clubs, parties, and events followed, but this first queer club possessed a quality where straight men (sometimes accompanied by their partners) would come and party in full drag all night long. The club was conceived as a space where one could forget that there was an outside. Being subject to the Dutch Afro condition, I experimented with stereotypes at a time when it was uncommon to have white runners, Black bartenders, drag performers, dancers, and DJs from different ethnicities and genders. While

I was unaware of the resonance this place had with what was going on in other urban clubs around the world, it facilitated a whole new social environment in the sense of what Nicholas Bourriaud would later call "relational aesthetics," when he theorized this early 1990s period in his eponymous monograph.[1] The combination and contrast of club life with "real" life made me question the sort of agency that was available to me as a club kid. Several clubs, parties, and events later, I concluded that my Surinamese cultural background related to the majority group culture in the same way that my club culture identity related to common daytime society. Being embedded in all these environments created a culturally hybrid individual whose agency depended on the space in which he operated. It is in this context of Dutch nightlife that the question emerged as to whether it was possible to be permanently self-evident in all social environments. Understanding that nightlife agency did not translate outside of that context, I decided to quit nightlife and pursue an education in art.

In my Fulbright application in 2007, I argued that it was time not to speak *about* Dutch Afro subjects, but time for us to speak *for ourselves*. Starting from this principle, this book contributes to the wider contemporary production of continental European thought emerging from the experience of Europeans with a migrant background. Being part of this group allows me to formulate questions that are relevant to this particular experience. The centering of Afro-ness is deliberate, as skin color cannot be "unseen." As a consequence of this hypervisibility, Afro artists have developed a sophisticated set of skills to navigate through the Dutch art system. Ultimately, variations of these skills can be seen in other artistic minority groups and in society at large. This book emerges from my own history, practice, and personal experience with the issues discussed. Being invited to speak at conferences, seminars, and public discussions, I found that issues surrounding my position and how it is perceived in society resonated with other Afro subjects from different back-

---

1   Nicolas Bourriaud, *Relational Aesthetics* (Les Presses du réel, 2002).

grounds in the Netherlands. Together with my work as an arts and policy advisor, writer, visual artist, educator, and curator, the need to address these questions in greater depth became both apparent and urgent. As it turned out, the current theoretical and aesthetic models that are available to contextualize Dutch Afro artistic production were not adequate as a framework to signify its importance in the development of a contemporary Dutch subjectivity projecting into the future. To remedy this, the present work proposes an initial framework to contextualize the work of my colleagues and myself.

This research is relevant to the identification of how and where Dutch Afro artists locate their practices internationally, locally, and personally. Where the Dutch artistic landscape locates these artists provides the starting point, because this location strongly determines the basic principles of the work environment, providing insight into the Dutch relation to its colonial history and attitudes toward art produced by people with a migrant and migrant worker background from the 1970s onward. With this in mind, the central question of this book appears: *Is it possible to locate Dutch Afro artists as native to the Dutch artistic landscape?* Answering this question also provides us insight into the current overarching societal question of what it means to be Dutch. Being primarily informed by aesthetics and sensibilities that come along with Dutchness and the Dutch Afro condition, art is one of the methods to rethink ideas of belonging in the twenty-first century, offering a meditation on a different sort of artistic environment designed around the current and future mix of people that make up the Netherlands.

The Need for a Dutch Afro Language

My early understanding of the world was informed by Afro-Surinamese, and consequently West African religion, metaphysics, and traditions that paint a philosophical picture of the world, based on the idea of striving for balance.[2] During my education in London and New York, twentieth-century French philosophy, particularly structuralism and poststructuralism, provided a framework within which to apply African American and Black British theoretical frameworks emerging from cultural movements of the twentieth century. These movements were the generous aunts that cultivated my understanding of Afro-ness in the Netherlands. In the process of applying these general insights on Blackness that led to an interpretation of Afro-ness in the Dutch situation, I realized that they were not applicable without complications. Hailing from and living on a different continent, with a history and generational arrival distinct from the African American and Black British, I found it important to listen and learn while understanding the facts that inspired theoretical frameworks that were comparable but not the same.

Therefore, this book needs to be read within the wider continental context of the contemporary discourse on what it might mean to be European in the twenty-first century. Considering the French philosopher Étienne Balibar's *We, The People of Europe?* and collections such as *Do I Belong? Reflections from Europe* and *Re: Thinking Europe,* a variety of disciplines deal with this question.[3] The imagining through visual arts and the curatorial opens up possibilities akin to the concept of *Leitkultur* as proposed by the German political scientist Bassam Tibi in 1998.[4] In the European context, this book is one of those "Euro-

---

2   J. Lorand Matory, *Black Atlantic Religion: Tradition, Transnationalism, and Matriarchy in the Afro-Brazilian Candomblé* (Princeton University Press, 2005), and Pieter Hendrik Coetzee and A.P.J. Roux, eds., *The African Philosophy Reader,* 2nd ed. (Routledge, 2003).

3   Étienne Balibar, *We, The People of Europe? Reflections on Transnational Citizenship,* trans. James Swenson (Princeton University Press, 2004); Antony Lerman, ed., *Do I Belong? Reflections from Europe* (Pluto Press, 2017); and Mathieu Segers and Yoeri Albrecht, eds., *Re: Thinking Europe: Thoughts on Europe: Past, Present and Future* (Amsterdam University Press, 2016).

4   Bassam Tibi, *Europa ohne Identität: Die Krise der multikulturellen Gesellschaft* (Bertelsmann, 1998).

pean others," following the eponymous monograph of German historian Fatima El-Tayeb.[5] From that broader European overview, my research also resonates with national conversations such as the *Black France/France Noire* discussion on what Afroness might mean in France.[6] With regard to the Netherlands and its history, it is in conversation with British historian Simon Schama's interpretation of Dutch culture following the onset of its colonial expansion in the "Golden Age,"[7] which brought forth the Afro artist Gerrit Schouten (1779–1839) who portrayed life in Suriname.[8] My treatment of the Dutch colonial past also aligns closely with cultural anthropologist Lizzy van Leeuwen's *Ons Indisch Erfgoed* (*Our Indonesian Heritage*),[9] as well as contemporary novels such as Rihana Jamaludin's *De Zwarte Lord* (*The Black Lord*) which is set in nineteenth-century Suriname, and Annejet van der Zijl's *Sonny Boy*,[10] about the life of a Black man in the Netherlands during the Second World War. Looking at the specifics of Afro literature in the Dutch context, I also relate to *Wij Slaven van Suriname* (*We Slaves of Suriname*) by communist resistance fighter Anton de Kom, who said that "Not one people that stays with a hereditary sense of inferiority can come to full maturity."[11] The legacy of this sentence and the undoing of this sense of inferiority it refers to are taken up in the literary heritage of Astrid Roemer, Edgar Cairo, and Frank Martinus Arion, among others, and this book follows suit. The

---

5   Fatima El-Tayeb, *European Others: Queering Ethnicity in Postnational Europe* (University of Minnesota Press, 2011).

6   Trica Danielle Keaton, T. Denean Sharpley-Whiting, and Tyler Stovall, eds., *Black France/France Noire: The History and Politics of Blackness* (Duke University Press, 2012).

7   Simon Schama, *The Embarrassment of Riches: An Interpretation of Dutch Culture in the Golden Age* (University of California Press, 1988).

8   Clazien Medendorp, *Gerrit Schouten (1779–1839): Botanische tekeningen en diorama's uit Suriname* (Koninklijk Instituut voor de Tropen, 1999).

9   Lizzy van Leeuwen, *Ons Indisch erfgoed: Zestig jaar strijd om cultuur en identiteit* (Uitgeverij Bert Bakker, 2008).

10   Rihana Jamaludin, *De Zwarte Lord* (KIT Publishers, 2012), and Annejet van der Zijl, *Sonny Boy* (Nijgh & van Ditmar, 2005).

11   Cornelis Gerard Anton de Kom, *Wij slaven van Suriname* (Contact, 1972), 50.

cultural anthropologist Philomena Essed, with her book *Understanding Everyday Racism,* and her colleague Gloria Wekker, with *White Innocence,* have taken up the workings of racism and discrimination in the Dutch context and with their work support my assumption about the difference in experience with the English-speaking diaspora.[12] Because this work looks at where art and the artists are located and what emerges from this, I also take note of a possible line of interpretation through World Art Studies,[13] as well as the important decolonization work that is being done by scholars such as Alanna Lockward and Walter Mignolo.[14]

Nevertheless, I want to emphasize that this book is invested in theorization *from the inside* toward a model based on the lived experience of Dutch Afro artists with a migrant background. Therefore, I do not offer a comparative study but rather an analysis of the Dutch situation by casting a different light on how diaspora are understood, while investigating ideas about a Dutch Afro condition, its art production, the language that contextualizes it, and curatorial practices involved in this condition. This book renders the twentieth-century project of the Western/non-Western power dialectic in the Dutch local arts environment intelligible, while also aiming to transcend it by means of the imagination.

Because English-language discourse is not sufficient to address its specificities, the Dutch context needs to be articulated specifically in relation to Dutch history, public policy, and artistic practices, and thus needs its own language to move for-

---

12 Philomena Essed, *Understanding Everyday Racism: An Interdisciplinary Theory* (SAGE, 1991), and Gloria Wekker, *White Innocence: Paradoxes of Colonialism and Race* (Duke University Press, 2016).

13 Kitty Zijlmans and Wilfried Van Damme, *World Art Studies: Exploring Concepts and Approaches* (Valiz, 2008).

14 Alanna Lockward, "Call and Response: Conversations with Three Women Artists on Afropean Decoloniality," in *A Companion to Feminist Art,* ed. Hilary Robinson and Maria Elena Buszek (Wiley, 2019), and Walter D. Mignolo and Catherine E. Walsh, *On Decoloniality: Concepts, Analytics, Praxis* (Duke University Press, 2018).

ward. With that in mind, the question of this book — whether it is possible to locate the Dutch Afro artists as native to the Dutch artistic landscape — has been perhaps best articulated during a conversation I had at "Cinema Olanda: Platform" in contemporary art center Witte de With, Rotterdam.

> We had artists of color representing the Netherlands; stanley brouwn is one of them. However, they have done so under the then prevailing modernity. So, what we have not had is an artist of color representing the Netherlands, and their color, so to speak being self-evident. Now, the question that I would like to see answered, is: Could we have an artist [...] be presented at the Venice Biennale, in all their fabulous blackness, and that presented as Dutch?... We're getting there.[15]

Dutch Afro Becomings: Overview

In Chapter One, "It's Not About Emancipation: Dutch Afro Artists in the Dutch Artistic Artworld," I take racial, ethnic, spatial, and geographical *hybridity* as a point of departure, showing how within the current art-theoretical discourse this concept is misconstrued as not being native to any nation in particular. Based on the idea that Dutch Afro-ness is constituted differently from what the African American and Black British discourses on Afro-ness have proposed, I demonstrate that contemporary Dutch Afro-ness is in a state of pre-Blackness ("becoming-Black"). This state of being, in turn, opens up the possibility of thinking of Dutch Afro-ness along the axis of cultural belonging rather than of racial difference. From a Dutch perspective, this proposition allows us to explore an artistic environment that moves beyond questions of representation.

Corporal, geographical, and cultural hybridity thus become givens from which we may start to imagine the placement of the

---

15 Charl Landvreugd, "Public-Platform-Open-Letter," in *Blessing and Transgressing: A Live Institute (2012–2017)*, by Wendelien van Oldenborgh, ed. Defne Ayas (Witte de With Center for Contemporary Art, 2018), 269.

Netherlands within this constellation. From the perspective of its cultural and artistic history, American, British, and Caribbean languages and concepts prove not always to be sufficient to speak or support the Dutch Afro context, as we are in a state of "becoming" Black, which may mean that we are moving from the Dutch Afro condition to Blackness as a racial category and political tool. However, through Édouard Glissant's idea of spiral retelling,[16] these (race-based theoretical) languages and concepts move into the Dutch context and become tools to unpack the Dutch artistic and cultural environment in which there is a strong focus on cultural difference. In order to move toward the end of an essentialized culture where this subject is culturally native, it is imperative to imagine a space of inherent hybridity where difference is the default. In this *imagined normal space,* the artistic subject is invested in the paradox of simultaneously becoming and refusing to be "Black."

What this Blackness has meant thus far is explored in Chapter Two, "A No-Man's-Land Patrolled by the International Art World: The Dutch Afro Problem Space in the Late Twentieth Century," which surveys issues of the Dutch contemporary art magazine *Kunstbeeld,* exhibition catalogs, cultural policy papers, and interviews to construct a view of the developments within the Dutch art scene over the past fifty years. It maps the changes in views on, and interaction with, non-Western visual culture from *transculturality* (1970s) to *diversity* (1990s), leading to the moment Dutch Afro artists affirmed their own imagined normal space within the Dutch context, an affirmation of being native to the Dutch art world. This imagined normal space is a response to the imposition of a *problem space,* as defined by David Scott: "a conjunctural space, a historically constituted discursive space. This discursive conjuncture is defined by a complex of questions and answers — or better, a complex of statements, propositions, resolutions and arguments offered in

---

16 Max Hantel, "Rhizomes and the Space of Translation: On Edouard Glissant's Spiral Retelling," *Small Axe: A Caribbean Journal of Criticism* 17, no. 3 (2013): 111.

answer to largely implicit questions or problems."[17] The Dutch government's understanding of the Dutch Afro subjectivity as non-Western, on socio-economic grounds determined by the (postcolonial) country of origin, dictates how its discourse and the problem space are construed.

This chapter brings together the views that have been consequential for the self-image of Dutch Afro artists and the reception of their artistic production in the Dutch art world, while mapping the discursive shifts from *world art* to *diversity,* which resulted in locating Dutch Afro art production not as native to the Netherlands but rather affirmed its geographical location outside the West.

Chapter Three, "*Be(com)ing Dutch*: Between Institutional Desire and Exclusion," builds on the developments and outcomes of consecutive cultural policies in the Dutch cultural milieu, leading to the pivotal moment when the Mondriaan Fund, the national Dutch arts and culture foundation, initiated the Stimuleringsprijs voor Culturele Diversiteit (Development Prize for Cultural Diversity) (2005–2008). I explore this particular moment through the institutional lens of the Van Abbemuseum in Eindhoven, because of the role of its then director Charles Esche and curator Annie Fletcher in transforming a Dutch public museum, with its grounding in Western art, into the leading institution with an "experimental approach towards art's role in society"[18] today. Looking at this moment through the viewpoints of those involved, their experience of this process, and their agency in this assignment toward "cultural diversity" within the museum illuminates how the different actors grappled with this question within the Dutch institutional context,

---

17 Stuart Hall, "David Scott by Stuart Hall," *BOMB,* January 1, 2005, https://bombmagazine.org/articles/david-scott/. The concept of *problem space* is more fully developed in David Scott, *Conscripts of Modernity: The Tragedy of Colonial Enlightenment* (Duke University Press, 2004).

18 "Who We Are," *Van Abbemuseum,* archived at https://web.archive.org/web/20190327135114/https://vanabbemuseum.nl/en/about-the-museum/organisation/who-we-are/.

demonstrating how diversity is a problem of the majority group coming to terms with a changing definition of art.

The public assessment of Van Abbe's *Be(com)ing Dutch* project evidences that Dutch art critique was measuring artistic diversity along the lines of the so-called *quality argument,* the misguided idea of a dominant class of white critics that the absence of nonwhite artists and cultural workers was not the result of colonial or racist mentalities, but because these artists "objectively" did not adhere to particular aesthetic and conceptual standards. In this post-9/11 artistic environment, where the focus was not on Afro-ness due to the larger art system's focus on Islam, Afro subjects and artists found the space to think constructively about their position in the landscape.

Chapter Four, "He Who Moves in All Spaces: The *Wakaman* Project (2005–2008)," then turns its gaze to the impact of the Mondriaan Fund's Stimuleringsprijs voor Culturele Diversiteit from the perspective of the Dutch Afro artists, showing the efforts of these artists to create a space beyond the confining discourse of natives and immigrants. This is exemplified by Wakaman, a movement of Surinamese Dutch artists reclaiming both a theoretical and artistic language to define their nativity to multiple origins, including the Dutch art world. An examination of the Dutch Afro condition that produced artistic, curatorial, and linguistic agency before and during this movement clearly brings into view why these artists thought the new space was necessary and how Wakaman tried to carve out this space by establishing a distinct presence in the Dutch art world.

From this effort two ways of curating emerged. One followed the logic of the existing model, geographically locating artists outside of the Western canon, with the understanding that their cultural and artistic relevance was not rooted in the Dutch art world but in their country of origin. The other followed the logic of "diversity" into "superdiversity" and proposed to "Eat the Frame!," a slogan coined by artist Michael Tedja that demands the undoing of the frame imposed upon Dutch Afro artists and cultural workers. Wakaman resulted in the emergence of "action research" as a curatorial practice, with the specific aim of changing the status quo, which I call *action curating*. The aim of action curating is to change not only the position of Dutch Afro artists in the landscape but also the institutional approach toward their work.

Chapter Five "Cultural Multiplicity as Default: Action Curating Dutch Afro Subjectivity" investigates the practical side of this action research as a curatorial practice within a larger institutional framework, at the moment this method projected into the future from a shared lived experience that embraced its inner multiplicity as the default. This approach allows for an exploration of the imagined normal space's ephemeral quality, providing a way to imagine beyond existing spaces that hinder overcoming the representational. My aim is here to highlight aesthetic articulations and sensibilities that enable what emerges from the edges of the imagined normal space without being primarily steered by the English-language race discourse. What surfaces from approaching the subject from this point of view is the agency that is obtained from artistic production while being subject to the social and political structure, or what I call the *Dutch Afro condition,* whose perception from inside and outside of the cultural community is heavily influenced by racial comparison with the United States and Great Britain. This comparison shows a difference in generational arrival and development in time, linking to a broader diaspora history through digital media.

By taking hybridity as a starting point, different cultural practices can be merged into action curating, rendering the edges of the imagined normal space visible. Geographically locating this subjectivity in the Netherlands means considering the specific sensibilities that are embedded within the Dutch language. Because of the lack of a local language to address our issues, the use of the Dutch language as a method may be exhausting, but so is translation to and from English. What is important in the discussion toward the imagined normal space is the cultural entitlement felt by those with a migrant background, yet this understanding of the self vis-à-vis Dutch culture is not widely shared with art institutions. Therefore, a different language has to be invented and this is one of the responsibilities of action curating. In the process, the normal space is altered in such a way that artists' work is considered native to the artistic landscape, without having to culturally pass to be appreciated. Action curating thus is a curatorial development where the artists and cultural makers that are the topic of my investigation here shape the normal space through active engagement on their own terms.

This is a narration of becoming Dutch Afro.
Of being native to the Dutch art scene.
Of a quest for an imagined normal space.

Of self-evident hybrid being.

1

It Is Not About Emancipation: Dutch Afro Artists in the Dutch Art World

I was born in hybridity.

Allow me to explain.

I was born on the northern edge of the Amazon in Paramaribo, Suriname. My birth is the historical result of centuries of forced and voluntary migration from Iberia, West Africa, India, and China to South America. My current work as an artist, researcher, curator, writer, and policy advisor dictates the conditions that inform how I understand this history.

Modernity gave birth to the New World and to the Creole. In Suriname, Creole is understood as African diaspora with ethnic backgrounds from different parts of the world. The racial and cultural mixing of Europeans, Africans, and Native Americans first happened during the times of slavery. After the abolition of slavery in 1863, male laborers were imported to Suriname from India, China, and Indonesia. Some of these laborers had children with, or started families with the local non-European women. Like other countries in the Caribbean, over the centuries Suriname developed as a society where different ethnic groups intermingled and created a communal existence. Not without any reciprocal discrimination, the various groups had to adapt and relate to each other based on cultural differences and similarities. Together they formed a society whose traditions, customs, and social relations derived from the different areas of ethnic origin.

The Creole practice of explicitly naming one's ancestry in addition to African evolved from this ethnic, social, and cultural entanglement. In Suriname, it is a way of explaining the specifics of one's physique and can be used as a lever when indicating a person's or a family's (historical) social position in a (post-) colonial society that is infused with colorism (discrimination based on skin tone) and classism. On a more positive note, in the context of the family, this naming was and is also a tool to orally remember genealogy, family history, traditions, and the reason for social and religious practices and rituals. This second usage, which establishes a physical, social, religious, and, specifically, cultural hybridity that emerges from a history of (forced) migration became my starting point for thinking through how the Dutch Afro artists fit into the Dutch artistic landscape.

Inspired by this Creole (hybrid) subjectivity mainly being racially categorized by its African appearance, my search for an African cultural identity began around 2005 while studying at Goldsmiths. On the internet I uncovered a history, never taught at Dutch schools, stretching further back than slavery and revealing ancient African kingdoms and empires, which countered the common trope of illiterate African savages to whom civilization was brought by the Europeans. I fantasized about an Indigenous African cultural identity that could only exist and materialize through the obvious bodily presence and blurred cultural remains that were inherited from ancestors who lived in an imagined empire and of whom no record existed.[1]

It occurred to me that to find a truly original cultural identity I had to return to Suriname.

Going to the most reliable source of my racially, ethnically, and culturally hybrid roots raised high expectations in me. After

---

1   In 1821 and 1832 fires occurred in Paramaribo that destroyed archives about the enslaved people brought in from Africa.

arrival, the first thing that struck me was that everybody was brown, like me. I felt a sense of belonging. The burden of representation, of which I had not been aware until that moment, disappeared. However, even though I am natively proficient in Sranan Tongo, the *lingua franca* of Suriname, my Dutch accent with its rolled *r* gave me away. Having not grown up in the country, cultural clashes occurred, and within days my sense of belonging disappeared. I realized that although I was *des lands kind* ("a child of the land"; a term used to indicate that one is born in Suriname), I was ethnically but not culturally Surinamese. This "homecoming" experience of both losing the representational burden of my skin color and the cultural dissimilarity problematized my search for cultural belonging.

Against the grain, identifying as a Dutch person that is part of the African diaspora, with a direct cultural and embodied genealogy to Africa by way of Suriname, was a far more logical option for the location of my cultural identity. As part of this Dutchness, my diasporic Creoleness was established through enslaved people, free Blacks, contract workers, and slave traders. What they all shared was a history of oppression, migration, survival, and adaptation. Whatever genealogy we may follow, a diasporic and culturally internal other-ness that is experienced as one-ness is foundational to the Creole subject that identifies as Dutch. In response to my African appearance, the intricacies of the Surinamese ethnic Creoleness are met with skepticism within the Dutch context where most non-Creole Dutch expect me to identify as what they consider Surinamese or Caribbean. The historical significance and lived experience of the multiplicity that defines Creoleness is lost in translation and loses its social weight in the Dutch context.

The identity of previous generations of Afro-Surinamese people has not been construed in opposition to the Dutch majority group but rather reflected in it. Through colonialism, migration, and integration, Afro-Surinamese (postcolonial) subjects have come to inhabit Dutch cultural standards while their Surinamese-ness and Creoleness faded to the background.[2] Yet even though people of Surinamese descent in the Netherlands are considered to be the most "successfully" integrated in Dutch society, I am still today perceived as having an immigrant background. This social perception obstructs the process of, and contrasts with, identifying as Dutch.

How then is one to gain a contemporary Dutch sense of self, beyond the Creole understanding, of the "I" as a "kaleidoscopic, ever-moving sequence"?[3] The result is a Creoleness augmented and complicated by a continental European cultural supplement that results in a particular sense of Dutchness, a multiple subjectivity that shifted my perspective from fixed-identity thinking to a thinking of multilayered subjectivity. This understanding of subjectivity as inherently layered is in line with the multicultural environment of my upbringing. It includes a layering that is not only the result of a domestic culture embedded within a larger social culture, but also because these two cultures originate in different principles. Customs, sensibilities, and concepts from the country of origin lose their meaning or are altered in this new constellation of lived cultural heritage.

The sense of one's own subjectivity also shifts in other environments. My travels revealed that in Great Britain perception of me points toward Black British, in the USA to African American/Black, in Egypt to Nubian or European, and in Senegal to Wolof. My Afro-ness is always leading, while, depending on the location, my assumed cultural identity as an ethnic construct varies. From my own perspective, the interplay between being perceived as racially African, ethnically South American, and culturally European in these spaces demands a rethinking of the contemporary subjectivity formerly known as Creole in order to resolve a sense of self that matches one's current condition. This

---

2   Robin Fransman, "Het gaat ook heel goed met de integratie in Nederland," *Centraal Bureau voor de Statistiek*, December 22, 2016.

3   Gloria Wekker, "One Finger Does Not Drink Okra Soup: Afro-Surinamese Women and Critical Agency," in *Feminist Genealogies, Colonial Legacies, Democratic Futures*, ed. M. Jacqui Alexander and Chandra Talpade Mohanty (Routledge, 1997), 336.

process reveals that self-identification doesn't necessarily mirror how one is perceived by society. The case of my personal subject position is merely an example of the complex multilayered hybridity that subjects with an immigrant background experience in the Netherlands.

Contemporary subjects, the (grand)children of the first generation of immigrants to the Netherlands (1963–1975), who are considered foreign due to their skin color or religious background, are carving out a space for themselves in the Dutch cultural landscape. They are imagining their cultural or ethnic subjectivity beyond the binary spaces that, as a form of control, demand submission to historical or (post)colonial relations. In the process of becoming, unraveling the terms that already exist, they are concerned with shaping their presence through the imagination. Their coalescing cultural backgrounds model these subjects into a new form, leaving identifiable marks on their surroundings. Difference is constitutive in imagining this twenty-first-century subjectivity with a migrant background that becomes self-referential by embracing its *hybridity*. Being part of this generation, and from a personal and artistic subject position, I take the idea of hybridity as the inevitable starting point from which to jump into the unknown, exploring how coalescing cultures are modeling a new artistic environment beyond the representational by pushing the boundaries of the confining spaces of historical circumstances. With the training wheels of existing ideas around African diaspora history and identity, this treatise reflects the process of what it is to become rather than follow prevailing cultural standards.

Problem Spaces: Calling Forth a People-Yet-To-Come

Embracing hybridity as a launching pad into the future needs a reconceptualization of the past that enables imagining a future that internalizes this thought. David Scott's concept of the *prob-*

lem space, which is "a discursive context, a context of language,"[4] provides a tool for this conceptualization. To understand the possibilities of imagining a self-referential subjectivity that embraces its hybridity, I propose to deploy this concept of the problem space. Stuart Hall describes this as follows:

> [A] "problem space" [...] is first of all a conjunctural space, a historically constituted discursive space. This discursive conjuncture is defined by a complex of questions and answers — or better, a complex of statements, propositions, resolutions and arguments offered in answer to largely implicit questions or problems [...]. [T]hese statements [...] are moves in a field or space of arguments and to understand them requires reconstructing that space of problems that elicited them.[5]

Hall further expands on this problem space as conjunctural space in his 2004 lecture "Black Diaspora Artists in Britain: Three 'Moments' in Postwar History":

> Evoking a "problem space," then, is to think of a conjuncture epistemologically. It is as if every historical moment poses a set of cognitive, political — and I would add, artistic — questions which together create a "horizon" of possible futures within which we "think the present," and to which our practices constitute a reply; a moment defined as much by the questions posed as by the "answers" we seem constrained or "conscripted" to give. When the historical conjuncture changes — as it did significantly between the 1960s and the 1980s and again, between the 1990s and the present — the problem space, and thus the practices, also change since, as David Scott puts it, what was a "horizon of the future" for

---

4   David Scott, *Conscripts of Modernity: The Tragedy of Colonial Enlightenment* (Duke University Press, 2004), 4.

5   Stuart Hall, "David Scott by Stuart Hall," *BOMB,* January 1, 2005, https://bombmagazine.org/articles/david-scott/.

them has become *our* "futures past" — a horizon which we can "no longer imagine, seek after, inhabit," or indeed create in, *see* or *represent* in the same way.[6]

The historical horizons for the future in other diaspora areas show that the current Dutch conjunctural space of "calling forth a people-yet-to-come who in some senses are already here"[7] is not new and has always happened in different contexts, producing different outcomes. Because the Dutch conversation on the role of Afro-ness in society is overdetermined by African American and Black British discourses, it is useful to touch upon their historical social and artistic horizons. This will bring into view the differences with the Dutch situation, confirming the importance of imagining an artistic space in the Netherlands where Dutch Afro art production is understood as an integral part of the Dutch artistic landscape.

Pre-Blackness: A Spiral Retelling of Language

As the Netherlands lacks a strongly developed (visual) language to articulate its internal ethnic differences, it is important to acknowledge that all Dutch people depend on understanding and translating foreign languages in pursuit of concepts that explain our situation. As an obvious consequence of linguistic and cultural translations, the meaning of concepts and visual tropes changes to be matched with local sensibilities. These modified terms then gain new meanings within the local context in such a way that they need explanation when translated back into the language from which they originated. As Max Hantel notes, the meaning of borrowed terms and visual forms from a specific culture only functions as a "natural referent" to

---

6 Stuart Hall, "Black Diaspora Artists in Britain: Three 'Moments' in Postwar History," *History Workshop Journal* 61, no. 1 (2006): 4. Emphases original.

7 Simon O'Sullivan, "Notes towards a Minor Art Practice," *Drain: Journal of Contemporary Art and Culture* 2, no. 2 (2005).

that culture.[8] Rather than producing a "carbon copy of equivalence or the linear projection of progress,"[9] in this new environment, these translations and transformations are like Édouard Glissant's *spiral retelling*: the movement from the One out to the multiple.

For the Dutch Afro cultural producer, the access to the texts that set out and determine the area of discussion and its borders follows the historical, academic, and popular culture route established through African American, Black British, and Caribbean cultural outputs. Therefore, I understand spiral retelling as the way in which, in particular owing to English language proficiency, American and British discourses are activated and translated toward an understanding and reconsideration of Dutch Afro-ness in the arts. This is a rhizomatic understanding "in the sense of producing a rootedness in the world."[10] Thus, a concept such as *Black(ness)* cannot be faithfully translated but only recontextualized. This awareness "undermines the illusion of global translatability and the possibility of pure transparency because we move through and across scales only by way of the opacity of others and their language."[11]

Ethnicity, which is marked as cultural, entangled with the implicit Dutch native cultural superiority, is so strongly rooted in the overall consciousness of the Netherlands that it conceals ideas about race. Knowing this, it is useful to explore the Dutch position toward race when unraveling the idea of Blackness as an indicator of the artist's social, legal, and cultural position in comparison to the United States and Great Britain. A starting point is the particular Dutch eagerness to point out the United

---

8 Max Hantel, "Rhizomes and the Space of Translation: On Edouard Glissant's Spiral Retelling," *Small Axe: A Caribbean Journal of Criticism* 17, no. 3 (2013): 104. "The art of translation [...] is creolisation at work, the unpredictability of Relation." "In other words, the way two languages interpenetrate in a specific act of translation actualises the network of unpredictable ties that every single language has to every other language in cultural, geographical and affective terms" (108).

9 Ibid., 110.

10 Ibid., 111.

11 Ibid., 112.

States's problematic racial politics combined with, as Gloria Wekker remarks, the collective denial of the racial and ethnic issues in the Netherlands.[12] With racial bias disguised as "cultural difference," race has been displaced onto the axis of culture. However misleading this may be, the currently prevailing paradigm is that Dutch Afro art production should not be understood as *racially marked,* but as *culturally different.* This idea of nonracist equivalence and tolerance, however, does not translate to ethnic equality.

I see this as an opening to work toward an imagined normal space, a conjunctural space born from cultural hybridity. To get there, I deliberately choose to occupy a self-referential cultural space that accommodates the whole spectrum of multilayered Dutch subjectivity. From a local Afro and diaspora perspective, my position may seem politically unsustainable due to the systematic and everyday racism[13] and micro-aggressions that are fully present in the visual arts. Because of this reality I am thankful to my colleagues who are impassioned about eradicating Dutch anti-Black racism within their work. By contrast, my position as someone thinking through the idea of culture rather than race might even be considered as giving in to the Dutch cultural superiority thinking or give white readers the idea that I am trying to eradicate color. This, in turn, may raise questions about my internalized colonization. These objections and considerations derive from an either–or binary system and the refusal to understand that it is possible to operate from a space that embraces the full multiplicity that is Dutch Afroness, including being coconstituted through the same cultural paradigms as the majority group. Effectively, this position is a recontextualization of the Creole subject that is inherently multilayered. Accepting this postcolonial condition as degree zero allows me to create an environment that originates in an Afro

---

12 Gloria Wekker, *White Innocence: Paradoxes of Colonialism and Race* (Duke University Press, 2016), 16.

13 Philomena Essed, *Understanding Everyday Racism: An Interdisciplinary Theory* (SAGE, 1991).

(migrant) experience rather than a space that is occupied with fighting majority group shenanigans, even if these affect me on a daily basis.

The issue with this position is that in the Dutch environment, where many different Afro (and other) ethnicities with a variety of histories live together, each group has different ways of dealing with everyday and institutional racism. Different from 1980s Great Britain, the variety of social — and political — agendas prevent a unification under the political umbrella "Black" — or any other term, for that matter. There is not enough of a generally felt shared history or feeling of oppression to encourage or create a Black Dutch (cultural) nation based on the idea of race and plurality of Afro ethnicities. This idea of a Black Dutch nation promotes a divide that leads to a cultural separation which in the context of the Netherlands is not necessarily desired. The way "Black" is understood as an umbrella term for Afro people outside of the Netherlands does not work in the effort of imagining this Dutch subjectivity, not until the emergence of the Black Lives Matter movement that is.

Allison Blakely concurs that the current language does not suffice to speak about being Black on the European continent.[14] Because of the historical diversity in Afro ethnicity in the Netherlands and the resulting variety of social and political positions, I argue that we have to ask ourselves whether following the American and British examples leads us in the right direction. Let us therefore first inspect their respective contexts.

Self-Actualization and Self-Definition: Black Arts and Culture in the United States

Although this is not the place to delve deep into the African American art movements, the historical context sketched out

---

14 Allison Blakely, "Coda: Black Identity in France in a European Perspective," in *Black France/France Noire: The History and Politics of Blackness*, ed. Trica Danielle Keaton, T. Denean Sharpley-Whiting, and Tyler Stovall (Duke University Press, 2012), 290.

below confirms how horizons for the future inspired new artistic spaces in the United States, underpinning the role of arts and culture in the formation of US Black discourse around self-image and representation. With this in mind, it is crucial to understand that, even though the predicament of Afro-ness is comparable, the way in which it became part of the national fabric is radically different. Whereas African physical presence is a constituent element of what we know as US culture, the Dutch enjoyed colonialism without a significant African presence in their own country. Therefore, in the cultural imagination of the Netherlands, Afro contributions to Dutch culture are negligible, if not nonexistent. This crucial difference is fundamental to understanding how Dutch sensibilities are mobilized when people of African descent identify as Dutch and claim cultural citizenship.

Between 1910 and 1930 many African Americans from the US South moved to the urban North seeking economic and political advancement. Those who moved to New York settled in Harlem where a Black presence was already in place. With a large Black population, "Harlem represented a spirit of advancement" and the motivation to "improve the social position of all blacks."[15] With the move from a rural to urban environment, the philosophies of Black leaders also changed with regard to self-expression and gaining political power. W.E.B. Du Bois's work led from Booker T. Washington's Atlanta Compromise (1895)[16] to the formation of the Niagara movement (1905)[17] and subsequently the National Association for the Advancement

---

15 Eva Lenox Birch, "Harlem and the First Black Renaissance," in *The Harlem Renaissance*, ed. Harold Bloom (Infobase Publishing, 2004), 116.

16 Booker T. Washington, "The Cotton States and International Exposition Speech" [Atlanta Compromise speech 1895], in *The Booker T. Washington Papers*, vol. 3: *1889–95*, ed. Louis R. Harlan (University of Illinois Press, 1974).

17 W.E.B. Du Bois and William Monroe Trotter, "The Niagara Movement's 'Declaration of Principles,'" *Black History Bulletin* 68, no. 1 (2005): 21–23. The Niagara Movement advocated for a strategy that was not based on patience and submission to white political rule, but on active demands on political, social, and economic levels.

of Colored People (NAACP) in 1909.[18] An identity beyond that of formerly enslaved persons, which was previously denied to Black Americans, was found in this environment.[19] As a consequence, the Great Migration in the United States gave birth to the Harlem Renaissance. Henry Louis Gates, Jr. describes the Harlem Renaissance as having taken its artistic inspiration from the Europeans. He references Antonín Dvořák's declaration that the spirituals are America's authentic contribution to world culture and the transformation of European art through its appreciation of African art by means of Pablo Picasso and the creation of Cubism. He concludes that the appreciation of African art from debased to sublime in a short period of time in the "cultural imagination of the West"[20] opened up its potential for political use. Du Bois and Alain Locke, who both trained in Europe during this period, were inspired by these events. Gates explains:

> If European modernism was truly a mulatto, the argument went, then African-Americans would save themselves politically through the creation of the arts. The Harlem Renaissance, in so many ways, owes its birth to Euro-African modernism in the visual arts. This Renaissance, the second in black history, would fully liberate the Negro — at least its advance guard.[21]

The Harlem Renaissance's major events are placed between the first publication of the NAACP magazine *The Crisis* in 1910

---

18 Patricia Sullivan, "Civil Rights Movement," in *Africana: The Encyclopedia of the African and African American Experience,* ed. Anthony Appiah and Henry Louis Gates, Jr. (Running Press, 2003).
19 Birch, "Harlem and the First Black Renaissance," 115.
20 Henry Louis Gates, Jr., *The Henry Louis Gates Jr. Reader* (Basic Civitas Books, 2012), 453.
21 Henry Louis Gates, Jr., "Harlem on Our Minds," in *Rhapsodies in Black: Art of the Harlem Renaissance,* exh. cat. (University of California Press, 1997), 163–64.

and Langston Hughes's publication of *The Big Sea* in 1940.[22] The outburst of creative output that launched the period took place between 1920 and 1930 during the economic boom in the United States. It happened at the same time as the Jazz Age, the Roaring Twenties, and the Lost Generation. A wealth of Black-owned magazines and newspapers producing thought around the "New Negro" and the support of white publishers launched careers that furthered the ideas of Du Bois and Locke, among others.[23] The period produced artists, musicians, dancers, performers, actors, writers, and poets, with an influence far beyond national borders. Locke's *Enter the New Negro* (1925) was the piece of writing that brought together ideas by previous intellectuals and defined the term for future generations. The "New Negro" argued for transformation. Locke's mandate was "that the 'New Negro' had to 'smash' all of the racial, social and psychological impediments that had long obstructed black achievement."[24] The goal was social progress through racial solidarity and transcendence of racial difference. These ideas were promoted through literature, painting, film, and all other available forms of cultural expression and were heavily influenced by women and queer artists. The cultural production of the Harlem Renaissance was recognized by the "mainstream" and gave Black people more control to represent themselves and speak about their own experiences. The critique for and against the

---

22 Ella O. Williams, *Harlem Renaissance: A Handbook* (Authorhouse, 2010), 8–9.

23 Alain Locke, "Enter the New Negro," *Survey Graphic*, March 1925, 1, http://nationalhumanitiescenter.org/pds/maai3/migrations/text8/lockenewnegro.pdf: "In the last decade something beyond the watch and guard of statistics has happened in the life of the American Negro and the three norms who have traditionally presided over the Negro problem have a changeling in their laps. The Sociologist, The Philanthropist, the Race-leader are not unaware of the New Negro, but they are at a loss to account for him. He simply cannot be swathed in their formulae. For the younger generation is vibrant with a new psychology; the new spirit is awake in the masses, and under the very eyes of the professional observers is transforming what has been a perennial problem into the progressive phases of contemporary Negro life."

24 Richard J. Powell, "Re/Birth of a Nation," in *Rhapsodies in Black*, 18.

success and effectiveness of the Harlem Renaissance mostly has to do with the interracial dynamics of the movement, and its appeal to Black middle-class and white audiences. However, this movement succeeded in placing the Black experience within the frame of the US experience and changed forever how African Americans are viewed in the world. With its political message and core of racial consciousness, it helped lay the foundation for the civil rights movement. Simultaneously it presented a precedent for cultural adulation, as white middle-class Americans flocked to Harlem to hear the "erotic Black jazz," and the adoption of jargon such as "cool" and "heavy" by the white marginal groups.[25]

Racial inequality, segregation, and exclusion drove the shift in horizon after WWII that gave birth to the civil rights movement. It was a system of "racial domination — economic, political, and personal oppression — [that] was backed by legislation and the iron fist of Southern governments."[26] In this environment of segregation, Black institutions (colleges, churches, societies) were established where color was more important than social class and the weight of separation could be left behind.[27] Consequently, it was in these spaces that discussions could take place and collective resistance organized. By the 1950s Blacks in the South were ready to challenge Jim Crow laws.[28]

What we have come to know as the civil rights movement of the 1950s and 1960s is a collection of incidents and a plethora of organizations trying to undo the disenfranchisement of Blacks in the United States, following in the footsteps of previous activists. Organizing boycotts, protests, sit-ins, freedom rides, marches, nonviolent and violent action, and court cases was part of the strategy of civil resistance to change the situa-

---

25 Cathy Covell Waegner, "Rap, Rebounds and Rocawear: The 'Darkening' of German Youth Culture," in *Blackening Europe: The African American Presence,* ed. Heike Raphael-Hernandez (Routledge, 2003), 176.

26 Aldon D. Morris, *Origins of the Civil Rights Movement* (The Free Press, 1986), 3.

27 Ibid.

28 Ibid., 4.

tion for African Americans. It was "the intersection of art and activism."[29] The movement was made up of all layers in the Black community, and also this time supported by the US Jewish community and white sympathizers. From the civil rights movement emerged the Black Power movement that was prominent in the 1960s and 1970s. The use of the term "Black Power" popularized by Stokely Carmichael in 1966 was a challenge to the philosophy of nonviolence put forward by leaders such as Martin Luther King.[30] It was a terminology that was in accordance with other cries for power in the diaspora, such as the African National Congress (ANC) in South Africa's claim to *amandla* (power) from that same period. The civil rights and Black Power movements are interconnected and may be seen as a single Black Freedom Movement.[31] As early as 1964, the Black Power movement's effect could be also seen in popular culture such as the live album *Nina Simone in Concert,* particularly in the song "Mississippi Goddam" (1964). As Historian Ruth Feldstein states:

> Contrary to the neat historical trajectories which suggest that black power came late in the decade and only after the "successes" of earlier efforts, Simone's album makes clear that black power perspectives were already taking shape and circulating widely [...] in the early 1960s.[32]

---

29 Dawn Levesque, "Artists of the Civil Rights Movement: A Retrospective," *Guardian Liberty Voice,* March 2, 2014, http://guardianlv.com/2014/03/artists-of-the-civil-rights-movement-a-retrospective/.

30 The Martin Luther King, Jr. Research and Education Institute, *King Encyclopedia,* s.v. "Carmichael, Stokeley," https://kinginstitute.stanford.edu/encyclopedia/carmichael-stokely.

31 Barbara Ransby, *Ella Baker and the Black Freedom Movement* (University of North Carolina Press, 2003).

32 Ruth Feldstein,"Nina Simone: The Antidote to the 'We Shall Overcome' Myth of the Civil Rights Movement," *History News Network,* March 3, 2014, http://historynewsnetwork.org/article/154884.

As the Black Power movement's "aesthetic and spiritual sister,"[33] the Black Arts movement emerged in the mid-1960s and lasted into the 1970s. In 1968 Larry Neal claimed:

> The new aesthetic is mostly predicted on an Ethics which asks the question: Whose vision of the world is finally more meaningful, ours or the white oppressors'? What is truth? Or more precisely, whose truth shall we express, that of the oppressed or the oppressors?[34]

And in the same year Ron Karenga stated: "All Black art, irregardless [*sic*] of any technical requirements, must have three basic characteristics which make it revolutionary. In brief, it must be functional, collective and committed."[35] It was a Black aesthetic that was never precise in its definition and was concerned with "literature, music, visual arts, and theater,"[36] emphasizing "racial pride, an appreciation of African heritage, and a commitment to produce works that reflected the culture and experiences of black people."[37] Out of the Black Arts movement

---

33 Larry Neal, "The Black Arts Movement," *The Drama Review: TDR* 12, no. 4 (1968): 29.

34 Ibid., 30.

35 Ron Karenga, "Ron Karenga and Black Cultural Nationalism," *Black World/Negro Digest* 17, no. 3 (1968): 5.

36 *Encyclopedia.com*, s.v. "Black Arts Movement, https://www.encyclopedia.com/history/biographies/historians-miscellaneous-biographies/black-aesthetic-movement.

37 Ibid. Even though the Black Arts Movement is the most well known, there were prior groups, such as Karamu Playhouse in Cleveland, the National Conference of Artists (1959), the Umbra Writers Workshop (1963), the Association for the Advancement of Creative Musicians (AACM, 1965), and the Organization of Black American Culture (OBAC, 1967), from which emerged Third World Press and the Institute for Positive Education (1967). "The most dramatic public statement by OBAC was *The Wall of Respect,* a Black Power mural painted on a building at the corner of 43rd Street and Langley Avenue on Chicago's South Side by Jeff Donaldson, Eugene Wade, Bill Walker, and other members of the visual arts workshop in 1967. The wall depicted various historical and contemporary black heroes such as Muhammad Ali, W.E.B. Du Bois, Malcolm X, Marcus Garvey, Nina Simone, Amiri Baraka, and Gwendolyn Brooks. This mural galvanized

emerged dance companies such as the Alvin Ailey Group that traveled to Africa and the diaspora. "[T]heir challenge was not to introduce new forms to American dance but rather to refine and extend a firmly established tradition" of African and diaspora dances in the United States.[38]

After the Harlem riots of 1964, the Black Arts Repertory Theatre/School (BART/S) of LeRoi Jones (Amiri Baraka) received funding from the New York City government via the Harlem Youth Opportunities Unlimited. This was a consequence of the "war on poverty" legislation introduced by then President Lyndon B. Johnson. Political scientist Jerry G. Watts argues that the school was one of the "key launching pads for the crystallization and emergence of the Black Arts Movement."[39] He goes on to say that "while Jones believed that his dramatic productions and jazz concerts were educational, it seems clear that the state viewed them as tranquillizing entertainment."[40] This school

---

the imaginations of community people, and based on their comments, the artists made various revisions on the mural. The appeal of public art notwithstanding, this privately owned building was eventually razed, and *The Wall of Respect* passed into legend. Despite its brief existence, the mural sparked a local and national movement. Numerous cities soon produced their own equivalents, such as The Wall of Dignity in Detroit, several murals by artists including Dana Chandler and Gary Rickson in Boston, and similar projects in New York, Philadelphia, and San Francisco, among others. Needless to say, the mural movement had roots going back to the 1930s in the WPA public art projects and especially in the powerful work created by the Mexican artist Diego Rivera. The Black Arts movement also echoed the 1930s in that the vogue of murals was seized upon by state and federal arts agencies. While black artists could see such murals as 'committed and committing,' government agencies saw them as a fine combination of public art and social control mechanisms for urban youths who could be organized into painting teams during the incendiary summers of the 1960s. Artists such as Bill Walker and Dana Chandler organized mural projects in several cities, but the political impact of these projects diminished as their frequency increased, and when government support evaporated in the arid 1970s, the mural movement withered away" (ibid.).

38 Ibid.
39 Jerry Watts, *Amiri Baraka: The Politics and Art of a Black Intellectual* (NYU Press, 2001), 160–61.
40 Ibid., 158.

thus occupied an "inauthentically autonomous" space where, when government funding stops, the broader political agenda is undermined.[41] Even so, Jones's concept was eventually copied as a model for "similar efforts in urban areas throughout the United States."[42]

A place, recognized by the large institutions, to exhibit works by African Americans was opened as the Studio Museum in Harlem in 1968.[43] How it came about was either because of the New York Museum of Modern Art's Junior Council, or the local Harlem Community that came together for chili dinners at the house of Betty Blayton-Taylor, resulting in the Committee to Form the Harlem Museum.[44] The committee argued that such a museum could contribute to the process of urban renewal. Andrea Allison Burns describes how on the museum's opening date there were protests in front of the building that reflected the "underlying apprehension within Harlem regarding the purpose and presence of such an institution."[45] With Black Power as its horizon, a point of critique was that the museum had many financial and governance ties to the white community.[46]

Many events and art works from this "second renaissance" are still referenced today. One of them is the "I Am a Man" signs used during the Memphis Sanitation Strikes in 1968. Artists such as Faith Ringold and David Hammons used the US flag

---

41 Ibid.

42 Ibid., 160.

43 The oldest African American museum in the United States is the Hampton University Museum (1868). Also there were several African American "neighborhood" museums, including the DuSable Museum of African American History in Chicago (founded in 1961); the International Afro-American Museum in Detroit (1965); the Anacostia Neighborhood Museum in Washington, D.C. (1967); the Studio Museum in Harlem (1968); and the African American Museum of Philadelphia (1976). See Alison Burns, "'Show Me My Soul!': The Evolution of the Black Museum Movement in Postwar America," PhD diss., University of Minnesota, 2008.

44 Ibid., 89.

45 Ibid., 92.

46 Ibid., 94.

to speak about the African American condition in the 1960s. With their actions these artists pushed the boundaries of what it means to be American by questioning the flag, thus pushing the horizon in the direction of where African American arts and artists are today. Groups emerged such as the arts alliance Spiral and AfriCobra and "Where We At" Black Women Artists, Inc., which worked on social change and the Black aesthetic.

From a common ancestral past, the Black Power movement used all forms of expression to advocate for self-actualization and self-definition.[47] It was a cultural and political movement, which gave rise, in turn, to the Black is Beautiful movement, celebrating Black skin, hair, and facial features, rejecting white beauty standards. This development generated a celebration of Blackness, notably with the Afro/natural hairstyles, name changes, and handshakes. William Van Deburg states that

> Recognizing that culture sometimes took the role of politics among the disfranchised, they hoped to reconcile ethics and aesthetics. Serving as a communication link between advocates of various "political" persuasions they articulated a new black consciousness.[48]

The problem space that shifted through time, from acquiescence to Atlanta Compromise to Black Power, also shifted the horizons of what was possible for African Americans, from the derogative "boy" to the self-affirmative "I Am a Man" and "Black Is Beautiful." Building on historical precedents, Black artists pushed the boundaries of how collective and individual subjectivities were produced, inspiring other minorities to do the same. There were also deviating voices, notably that of the jazz musician and composer Sun Ra (Herman Poole Blount), who initially felt closely related to the ideas in Black Power and saw his music as part of liberating and educating Black people. He ultimately felt disil-

---

47 Ibid., 192.

48 William L. Van Deburg, *New Day in Babylon: The Black Power Movement and American Culture, 1965–1975* (University of Chicago Press, 1992), 191.

lusionment and that he "couldn't approach black people with the truth because they like lies."[49] Over the years he created a personal mythology from another dimension and has since been considered an early pioneer of Afro-futurism.

All of this happened during a time when the whole world was changing. Decolonization of Africa and parts of the Caribbean infused the Black Power movement with energy and fueled Afro-centrism and Pan-Africanism in all parts of the diaspora. Even though Black Power has been described as antisemitic, misogynist, and racist, it inspired and provided the tools to other minorities to excavate their background.

> I think what Black Arts did was inspire a whole lot of Black people to write. Moreover, there would be no multiculturalism movement without Black Arts. Latinos, Asian Americans, and others all say they began writing as a result of the example of the 1960s. Blacks gave the example that you don't have to assimilate. You could do your own thing, get into your own background, your own history, your own tradition and your own culture. I think the challenge is for cultural sovereignty and Black Arts struck a blow for that.[50]

---

49 John F. Szwed, *Space Is the Place: The Lives and Times of Sun Ra* (Perseus Books Group, 1998), 313. "I couldn't approach black people with the truth because they like lies. They live lies… At one time I felt that white people were to blame for everything, but then I found out that they were just puppets and pawns of some greater force, which has been using them… Some force is having a good time [manipulating black and white people] and looking, enjoying itself up in a reserved seat, wondering, 'I wonder when they're going to wake up'" (ibid.).

50 Ishmael Reed, quoted in Kalamu ya Salaam, "The Black Arts Movement," in *The Oxford Companion to African American Literature*, ed. William L. Andrews, Frances Smith Foster, and Trudier Harris (Oxford University Press, 1997), 70.

The Production of a New Black Subject: Black Arts and Culture in Great Britain

What looks like a closer historical and social match, due to its immigration dynamics, is the British context. This is caused by the similarities between British and Dutch colonial rule, which included overseas territories and resulted in a moment of (post-) colonial immigration to the motherland. The circumstances that brought about horizons for the future were, however, different. Without implying that there was no Black presence in Great Britain before WWII, I would like to start after the war when the British needed to expand their workforce and started looking at its colonies.

The British artistic development is clarified in Stuart Hall's 2004 speech at London's Conway Hall as three moments in postwar Black visual arts in the UK. According to Hall, there is no single movement to which "all the artists [...] can be said to belong"[51] but rather moments in which different kinds of elements, generations, and kinds of work converge. Hall spotlights the "last colonials" who were born in the early 1900s and came to Great Britain after WWII in the 1950s and '60s just before the onset of decolonization. This "first" generation entered Great Britain "to fulfil their artistic ambitions and to participate in the heady atmosphere of the most advanced centres of artistic innovation at that time and produced writers and artists."[52] He argues that they came as subjects of the modern movement with the "promise of decolonization" firing their ambition, their sense-of-self as "modern persons" that "liberated them from any lingering sense of inferiority."[53] "'[M]odern art' was seen by them as an international creed, fully consistent with anti-colonialism which was regarded as intrinsic to a modern consciousness."[54] Their attitude toward "the modern" was mirrored in other colo-

---

51 Stuart Hall, "Black Diaspora Artists in Britain: Three 'Moments' in Postwar History," *History Workshop Journal* 61, no. 1 (2006): 3.

52 Ibid., 5.

53 Ibid.

54 Ibid.

nial spaces such as Brazil and South Africa. Their "horizon of the future" was independence and a new era of progress in which, according to Hall, they seemed to consider the sights and sounds, cultures and tradition, histories and memories of their places of origin "within a modern vision-field, via the modern consciousness of a certain 'de-territorialization' of colour and form."[55]

In 1967, after Jamaica, Trinidad & Tobago, Guyana, and Barbados gained independence from the United Kingdom, Black Power, through Stokeley Carmichael's speech at Speakers' Corner, leaped across the Atlantic and was adopted in Great Britain. This intersected with Michael X and the London Free School's involvement in the "Carnival of the Poor," which developed from a "jump up" street party for children in 1966 to an organized strengthening of community cohesion in 1967.[56] According to Hall, by the 1970s this first group, who for a while were "central to the avant-garde of the day,"[57] became disenchanted due to "institutional indifference" and the shift in attitudes toward modernism, among other things. The situation changed and politically the "shadow of race" fully entered the discussion by the mid-1970s.[58]

The "second generation" — the first "postcolonials" — who were born in Great Britain emerged with this horizon of race instead of anticolonialism. Politically and artistically active artists stormed the scene in a reaction to racial discrimination. They pioneered the Black Arts movement and the creative explosion of the 1980s, and were "anti-racist, culturally relativist and identity-driven."[59] It was with the beginning of the BLK Art Group and the landmark exhibition *Black Art An' Done* (1981) that the period of many independent exhibitions concerning these matters started. Who are we? Where do we come from?

---

55 Ibid., 7.
56 Notting Hill Carnival. Before this a Caribbean Carnival (1959) was organized in London as a reaction to the 1958 Notting Hill race riots.
57 Hall, "Black Diaspora Artists in Britain," 7.
58 Ibid., 16.
59 Ibid., 1.

Where do we really belong? These were central questions in this period of identity politics, which surfaced from the 1970s onward.[60] This new horizon

> produced a polemical and politicized art: a highly graphic, iconographic art of line and montage, cut-out and collage, image and slogan; the "message" often appearing too pressing, too immediate, too literal, to brook formal delay and, instead, breaking insistently into "writing."[61] Black art became a tool to "assist in the struggle for liberation."[62]

Hall further argues that

> the emergence of the identity question constituted a compelling and productive "horizon" for artists: not so much the celebration of an essential identity fixed in time and "true" to its origins, but rather [...] what we would now call "the production of a new, black subject."[63]

He continues: "And since that is a conception of identity and subjectivity which can only be constituted within, rather than outside, representation, the 'answers' in practice, which music and the visual arts provided, were absolutely critical."[64] Through different practices of this era, the "Black body" became central and its belonging was put into question. It resulted in what Hall called "the end of the essential black subject" as we entered the 1990s.[65]

Taking the first generation of Black British immigrants as the point of departure, the idea of the end of the essential Black

---

60 Ibid., 9.

61 Ibid.

62 Eddie Chambers, artist's statement in the *Black Art An' Done* catalog, Wolverhampton Art Gallery, June 1981.

63 Hall, "Black Diaspora Artists in Britain," 10.

64 Ibid.

65 Stuart Hall, "New Ethnicities," in *Stuart Hall: Critical Dialogues in Cultural Studies,* ed. David Morley and Kuan-Hsing Chen (Routledge, 1996), 443.

subject in the arts at the start of the 1990s was reached over a period of forty years. Looking at the different social history, it is clear why the US arts needed much longer to come to a similar proposition in the form of "post-Black" art in the late 1990s. To connect the state of mind in the Netherlands to this moment, let us now turn to the Dutch generational difference with the British before returning to Hall's third and the final moment in postwar Black visual arts in Great Britain.

The Multiple Black Self: Black Arts and Culture in the Netherlands

The historical developments in the United States and Great Britain that gave rise to Black as a "sense of self" are not immediately pertinent to the Dutch situation. As a borrowed political denomination, this construction lacks historical context and, even though it is of service to Dutch Afro subjects, does not find consensus among the Dutch Afro population. A Dutch Afro awareness toward a distinctive cultural identity is growing but is in its infancy and still far from reaching a definitive form. It is in a stage of becoming, a political "pre-Black" state that opens up different possibilities of subject production.

When music television and hip hop started their conquest of the world in the early 1980s, the majority of Afro youths in the Netherlands were first-generation immigrants. Without a demonstrable local Black culture that went back for generations, the Dutch urban culture that developed at that time found much of its input in the local community. Starting with Michael Jackson's *Thriller* (1982), records and video clips on music channels provided teenagers such as myself with African American examples to imitate. The appeal of African Americans advancing themselves from a disadvantaged position into musical and athletic stars had a strong effect on us. How we produced a sense of self through dance, rap, graffiti, language, posturing, signs (tags), and symbols was a direct consequence of what was presented to us via electronic media. In short, music television and hip hop were among the major contributors in providing the tools for the necessary street credibility. Mixing with all the different migrant-background teenagers, an inherently hybrid street language developed, infused with Surinamese, Moroccan, Papiamentu, Dutch, and American slang.[66] Street language, with its distinctive style, finds its way into music and as such produces and speaks about our urban concerns in Dutch hip hop. It is evident how in the Netherlands the reinterpretation and development of hip hop, as a tool of self-affirmation and resistance, are located in a multi-ethnic urban community rather than in a "Black" one.

Éva Miklódy writes of the adoption of rap music in Hungary that "[w]ithout violating the unity of form and content, any art form including rap can be borrowed and applied in different sociocultural circumstances."[67] In France this is exemplified by the emergence of *le hip hop,* which was developed by African and Caribbean youths in French cities in the 1970s and '80s.[68] MC Solaar was the first star to emerge in 1991 and by the 2000s *le hip hop* and the image of the *banlieu* (immigrant suburb) were more popular than ever. Funded by national and local agencies, hip hop was used in France to accommodate political and social discussions around race, class, opportunity, and labor.[69] French artists involved in the hip hop dance movement pinned "their cause to the struggles of a people and art ghettoised in the United States"[70] and in this way encoded the issues connected to their (North-)African immigrant status.[71] Hip hop is one of the ways of speaking about such sensitive issues. In the visual

66 Jolanda van den Braak, "Met andere woorden: Straattaal in Amsterdam," in *Taal in stad en land: Amsterdams,* by Jan Berns with Jolanda van den Braak (Sdu Uitgevers, 2002).

67 Éva Miklódy, "A.R.T., Klikk, K.A.O.S, and the Rest: Hungarian Youth Rapping," in *Blackening Europe,* ed. Raphael-Hernandez, 191.

68 Samir Meghelli, "Between New York and Paris: Hip Hop and the Transnational Politics of Race, Culture, and Citizenship," Ph.D. diss., Columbia University, 2012.

69 Felicia McCarren, "Monsieur Hip-Hop," in *Blackening Europe,* ed. Raphael-Hernandez, 158–61.

70 Ibid., 160.

71 Ibid., 162.

arts, Dutch and French artists also used this strategy of adopting contemporary and historical African American martyrs and heroes to discuss local concerns. For the artist, the coding circumvented direct criticism of the situation in their country while deflecting direct criticism from themselves.

The influence of electronic media was amplified by internet penetration in the Netherlands starting in the early 1990s. In particular, African American histories were absorbed as cultural commodities that influenced the lives of young Dutch Afro people. With an increasing amount of information becoming available online by the early 2000s, this boost brought the examples of other diaspora closer. The local intellectual and embodied experiences found resonance in similar stories elsewhere in Europe and beyond. For young Dutch Afro people these developments created better self-understanding of their social condition.[72] In this sense, electronic media allowed other Afro experiences to become examples that proved to be useful tools for expression and self-analysis:

> The people are now the very principle of "dialectical and tacit knowledge reorganization" and they construct their culture from the (inter)national text translated into modern Western (European) forms of information technology, language, dress.[73]

When I left the Netherlands in 2004, the thorough analysis of the Dutch Afro condition by Dutch Afro citizens and artists was still at an early stage. In the following years, I participated in the Wakaman project (2005–2008) instigated by the artists Remy Jungerman, Gillion Grantsaan, and Michael Tedja. This project, which is extensively discussed in Chapter Four, was concerned with "the problems of categorization, recognition and interpretation that [the members] encounter as non-Western artists liv-

---

72 Charl Landvreugd, "Notes on Afro-European Aesthetics and Sensibilities #1: North and Western Europe," *ARC Magazine* 7 (2013): 60–67.
73 Homi K. Bhabha, *The Location of Culture* (Routledge, 1994), 55.

ing in the West."[74] By the time I returned to the Netherlands in 2010, electronic media, and the critical analysis of Blackness that could be found there, were encouraging Afro awareness in intellectual and artistic circles. For the radical Dutch Afro artistic community, borrowing the term "Black" as a self-identifier proved to be a useful, albeit problematic, way to connect to the African American and Black British diaspora theories.

With the aim of critically engaging with what I then called a "Black-Dutch consciousness in the visual arts,"[75] patricia kaersenhout and I organized the debate *Am I Black Enough?* on October 26, 2010 at De Unie as part of the public program accompanying the *Paramaribo Perspectives* exhibition in TENT Rotterdam.[76] In my talk, which was the basis for a conversation on how to give shape to a Dutch idea of "Black," I proposed the idea that "Black" already assumed exclusion, while at the same time consciously rooted in a multiple self without being concerned with emancipation. This is a position that claims, without reservation, the same space to which all Dutch believe they are entitled, and consequently results in a Black self-awareness that is Dutch (Afro). This self-awareness is not a multicultural self-awareness, because this has been a concept formulated by a middle class largely made up of white Dutch people. This, then, raises the questions as to how cultural producers contribute toward a broader Black awareness?[77] This conversation evolved into a discussion about the usefulness of explicitly mentioning Blackness in the work and in the work environment. The panel of cultural makers felt trapped between the private and the public and could not reach consensus as regards the use of

---

74 "Wakaman Walks," *Intendant Culturele Diversiteit,* archived at https://web. archive.org/web/20160802083053/http://www.intendant.nl/intendant/english/projecten/02/project.php.

75 Charl Landvreugd, "Notes on Black Dutch Aesthetics," in *Conversations on Paramaribo Perspectives,* ed. Mariette Dölle and Malka Jonas (TENT, 2010).

76 Participants were documentary maker Tessa Boerman, movie director Hesdy Lonwijk, writer and publicist Clark Accord, and fashion designer Marga Weimans. The debate was moderated by sociologist and writer Aspha Bijnaar.

77 Landvreugd, "Notes on Black Dutch Aesthetics."

any word drawing attention to their Blackness.[78] A conclusion drawn from this 2010 debate was that, at that time, self-identification with the idea of Black was a private matter that could not intervene in the overall public sphere. In line with the growing Afro awareness, there was a desire to break free from this confining circumstance. The general feeling was that drawing attention to the idea of Blackness was harmful to career opportunities. Overcoming reluctance to identify the self and the work as Black in the public sphere also had to do with the scale on which the artists were able to operate, or the position they felt they held in the arts scene.

It was and still is a question of economic and political tactics based on the discussions that the cultural makers choose, feel engaged by, or empowered enough to enter. As Hantel notes, "scale is always political."[79] For Dutch Afro cultural makers, the level of connecting their work to the idea of Blackness depends on whether they are aiming for the local ethnic scene, local general scene, international Black scene, or international art scene. Finding ideological support in US-centric discourse as a tool for legitimation and empowerment is a tactical and, because of the influence of digital media, a natural choice for contemporary Dutch Afro artists. As a consequence, terms such as "Black" inevitably enter the discussion in the Netherlands. However, as I will show below, by tactically encoding local issues through the US-centrism as a way of legitimation, the intertwining with local linguistic tropes proves not effective enough in supporting the Dutch situation and anticipates its potential political quality.

Both "Dutch Afro" and "Black," each for their own reasons, fall short of fully encapsulating the subjectivities I want to imagine, because they (unwillingly) position the subjects inside a (post)colonial and "US-centric discourse."[80] When what is con-

---

78 See also Trica Danielle Keaton, T. Denean Sharpley-Whiting, and Tyler Stovall, eds., *Black France/France Noire: The History and Politics of Blackness* (Duke University Press, 2012).

79 Hantel, "Rhizomes and the Space of Translation," 106.

80 Paul Gilroy, "Foreword: Migrancy, Culture, and a New Map of Europe," in *Blackening Europe*, ed. Raphael-Hernandez, xvi.

veyed by English terms does not always match Dutch sensibilities, how does that language function in terms of producing us? Of what use can it be when exploring the specific local language to speak about the self that is coming into existence as Dutch Afro and being solidified as such in the process of emerging?

The Dutch state and society have their own ideas about this. Thinking along the lines of cultural difference, the state maintains categories that do not always reflect lived reality. The Dutch Nationality Law of 2003 states that all those born from Dutch nationals or inside the kingdom are Dutch citizens. The fact that people of different ethnicities can become citizens is not reflected in the language used by government agencies such as the CBS (Central Statistics Bureau), which is not geared toward full cultural inclusion. Since the recent wave of different ethnicities claiming their rights as cultural, rather than merely legal, citizens, national identity has become a political issue. When talking about the population, a distinction was made between "native" and "nonnative" or, as it is was called until 2016, *autochthonous* (after 2016: "with a Dutch background"), originating from the country (but not necessary the wider kingdom, which includes the Caribbean islands) of the Netherlands; and *allochthonous* (after 2016: "with a migration background"), originating from a foreign country. The word "allochthonous" was used for immigrants and their descendants, while the law makes a distinction between first- and second-generation "allochthones." A first-generation allochthone is someone living in the Netherlands but born in foreign country, with at least one parent born in a foreign country. A second-generation allochthone is someone born in the Netherlands with at least one parent born in a foreign country. The country of the mother is the country of origin when both parents are from abroad, but in the case of the mother having been born in the Netherlands the father's country of origin becomes the country of origin for the child. When both parents are born in the Netherlands, the child is considered autochthonous.

This categorization was a response to immigration due to decolonization, the invitation of migrant workers, and the influx of asylum seekers. Furthermore, allochthones were divided into Western and non-Western.[81] The reason for this division was the different socio-economic and cultural position of the two groups. In general parlance, the word "allochthonous" has come to indicate all those whose culture is dissimilar to Dutch culture. In practice this means everybody who is not obviously white. Even though by law children whose parents were born in the Netherlands are autochthonous (culturally Dutch), in the public sphere those who are visually non-white are often approached as allochthonous (from a different socio-economic background). Consequently, Dutch legal and legally confirmed cultural citizenship does not automatically lead to inclusion in the fabric of society as a full and equivalent participant and contributor to Dutchness.[82]

Afropea: Natives to the Utopia of the Imagined Normal Space

The term "Dutch Afro" that I have used thus far is an overarching term that tries to encompass the intricacies of naming strategies for people of African and diaspora descent in the Netherlands. It is also the term that marks difference from traditionally used terminology as it deviates from, and refers to, the contemporary sociopolitical circumstances of the artists that I will discuss below. What I have in common with these artists is that we have developed strategies to incorporate cultural heritages and an embodied Dutchness into something new. In doing so we take an example from Afro writers such as the Surinamese–Dutch writer and poet Edgar Cairo. Cairo was a self-described "Euro-Creole" (centering the Creole) who advocated for, and in

---

81 If a group strongly resembles the Dutch population in socio-economic or cultural aspects they are considered "Western allochthonous": all countries in Europe except Turkey, as well as North America, Oceania, Japan and Indonesia. "Non-Western allochthonous" includes Turkey, all African Countries, Latin America, and Asia with the exception of Japan and Indonesia. Centraal Bureau voor de Statistiek, "Standaarddefinitie Allochtonen," August 1999, 1.

82 See also Gilroy, "Foreword," xi–xiv.

doing so foresaw, a doubly creolized "buffer culture"[83] in which Black and white would influence one another. It is at this point and with this horizon of the new that an imagined normal space as a utopian space where one can be culturally native emerges. It is with this horizon in mind, following Cairo and centering Afro-ness, that I use the term "Dutch Afro" instead of alternatives such as "Afro-Dutch." For this subject, the Dutchness is an addition to its multilayered Afro (Creole) cultural background.

Returning to Hall's argument concerning "the end of the essential black subject" at the beginning of the 1990s,[84] we can now fully grasp the imagined normal space in which the Dutch Afro artistic subject emerges as native. Hall states that this third moment after WWII was less politicized, but rather "artistically neo-conceptual, multi-media and installation-based."[85] It was the time when in the British context "'Black' by itself — in the age of refugees, asylum seekers and global dispersal — will no longer do."[86] Hall provides a horizon of going beyond Black, emerging from the specifics of the British artistic problem space. In the United States, this idea is echoed by the category of contemporary post-Black art coined by Thelma Golden and Glen Ligon. In post-Black art, race and racism are lined up while the interaction between these two is simultaneously rejected. As Golden remarks, the artists are "adamant about not being labeled 'black' artists, though their work was steeped, in fact deeply interested, in redefining complex notions of blackness."[87]

---

83 Wim Rutgers, 'The Netherlands and Its Colonies: Edgar Cairo," in *A Historical Companion to Postcolonial Literatures: Continental Europe and Its Empires,* ed. Prem Poddar, Rajeev S. Patke, and Lars Jensen (Edinburgh University Press, 2008), 326: "Cairo does not argue in favour of segregation nor assimilation or integration. What he wants is a doubly creolised 'buffer culture', in which black and white influence one another. Through his own migration from Suriname to the Netherlands, Cairo in the course of his career has evolved from a pure 'Sranan Man' to a 'Euro-Creole' who has had to learn how to survive as a minority in the Netherlands."

84 Hall, "New Ethnicities," 443.

85 Hall, "Black Diaspora Artists in Britain," 2.

86 Ibid., 13.

87 Thelma Golden, *Freestyle* (Studio Museum in Harlem, 2001), 14.

Effectively, the term tries to move beyond the ideas of Black and white toward imagining a different normal space. It is a horizon of going beyond Black, emerging from the specifics of the American artistic problem space.

All the steps of vindication, emancipation, and representation through art that have been taken in the past century in the United States and Great Britain are nowadays being repeated in the Netherlands. The difference is that, in addition to digital media, all the theoretical frameworks and knowledge that have been created in the past century are available. This allows for a rapid cultural development from barely any awareness to full-blown artistic activist action within ten years. Being fully aware of this Dutch spiral retelling in a contemporary environment of accelerated returns, I propose the idea of an imagined normal space. This space is in full accordance with the end of the essential Black subject and the ideas surrounding post-Black art but emerges from a different conjunctural space and has a different horizon for the future. Emerging from a pre-Black state, this conjunctural space is invested from its constitution as a Dutch space of inherent cultural hybridity rather than giving power to the twentieth-century race dialogue where Black is understood in opposition to whiteness.

This is a new environment that could tackle the predicament of Dutch Afro artists as a whole, separate space while being able to leave its concomitant structures, including the in-between space from which it originates, intact. This environment can do this because it is not in opposition to the diaspora, the majority group, or resulting friction between the two, but accepts all of these as elements in the multilayered, inherently hybrid, degree zero. It is the space where the rules that are in place on all sides of the hybrid spectrum do not apply while still exerting influence, where one can wander off, abandoning set paths. Rather than in a geographical region, the imagined normal space — in my earlier writings conceptualized as Afropea[88] — functions as

---

88 Charl Landvreugd, "Notes on Imagining Afropea," *Open Arts Journal* 5 (2016): 41–52.

a cultural space where one can locate continental Dutch Afro subjectivity as *native* rather than from elsewhere. The native Dutch Afro subject is consequently the cultural producer and native inhabitant of this imagined normal space. This native space is a utopian place where race and ethnicity are depoliticized because they lose their function as a markers of difference. Here Afro-ness is evident to itself as a universal point of departure. It is here where artists start to claim their place in society rather than as representations of otherness.

As shown, the subjects that are to inhabit this imagined normal space are driven by rejecting essentialization, carving out their own specific "end of the essential Black subject." At the same time, they cannot be post-Black as they are figuring out what it means to be Black in the Dutch context. Effectively, the Dutch Afro artistic subject is invested in the paradox of simultaneously becoming and refusing to be Black. By means of the imagined normal space, it is possible to maintain that position as self-evident while reserving the right to explore or develop a gesture that takes flight, creating a culture with a different horizon and shaping the future.

2

A No-Man's-Land Patrolled by the International Art World: The Dutch Afro Problem Space in the Late Twentieth Century

Ethnicity versus Quality: The False Binary of Dutch Art Critique

In 1982, recalling the historical relation between art from Africa and the Dutch, art critic Paul Faber draws attention to the fact that the Benin Bronzes and masks are admired for their "simplicity, force, and subtlety," despite having been produced by "primitive souls" who were "savages."[1] He further notes that the novelty of contemporary Nigerian art is not only surprising but, due to its affinities with other art forms, may be considered of interest to a Western audience.[2] This essay from art journal *Kunstbeeld*, which offers the first description of non-Western art within a twentieth-century Dutch art-critical context, further

---

1   Paul Faber, "De Goden zijn niet dood: Nigeriaanse Kunst in Zwolle," *Kunstbeeld* 6, no. 5 (1982): 12. Unless otherwise noted, all translations from Dutch sources throughout this volume are mine.
2   Ibid., 12–13.

explains that these contemporary Nigerian works break "the barrier of unfamiliarity and anonymity [...]. The first impression is confusing because of their diversity, richness in form, colorfulness, and exotic thematics."[3] Throughout this chapter, *Kunstbeeld,* since 1976 the longest running, locally distributed, self-sustaining Dutch contemporary art journal, will be our core resource. Together with documentation of Dutch national cultural policy, the articles on non-Western, non-white, and Dutch Afro art from the *Kunstbeeld* archive spanning 1976–2012 provide a sweeping view of the Dutch notions around the production of contemporary Dutch Afro artistic subjectivities, as well as an understanding of the developments leading to the moment of an imagined normal space described in the previous chapter.

In the years following this first essay, Faber develops a comparison and distinction between so-called "traditional" art practices around the world and Western art practices. These traditional art practices, operating in the realm of religion, are placed in the exotic context of magic and mysticism. Faber makes an effort to understand the works and notes about the Indian feast in honor of the goddess Durga, involving the immersion of religious sculptures and installations in the Hooghly river, a tributary of the Ganges: "Despite the prescribed iconography, the stylistic difference is great and the technical perfection is impressive."[4] The difference between Indian art and our (Western) art, he continues, not only concerns appearance but also "how it is used, its meaning, the sources of inspiration. When one explores non-Western art with these criteria, one meets extremely interesting phenomena, contemporary and alive, but not always fitting into our ideas of how or what art should be."[5] To demonstrate that this approach to art has not changed much in 1997, we may refer to an aricle by art critic Wouter Welling, who, when considering Yoruba altars as an art form, states that

---

3   Ibid., 12.

4   Paul Faber, "Kunst uit een andere wereld: Een niet-Westers vierluik," *Kunstbeeld* 12, no. 12 (1988–1989): 26.

5   Ibid., 27.

they are "an 'environment' that can reach theatrical splendor of which the Catholic Church can only be jealous."[6] He remarks that, unlike in contemporary Western art where context is necessary before it can be appreciated, this art form is immediately very compelling.[7] Welling then wonders whether these altars should be seen as art or whether they are "only interesting from an anthropological standpoint?"[8]

In an article on Venda sculptures in an exhibition of South African art, *Freedom Flight* (1997), Anne Berk explicated the contrast between "traditional" and Western art practices: "In contrast with Western conceptual art, which challenges the intellect, this art is corporeal, right from the heart."[9] South Africa, she claims, is a country of contrasts that is not only the economic engine of the continent but also plays an important role in the cultural field that produces both naïve sculptures (Black people) and oil paintings (white people).[10] She thus reduces the geographical difference between Western and African art practices to a cultural difference between Black and white artists living in the same environment.

Kunstbeeld's mapping of the art world in the rest of Africa also frames this cultural difference as an absence of art doctrines. As Welling notes, Benin presents a "different character" of the art world without infrastructure (academies, museums for contemporary art, galleries).[11] Concerning this difference, he cites artist Romuald Hazoumé (b. 1962), who states that there is no need for an academy, as "there we would only learn to mimic Western art."[12] Hazoumé thus reiterates the cultural difference and articulates a need for a contemporary Beninese artistic idi-

---

6   Wouter Welling, "Op de drempel van twee werelden: Altaarkunst uit Afrika en Afro-Amerika," *Kunstbeeld* 21, no. 5 (1997): 46.

7   Ibid.

8   Ibid.

9   Anne Berk, "De Apartheid voorbij: Vrije vlucht van kunst in Zuid-Afrika," *Kunstbeeld* 21, no. 2 (1997): 19.

10 Ibid.

11 Wouter Welling, "De vitale traditie van Benin," *Kunstbeeld* 22, no. 3 (1998): 50.

12 Ibid.

osyncrasy. He further states: "If there is something that the artists from Benin make clear, it is that the old [art from Benin] does not have to be a burden, but rather can form an excellent breeding ground for the new."[13]

Hazoumé here criticizes African art that builds on and is mediated through Western involvement. *Kunstbeeld* provides several examples of such developments, in which Western agents bring "quality" to African art practices. For example, Faber reviews the creation of contemporary art from Africa exemplified in Nigeria's Oshogbo where an "African renaissance" is triggered by the presence of the German linguist Ulli Beier and Austrian artist Suzanne Wenger.[14] The influence of Dutch teaching about the etching and *batik* technique as an influence on Nigerian art processes results in work that "is not heavy, theoretical art. It is illustrative, fairy-tale-like but above all indestructibly merry, this work [by Bruce Onobrakpeya] exudes a heart-warming charm."[15] In Zimbabwe's stonemason colony Tengenenge, "the sculptures stand disordered without pretence."[16] Here it is Tom Blomefield who migrated to "Rhodesia" in 1947 where he became a mineworker and later tobacco and maize farmer, providing the stones, hammers, chisels, and other tools to local artists while also taking care of the sales of the works in the capital Harare. The artist, teacher, and museum administrator Frank McEwen started the Zimbabwean "Workshop School" in 1955. This school was not designed as "formal training" but rather as a place where interested people were provided with "paint, pencils, and fabric. [...] Instead of stuffing an unformed mind with foreign information, examples, and prescribed subjects, it [the school] is concerned with the spirit, the *esprit,* of art that is nourished and expressed with care."[17] The result of these interventions is "an idiom of an unstoppable stream of fantasy and curious design, an expressive form-lan-

---

13   Ibid., 51.
14   Faber, "De Goden zijn niet dood," 13.
15   Ibid.
16   "Zimbabwe op de berg," *Kunstbeeld* 13, nos. 7–8 (1989): 19.
17   "Zimbabwe op de berg," 18.

guage without the burden of hyper- or post-modernism, with which young artists in the West are tormented."[18]

In 1982, Faber already observes that the success of African contemporary artists in the West is based on an "unquestionable idiosyncratic character,"[19] a certain "authentic African" feel that can be compared to the likes of Paul Klee and Cobra. He portrays an artist such as Twins Seven Seven (b. 1944) as someone who is not a "Western surrealist looking for individual dream-images," but as someone who recalls the "fairy tales and mythical world of the gods of his youth."[20] However, once his works become larger and move toward a "harmonious whole" — in other words, start dealing with the aesthetic concerns of Western art — it is considered to be less surprising and to have less tension.[21]

This particular line of Dutch art criticism revolves around the perceived inability of modern non-Western (particularly Afro) artists to attain the same quality standard as their Western counterparts, and develops into one of its cornerstones. In what follows, I will define this false binary between ethnicity and quality as the *quality argument*. Whereas, according to *Kunstbeeld*, in the 1989 art environment, the African "stone masons appear to be totally unaware of any European master whatsoever,"[22] they observe that in the appreciation of art from Africa "there is a strange tension between producers of contemporary art exhibitions and cultural anthropologists."[23] While this tension, which is constitutive of the quality argument, can be observed in Susan Vogel's *Africa Explores* (1991) and Clémentine Deliss's *Africa '95* (1995), these projects are not discussed in *Kunstbeeld*.

By 2000, Welling articulates the position of African artists on the world stage as one in which they want to be seen as artists

---

18 Ibid.
19 Faber, "De Goden zijn niet dood," 13.
20 Ibid.
21 Ibid.
22 "Zimbabwe op de berg," 19.
23 Ibid., 18.

first and not placed in the "ghetto."[24] The word "identity" is, in the words of the *Dak'Art 2004* director Rémi Sagna, considered "too burdened! Everybody is authentic and a world citizen at the same time. People have no more borders, it is a notion of a large open-ness to the world. Purity is a dangerous notion."[25] In his essay on *Dak'Art 2004* and *Africa Remix* (2004–2007) curator Simon Njami explains this development by identifying certain stages in the contemporary world art process from the position of the non-Western (African) artist. The first phase is becoming aware of one's own cultural background. Second is taking a distance from one's roots, due to perceived burden of the "exoticizing straitjacket."[26] In the third phase, "ethnicity is no longer an initial concept, but rather aesthetics and politics" become the central focus.[27] By identifying these stages, Njami effectively anticipates the imagined normal space I proposed in the previous chapter, echoing Stuart Hall's "end of the essential black subject."[28]

The African example illustrates the idea of difference in non-Western visual art production that is dependent on Western involvement to develop into what is considered "art." It reveals a strictly framed notion of art that is also assumed by modern and contemporary artists from these (colonized) areas. The demand for local authenticity and fitting into Western artistic doctrines leads to a double bind which in Dutch art criticism reinforces colonial beliefs of Western cultural superiority. For the artists, the possibility of passing as "art" in this framework not only sets up the vague borders of the indefinable space that is the quality argument but also locates them in this no-man's-land that is patrolled by the international art world.

---

24 Wouter Welling, "Dak'Art 2000: Globalisering van de Afrikaanse kunst," *Kunstbeeld* 24, nos. 7–8 (2000): 28.

25 Ibid.

26 Wouter Welling, "Afrikaanse kunst," *Kunstbeeld* (2005): 44.

27 Ibid.

28 Stuart Hall, "New Ethnicities," in *Stuart Hall: Critical Dialogues in Cultural Studies*, ed. David Morley and Kuan-Hsing Chen (Routledge, 1996), 443.

The White Perception of Local Authenticity in Australia, the Caribbean (Haiti), Latin America, and Indonesia

The form of "accommodating" locals to artistic production that is recognized as art in the West also happened outside of Africa. In Australia it was a white drawing teacher, Geoffrey Bardon, who stimulated Aboriginal Australians to start using canvasses and hardboard in 1971. This makes Aboriginal Australian art only several decades old when seen from the perspective of the hardboard carrier as a method recognized in the West.[29] In Haiti it was the American artist DeWitt Peters who arrived in 1943 as an English teacher and later opened an art center geared toward the Haiti elite. According to Faber, this development ignited a spark that passed over to the Black population of the island,[30] resulting in a "prairie fire" as artists were encouraged to examine their own possibilities.[31] As a result, Haitian artists produce work that ranges from "almost chaotic color trumpeting full of Voodoo symbolism [… to] carefully constructed monochrome."[32] "This jungle of images, combined with a cultural isolation, has produced paintings and sculptures that deserve more than the meagre term 'naïve art.'"[33] With this statement Faber acknowledges the development of a site-specific idiosyncratic formal language based on Western principles of art making. Whereas in Haiti it is "cultural isolation," as Faber puts it, in other parts of the world there is a significant precolonial visual language that is recognized as art informing local artists. Unlike African art, in these instances the "old" is not seen as something that hinders but rather enriches the new, that is, Western-influenced art.

In *Kunstbeeld,* apart from Indonesia which I will address below, the precolonial local influence on art is mostly discussed in relation to Latin America. Chilean poet Raúl Zurita writes

---

29 Wouter Welling, "Het Aboriginal Art Museum: De vitaliteit van een oer-oude kunsttraditie," *Kunstbeeld* 27, no. 3 (2003): 22.

30 Faber, "Kunst uit een andere wereld," 27.

31 Ibid., 28.

32 Ibid., 27.

33 Ibid., 28.

that the quest for identity and the continent's appearance in a new historical context is construed more based on "fantasy than on a concrete direct reality."[34] He states that it is a "subtle and ambivalent" reality that embodies an "unknown relation to Utopia."[35] British art historian Dawn Adès adds that the "identity question is not so much a problem but rather a source for the ideas of contemporary artists. They see their 'Americanness' as an idea to be investigated and tested against reality."[36] In this relationship to utopia, many artists are inspired by pre-Columbian cultures while others portray contemporary Indigenous cultures.[37] "Autochthonous art has contributed to the idea of a mixed mestizo culture, of which the origins are as strongly rooted in the Native American as the European world."[38] The works are not a "faint shadow of European painting, but a new and multifaceted development."[39]

Wim van Beek explains that "artists from those different countries, each in their own way, are trying to define their relationship to utopia: a 'common' Latin American art in which each country looks for its own identity with specific emphases."[40] An example of this is contemporary Latin American photography, where there is hardly any distinction between art photography and documentary photography.[41] Here, the developments lead to the issue of "stereotypical subjects [… which] in our Western world still determine the strong and emotional, romanticized image of these countries."[42] Even so, according to Adès,

---

34 Raúl Zurita, quoted in Willem van Beek, "U-ABC: Beeldende kunst uit Latijns-Amerika," *Kunstbeeld* 13, no. 10 (1989): 17.

35 Ibid.

36 Dawn Adès, "Kunst uit Latijns-Amerika," *Kunstbeeld* 13, nos. 7–8 (1989): 33.

37 Ibid.

38 Ibid. The Dutch term used for "Native American" is *Indiaans* (lit. Indian), which is distinct from *Indiaas* (Indian, from the Asian subcontinent) and *Indisch* (colonial, pre-independence Indonesian).

39 Ibid.

40 Van Beek, "U-ABC," 17.

41 Ibid., 15.

42 Ibid.

It is neither coincidence nor simply a reflection of international "good taste" that some of the impressive visual images and constructions in Latin American art are at the crossroads of folk art and environmental art, on the basis of which a true, original mestizo art develops.[43]

For Latin American artists such as Fredy Flores, working in the Netherlands in the 1980s, this form of art production implies the recognition of value in the pre-Columbian heritage, which Europeans often describe with terms such as "primitive," "exotic," or "folkloric."[44] It shows that the work attempts to grapple with this Latin American relation to Europe, between academia and "the spontaneity of its own culture."[45]

What this account reveals is how the perception of local authenticity is valued when it comes from an area that has historically been appreciated for its cultural achievements. Although content and form are questioned, in the case of Latin America, these historical cultural achievements are enlarged because they are canalized through European descendants. Therefore, the double bind of local authenticity and Western artistic doctrines works differently in this case because of the (mestizo) whiteness and cultural Europeanness of the artists. Consequently, the authority to measure the work against Western standards invokes the quality argument albeit without the notion of inherent cultural inferiority, because the artist is (unconsciously) perceived as part of the European diaspora.

Similarly, the Dutch art world and critique situate Asian art traditions as valuable practices from the former colonies. But when we look at the former Dutch colony in Asia, where there was already a thriving culture and pictorial tradition in place before colonialism, a different picture emerges. The Western influence on traditional art practices that transformed into local

---

43 Adès, "Kunst uit Latijns-Amerika," 33.
44 Rob Perrée, "Latijnsamerikaanse kunstenaars in Nederland 2: De dialoog van Fredy Flores," *Kunstbeeld* 12, no. 7 (1988): 54.
45 Ibid., 55.

contemporary art under Dutch colonial rule is exemplified in the accounts on modern and contemporary Indonesian art history. This history starts in 1936 when the artists S. Sudjojono and Agus Djaja established the association of painters Persagi, in which Sudjojono in particular rejected the *Mooi-Indië* (Beautiful Indonesia) style, which romantically idealized the landscape and traditional living.[46] As a result, an Indonesian Modernism developed that was "highly influenced by the social-political context."[47] Considering the fact that the formal idiom of this style was derived from the West but its content was not, Welling suggests that the main question in the 1930s was whether "modernization equalled to westernization."[48] Out of this question two schools developed. The one in Yogyakarta preferred "realistic or expressionistic painting, with an undertone of social sensitivity, based on 'Indonesian' subjects."[49] The other one, in Bandung, where the Dutch painter Ries Mulder was teaching, favored "an abstract, aesthetic style, deriving from Cubism."[50] According to art historian Helena Spanjaard, this difference played out in Indonesia as the Bandung school, where the community stayed Dutch-inclined in the 1950s, was accused of being a laboratory of the West.[51] The year 1975 saw the establishment of the Indonesia Art Movement, which made "an explicit distinction between higher arts and traditional art."[52] They drove the discussion to the brink by stating that "the possibility exists of syncretism, through which the modern and traditional can merge," resulting in "a modern art with an Indonesian charisma."[53]

What this review of articles in *Kunstbeeld* shows thus far is that different regions gained different forms of appreciation in

---

46 Wouter Welling, "Doorbraak en bloei in de Indonesische kunst," *Kunstbeeld* 22, no. 2 (1988): 48.

47 Ibid.

48 Ibid.

49 Helena Spanjaard, "Ahmad Sadali een religieuze abstract," *Kunstbeeld* 9, no. 4 (1985): 43.

50 Ibid.

51 Ibid., 43–44.

52 Welling, "Doorbraak en bloei in de Indonesische kunst," 48.

53 Ibid.

the West. Latin American and Asian art practices were looked at differently than practices with an Afro background. The coming into being of contemporary art in (former) colonial spaces was constructed through the intervention of Westerners who "encouraged" local artists. As the magazine argued, "All the attention that has been given to the influence of African expressiveness on European art [...] has little to do with declaring the contemporary art from third-world countries mature."[54] Even though, as in the case of Haiti, the art was appreciated as more than naïve art, the production emerging from this encouragement was viewed as lacking theoretical and formal grounding and was merely appreciated for its charm, naiveté, and expressiveness. At the same time, the role of precolonial influence on contemporary art production was regarded as valuable in the Latin American context. Here, people of European ancestry who were rooted in the Indigenous American and European culture produced a mestizo visual culture that could be measured on an international stage. As a whole, it is the European influence on all of these locations that provided the mandate to decide whether or not the work was valuable enough to be appreciated as part of the contemporary (Western and Dutch) art discourse.

A Cocktail of Surprises: The Fallacy of "World Art"

It was only in 1989 with the exhibition *Magiciens de la Terre* (1989) that the idea of non-Western art as "modern" would begin to gain a strong foothold. In his review of the show, Faber wonders about its purpose and content,[55] explaining that the curatorial team "did not choose for a general image of a culture but for the personal approach and intensity with which something is conceived and designed."[56] Faber concludes:

---

54 "Zimbabwe op de berg," 19.
55 Paul Faber, "'Les Magiciens de la Terre': Honderd tovenaars in Parijs," *Kunstbeeld* 13, nos. 7–8 (1989): 13.
56 Ibid., 14.

> Even though the presentations are organized in such a way that alternations are great and didactical side effects fail to appear, the observant visitor will make out interesting cross-connections [with regard to African cultural elements].[57]

With the previously discussed appreciation for Latin American art, the Stedelijk Museum in Amsterdam mounted the exhibition *U-ABC* (*Uruguay–Argentina, Brazil, Chile*) (1989), shortly after *Magiciens de la Terre*. This exhibition was an effort to give more attention to artists outside of the Cologne–New York international art axis.[58] The Groninger Museum subsequently hosted the exhibition *Africa Now* (1991–1992) with the curatorial argument that after *Magiciens de la Terre* "it did not seem justified anymore to present art from the West in art museums and leave art from the rest of the world to ethnographic museums."[59]

Magiciens de la Terre stimulated the discussion about art versus ethnography in the Netherlands. Welling stated that the accusation of the exoticizing character of *Magiciens de la Terre* resulted in the fact that now "only non-Western art which has familiarized itself with the Western (conceptual and/or technological) idiom, is shown in Western institutes. Everything with an explicitly cultural timbre is left to ethnographic museums."[60] Effectively, the quality argument had obtained a tool for separating out works by non-Western artists at the door. Nevertheless, the works that "passed" were still scrutinized on their mastery of Western-idiom art practices. A case in point is Welling's observation that the development of Australian Aboriginal art toward internationally oriented art, going beyond the political and [...] identity, while keeping the ties with the traditional background," is a development that inspires optimism.[61] However, urban Aus-

---

57 Ibid.

58 Raúl Zurita, quoted in Van Beek, "U-ABC," 14.

59 Frans Haks, qouted in Cas Bool, "Het museum als instituut staat ter discussie," *Framer Framed*, https://framerframed.nl/dossier/het-museum-als-instituut-staat-ter-discussie/.

60 Welling, "Afrikaanse kunst," 44.

61 Welling, "Het Aboriginal Art Museum," 20–21.

tralian Aboriginal "political art is rarely [considered] the best art."[62] In the same spirit he describes the *Dak'Art 2004* biennial as filled with cliché, politically correct work.[63] Welling passes judgment on those works, validating his authority by saying that the contextualization of the works by curators Okwui Enwezor and Salah Hassan "sound[s] critical and politically correct. But when putting pen to paper with the intent to write it down [...] it becomes more difficult."[64] Welling here applies the quality argument to scholarship about issues in contemporary art emerging from these Afro thinkers. In other words, colonial assumptions about ethnicity are applied to the quality of the intellectual labor based on a political position. This is what Lopez observed in 1996 as intellectual discrimination[65] originating in a patronizing Dutch position.

During *Documenta XI* (2002), with its theme of "cultural identity" in the postcolonial era, Enwezor's position was that "an artist 'produces knowledge.'"[66] Art critic Robert Roos wrote that the expectation was that Enwezor would "come with a procession of non-Western artists that would make political statements about the new, postcolonial world. Artists that would chastise the dominance of the Western art order. It turns out better than expected."[67] As Rob Perrée noted, Enwezor insisted that issues faced by African artists are similar to those faced by artists in the West,[68] and that "it is totally imaginable that *Documenta* is not the right platform for many artists."[69] With this line of thinking, Enwezor destabilized the quality argument by proposing that Western art institutions were insufficiently equipped to

---

62 Ibid., 20.
63 Welling, "Afrikaanse kunst," 47.
64 Ibid., 45.
65 "Vanwaar je dacht te vertrekken sta je geplant," *Kunstbeeld* 20, no. 2 (1996): 35.
66 Robbert Roos, "Documenta van Enwezor overtuigt," *Kunstbeeld* 26, nos. 7–8 (2002): 22.
67 Ibid., 25.
68 Rob Perrée, "Directeur Okwui Enwezor geeft visie op zijn Documenta: 'Ik dans niet voor geld,'" *Kunstbeeld* 26, no. 5 (2002): 7.
69 Ibid., 9.

grasp the full complexity of current cultural identities. As I will show below, such proposition is absent from the Dutch context, where Dutch Afro artists are expected to be validated by the quality argument that insists that their "ethnic" concerns have no place in an established art environment.

From the start of this development there was a tension in the Netherlands between international art and what would become known as "world art." With *Magiciens de la Terre* looking outside of the dominant axis of art, the idea of a general image of culture shifted toward the intensity with which artists conceived and designed their work. In *World Art Studies: Exploring Concepts and Approaches* Wilfried van Damme describes the historical development toward the moment when world art studies as a concept was first proposed by art scholar John Onians in 1996:

> Whereas scholars of music, despite changing opinions, would con-tinue [*sic*] to regard their multifaceted field as an intellectual unity under the flag of musicology [...], no "artology" developed that could have safeguarded scholars of the visual arts from seeing their shared subject matter fragmented into epochal, regional, and disciplinary specialties whose practitioners hardly communicate with each other. World art studies [...] may be considered an attempt to remedy this situation. [It is interpreted in this book as] to approach its subject matter from a global perspective across time and place and to study it from all relevant disciplinary viewpoints imaginable, ranging from evolutionary biology to analytic philosophy.[70]

When the modern international art world started looking beyond the Western axis of art, the outlines of world art started to emerge. As a result, according to curator Anne Berk, by 1997 contemporary art was no longer the exclusive domain of the

---

70 Wilfried van Damme, "Introducing World Art Studies," in *World Art Studies: Exploring Concepts and Approaches*, ed. Kitty Zijlmans and Wilfried van Damme (Valiz, 2008), 27.

West.[71] However, as we have seen thus far, this new form of contemporary art was not appreciated in the same way as Western contemporary art.

In her analysis Berk makes some poignant remarks about the changing art world, using the Dutch neologism *eigen-aardig*. When written unhyphenated, *eigenaardig* means "peculiar." But with the added hyphen, *eigen-aardig* can be read as a word play on *eigen aardig* which I translate as "pertaining to one's own nature." According to Berk, after *Magiciens de la Terre,* 'the advancement of exotic art is unstoppable. [The artists] pass by as a colourful procession, a cocktail of surprises.'[72] She explains this as a product of "third-world countries' emancipation."[73] Interestingly enough, in her article "Oriëntatie op het eigen-aardige" (Orientation on what pertains to one's own nature), she is the first, in 1996, to mention the internet in relation to artists of color: "Precisely now that the electronic highway wants to fuse us into global citizens, interest is revived in things that were once, as the source of all evil, discarded to the waste basket."[74] The *eigen-aardige* is a "favorite of the cosmopolitan art lover while the critic raises their finger in admonition: this is superficial exotism. Or worse: this is a form of ethnocentrism in which the West once again decides the criteria."[75] Berk sees this as a positive development: "Just as with the Indonesian *rijsttafel,* it is the variation of dishes that makes the delight. It is something different from *hutspot.*"[76]

In 1998 Welling declares that the West no longer has a monopoly on "the development of (post)modern art." Indeed, the artistic challenges of societal, political, and intellectual obstacles

---

71 Berk, "De Apartheid voorbij," 18–19.

72 Anne Berk, "Indonesiërs en Hollanders in Lakenhal: Oriëntatie op het eigen-aardige," *Kunstbeeld* 20, no. 5 (1996): 42.

73 Ibid., 43.

74 Ibid.

75 Ibid.

76 Ibid. *Rijsttafel* (rice table) is an invention of Dutch colonial cuisine, presenting a large variety of dishes from disparate Indonesian regions together in a singular composition. *Hutspot* (hotchpotch) is a staple of Dutch cuisine.

are, for the most part, representative of "all cultures outside of Europe and the United States."[77] By 2005 he observes that the keywords "globalization, identity, gender, post-colonialism, religion, spirituality, and life in the metropolis" are "on the agenda of curators and critics in Africa, Europe and the United States."[78] For Afro artists operating on the world stage this means that with the end of the essential Black British subject in the 1990s, the emergence of American "post-Black" in the late 1990s, and Okwui Enwezor's global *Documenta XI* in 2002, ethnicity is no longer a driving concept.

Looking at this context beyond the Netherlands gives us further insight into the framework that located most non-white artists in the Netherlands as originating "elsewhere." This elsewhere has a hierarchy that places European diaspora at the top of non-Western art production. This is followed by work from different regions that is produced using a carrier approved by the West, such as a canvas, albeit with a distinctive "ethnic" input. Works that use such carriers while grappling with the formal aspects of the discipline are considered less successful. Everything beyond this point falls under the domain of ethnography. Let us keep the development of this hierarchy in mind when looking at the Dutch cultural framework and see how some artists, by way of exeption, manage to find their way.

Legislating Post-Blackness in the Netherlands: From Transculturality in the 1980s to Diversity in the 1990s

Now that some insight has been offered into the Dutch view of the outside world, I turn to the local cultural framework in the last quarter of the twentieth century going into the twenty-first.

Faber argues that artists born outside the Netherlands such as stanley brouwn (1935–2017), Miguel-Ángel Cárdenas (1934–2015), Ulay (b. 1934), and Marina Abramović (b. 1946), who could be categorized as belonging to an ethnic minority,

---

77 Welling, "Doorbraak en bloei in de Indonesische kunst," 46.
78 Welling, "Afrikaanse kunst," 44.

were part of the Dutch art scene, playing a significant role. Yet their origins were of little significance, let alone incite special activities to perform their supposed "native" credentials.[79] He describes how the collective category of the "foreign" or "non-Western" artist only emerged in the 1970s, when the idea of the specifically "foreign artist" was not yet an issue. Faber notes that it was the migration streams from the 1970s, leading to larger communities of immigrants who permanently settled in the Netherlands, that led to policy-making. As a consequence, "Artists from these groups were pulled away from their profession and colleagues and were repositioned in the category of their countrymen and *cultuurgenoten* [cultural fellows]."[80] This change meant that their ethnicity was more meaningful to the policymakers, who were trying to manage the influx of new migrants, than their vocation. The artists were placed in the terminology that over the years "developed from 'guest-workers' and 'ethnic minorities' to 'allochthonous.'"[81]

In tandem with the new immigrant policies, another shift was taking place in the Netherlands. This was the Dutch development toward internationalism during the early 1980s in which modern art became recognized as a "worldwide, polycentric activity, executed by an ambitious and mobile top layer"[82] from Asia, Africa, and Latin America. According to Faber, the Dutch art world was questioning the idea of Western modern art on "theoretical and pragmatic grounds."[83] As these young artists were looking for "new locations with more possibilities,"[84] an increasing number of them also started to attend Dutch art academies. Faber states that these two contradictory develop-

---

79 Paul Faber, "25 mei 1991. De opening van de tentoonstelling Double Dutch: Van allochtoon naar kunstnomade," in *Cultuur en migratie in Nederland: Kunsten in beweging 1980–2000*, ed. Rosemarie Buikema R. and Maaike Meijer (Sdu Uitgevers, 2004), 173.
80 Ibid.
81 Ibid.
82 Ibid., 174.
83 Ibid., 173.
84 Ibid., 174.

ments of, on the one hand, integration politics and, on the other, the discussions about modern art created confusion.[85]

The solution developed around 1985 was to map these changes as well as the artists living in the Netherlands that may prove to be an enrichment to the Dutch or Western perspective on art.[86] This investigation, known as the KEM-Project (Art by Ethnic Minorities Project), was instigated by the Centrum Beeldende Kunst (Center for Visual Arts), De Rotterdamse Kunststichting (The Rotterdam Art Foundation), and the Museum voor Volkenkunde (Museum of Ethnography).[87] The investigators, some of whom had non-Dutch backgrounds, compiled a list of hundreds of artists, together with addresses and slides. Yet the final report from 1987 did not result in any concrete action, and part of the archive was taken over by the Gate Foundation, whose work we will discuss below. In her analysis of government policy for culture and migrants, Eltje Bos states that, "It is only after 1987 […] that the tension between the existing cultural policy and the one designed around migrants becomes clear."[88] By then, due to the existing cultural policies focused on welfare and initiatives focused on bringing out the high-quality "allochthonous" artists, it proved to be hard to integrate art by migrants into the existing high art system.

Bos explains that there was a certain ambivalence in the government's intervention, derived from romantic, universal ideas, as well as the contextual and participatory approach toward art that focused on quality, removal of obstacles, and participation.[89] She argues that, due to their immigrant status being more prevalent than their vocation, cultural expressions coming from immigrants were positioned somewhere between amateur and professional. Essentially, the difference was between those who were recognized in the official art circuit (of internationalism),

---

85 Ibid.

86 Ibid.

87 Ibid.

88 Eltje Bos, "Beleid voor cultuur en migranten: Rijksbeleid en uitvoering-spraktijk, 1980–2004," PhD diss., University of Amsterdam, 2011, 72.

89 Ibid.

such as stanley brouwn and Erwin de Vries (1929–2018), and those working in the exhibitions coming out of the Srefidensie gallery or Cosmic Illusion, whose initiatives, according to Faber, were designed around "going on a voyage of discovery," through which "they wanted to show their environment these unknown treasures."[90] Bos concludes that these initiatives not only put these artists in a "separate category but also excluded them from the facilities that were in place for professional arts and artists."[91]

By 1989 the Raad van de Kunst (Dutch Arts Council) had produced a report entitled "De kunst van het artisjokken eten" ("The Art of Eating Artichokes"), which looked into the developments concerning "foreign" and "non-Western" arts in the Netherlands since 1982. The report, whose title suggests both foreigness and multi-layeredness, states that "Despite the initiatives mentioned here it was established that more support was needed for the 'allochthonous artists' and that, from all the disciplines, the possibilities for support were least utilized in the visual arts."[92] Several methods that placed art made by people of color in the non-Western category were investigated to articulate the "difference" between Western and non-Western art. Despite this terminology and a specific interest in promoting cultural relativism, the report inadvertently resulted in a particular mapping which placed different values on different regions at a time when, according to Faber, contradictory developments of integration politics combined with discussions about modern art created confusion about the location of migrant artists in the Dutch art world.[93]

To locate these artists and their artistic production within the Dutch context, the report drew parallels with how artists' work was valued and how they were framed in other Western countries. The outcomes of this exercise were merged with Dutch ideas about art from elsewhere, meaning that the mode

---

90 Faber, "25 mei 1991," 175.
91 Bos, "Beleid voor cultuur en migranten," 72.
92 Faber, "25 mei 1991," 175.
93 Ibid., 174.

of questioning which declared exoticism, magic, and mysticism to be a site for an anthropological approach toward understanding art also became applied to non-white artists from Western countries.

As a consequence, the way in which African American artists in particular were understood inevitably had an influence on the Dutch understanding of their own artists with an Afro background. Speaking about Martin Puryear's (b. 1941) work in the catalogue for the *Black USA* (1990) exhibition that was mounted in the Overholland Museum (1987–1990), Marijke Beek concludes that the African American artist's work "evokes confusion in the eyes of a Westerner, because, in Western culture, the function of nearly every object is fixed."[94] When it comes to non-white Western artists of African descent, the "magic" and incomprehensibility of the works are sometimes characterized as innate. Beek describes an African American artist such as Bill Traylor (1854–1947) as an "archetypical [...] naïve prodigy,"[95] who has gotten down to the primal score of things,"[96] a *"bon sauvage"*[97] breaching time and place in a way that links him straight to ancient times. In short, Traylor is portrayed as a Romantic artist and magical "negro" archetype who works straight from the soul. Such exoticizing language reassigns the art work to the sphere of the magical, and even bleeds into translations from English. For example, when writing about the artist Romare Bearden (1911–1988) Beek translates the "Negro experience" into *zwart levensgevoel,*[98] rendering "experience" with *gevoel* (feeling) rather than *ervaring* (experience). In another instance, Benny Andrew's idea of living a "dual existence"[99] is translated as *schizofreen bestaan* (schizophrenic existence),[100] which in essence removes him from normalcy and constructive intellectual labor.

---

94 Marijke Beek, *Black USA: Overholland* (Lecturis, 1990), 75.
95 Ibid., 8, 10.
96 Charles Shannon, quoted in ibid., 9.
97 Ibid., 11.
98 Ibid., 24.
99 Ibid., 57.
100 Ibid., 56.

Until today, this supposed "innate incomprehensibility" of work dealing with Dutch Afro "life-feeling" (i.e., Negro experience) proves to be an impregnable fortress for Dutch art critique and curatorial practices.

The development of the Dutch framework differs from that of the United States and Great Britain as regards the parallel appreciation of Afro-ness in contemporary arts. Cultural policies, an advancing understanding of non-Western art through art criticism, and the emergence of world art prompted the active move from *transculturality* in the 1980s to *diversity* in 2005. This transition away from ethnicity as a driving concept will prove to be consequential for Dutch artists.

Leading up to this moment where the arts were "global in orientation but multidisciplinary in approach,"[101] we can discern several episodes in the Netherlands where the cultural identity of the artist took center stage. Art historian Nanda van den Berg, who is a regular contributor to the cultural and literary magazine *De Gids* (*The Guide*) and the director of the photography museum Huis Marseille, wrote a 1994 article on the position of allochthonous artists in the Netherlands, in which she explicates how the word "allochthonous" does not refer to artists such as Sigurður Guðmundsson (Iceland) or Marlene Dumas (South Africa) who are successfully working in the Netherlands.[102] She observes that "allochthonous artists" belong to the group of "acknowledged minority groups" such as "Antilleans,[103] Surinamese, Turkish, Moroccans, and artists from places such as South America, China, or Iran."[104] She further notes that the label "implies that the artist is 'amateuristic' and delivers 'bad

---

101 Kitty Zijlmans and Wilfried van Damme, "World Art Studies," in *Art History and Visual Studies in Europe: Transnational Discourses and National Frameworks*, ed. Mathew Rampley et al. (Brill, 2012), 220.

102 Nanda van den Berg, "De kunst van het weglaten: De positie van allochtone beeldend kunstenaars," *De Gids* 157 (1994): 69.

103 An ethnic term specifically referring to people with a background from the former Dutch colonies in the Caribbean: the Leeward Islands of Sint Maarten, Saba, and Sint Eustatius, and the Leeward Antilles of Aruba, Bonaire, and Curaçao.

104 Van den Berg, "De kunst van het weglaten," 69.

work,' which is the reason why the artist is not admitted into the 'acknowledged circuit.' Furthermore the allochthonous artist is usually Black or colored."[105]

Van den Berg's article provides further understanding of the racial and ethnic division as it applies in the Dutch context in relation to art history, museology, and the art-market-driven approach to "quality."

> The first initiative in the area of "allochthonous arts" stems from the social welfare context: in 1971 Srefidensie (Independence) was established in Amsterdam, a "gallery for Surinamese, Antillean, and Caribbean artists." The gallery was established single-handedly without [government] subsidy on the third floor of the Surinamese welfare organization Welsuria. There were no high art goals set, but according to Eugène Chateau, one of the founders, it simply provided a stage for the creativity and expression of the people. [...] The first exhibiting artists were drawn from the artist cafés on the Leidseplein.[106] [...] The exhibitions in the gallery eventually mapped the Surinamese and Antillean artists that were present in the Netherlands. That this gallery policy helped to define the image of the allochthonous artist can be deduced from the fact that the core exhibitors were part of the exhibition *Farawé: Acht kunstenaars van Surinaamse oorsprong* [*Farawé: Eight Artists of Surinamese Origin*] that was organized by people of Surinamese descent in the Nieuwe Kerk in Amsterdam in 1985.[107]

Van den Berg notes that at that point, in 1994, the exhibition catalog[108] of *Farawé*, a Surinamese word meaning "far away," was the only art-historical description of Surinamese art in the Neth-

---

105 Ibid.

106 A popular square in central Amsterdam.

107 Van den Berg, "De kunst van het weglaten," 69–70.

108 Emile Meijer, *Farawé: Acht kunstenaars van Surinaamse oorsprong* (Aldus Uitgevers, 1985).

erlands at that time. At the time the artists[109] were, like all Dutch artists, subsidized through the national Beeldende Kunstenaars Regeling (Visual Artists Regulation), and that as a result of the discontinuation of this subsidy in 1987 several of the artists were referred to the "allochthonous subsidy" that was handed out by the Ministry of Welfare, Public Health, and Culture.[110] As a result, "the designation 'allochthonous artist' consequently became less informal,"[111] and support points for allochthonous artists were established by organizations that focused on different ethnic groups, united in a single third-world category.[112]

An important example of such organizations was Cosmic Illusion, which was founded in 1976 in Curaçao by Felix de Rooy and Norman de Palm. By way of New York they found a base in Amsterdam and became one of the leading organizations in the area of allochthonous arts, with independent departments focusing on performing arts, visual arts, literature, and film.[113] They organized several exhibitions such as *Schaduw, Licht, Vorm* (*Shadow, Light, Form*) (De Balie, Amsterdam, 1987), *Beeld, Vorm, Kleur* (*Image, Form, Color*) (Galerie Inkt, Den Haag, 1988) and *Structuurenvorm/Vormenstructuur* (*Structure-andform/Formandstructure*) (Volkshogeschool Drakenburgh, Baarn, 1990).[114] Van den Berg remarks that all these exhibitions took place in "secondary exhibition spaces."[115]

As she observes, "There is a clear principle at the basis of all these exhibitions as can be seen on the leaflet of the exhibition *Schaduw, Licht, Vorm*":[116]

---

109 The artists were Armand Baag, Frank Creton, Eddy Goedhart, Hans Lie, Guillaume Lo A Njoe, Sam Parabirsingh, Q. Jan Telting, and Erwin de Vries.
110 Meijer, *Farawé*, 70.
111 Ibid.
112 Ibid.
113 Ibid.
114 Ibid.
115 Ibid.
116 Ibid., 71.

> The works of the artists in this exhibition who are brought together are an example of the imagery that originates from the melting pot of modern society. A melting pot that emerged from the blending of races and cultures [...]. In this way, through their work, they speak a visual "Esperanto." The emotions of the modern human are visualized in a universal imagery, detached from cultural-historical backgrounds and other limitations. A panorama of artists in the Netherlands united through the universal theme of Shadow, Light, Form.[117]

Van den Berg notes that the artists in these exhibitions did not belong to the invisible center of power dominated by the mythical norm of white men of a certain class, religious background, and financial status, and that the process of exclusion was in many ways comparable to that of their colleagues in the United States.[118] Whereas most of these artists, in line with Stuart Hall's "last colonials," called themselves "universal artists,"[119] Dutch art critique struggled with the work they produced, as the imagery was unfamiliar. Even though these artists saw modern art and their quest for a universal language as "intrinsic to a modern consciousness,"[120] it is safe to say that the Modernism emerging from these artists was not understood because it failed to be recognized as such.

The artists exhibited by Cosmic Illusion were dealing with Modernism rather than with a vague Dutch Afro "life-feeling," but the seeming "innate incomprehensibility" of their work made that impossible. Van den Berg speaks of the newly emerging variety of exhibiting allochthonous artists, which seemed to come from a sense of "Dutch (autochthonous) amicability. In these exhibitions it was not about detaching from the cul-

---

117 Ibid.
118 Ibid., 72.
119 Ibid., 74.
120 Stuart Hall, "Black Diaspora Artists in Britain: Three 'Moments' in Postwar History," *History Workshop Journal* 61, no. 1 (2006): 5.

tural-historical backgrounds but about cultivating them [as different]."[121]

Faber recounts that there was a "wave of activities that started half-way into the 1980s and ebbed away halfway into the 1990s,"[122] which were developed to "discover, present and integrate"[123] the "allochthonous artist as they were called in those days."[124] One of the instigators of this process of "discovery" was Els van der Plas. She had studied art history in Utrecht, founded the Gate Foundation in 1988, and would go on to establish the Prins Claus Fund in 1997. Van der Plas started the Gate Foundation (1988–2006) "to stimulate intercultural exchange in the area of modern and contemporary art."[125] This organization was initially interested in promoting "Japanese and Asian artists"[126] and later on developed an interest in other non-Dutch artists in the Netherlands.[127] The Gate Foundation organized exhibitions with "foreign artists living in the Netherlands"[128] such as *Het land dat in mij woont* (*The Country That Lives Inside of Me*, Museum voor Volkenkunde, Rotterdam, 1995), *Indonesian Modern Art* (Oude Kerk Amsterdam, 1993), and *Orientation* (Museum De Lakenhal, Leiden, 1996).[129] Most notable is *Het Klimaat* (*The Climate*) (Museum De Lakenhal, Leiden, 1991), which was initiated by Centrum Buitenlanders Dordrecht (Foreigners' Center Dordrecht) in collaboration with similar organizations in the province of South Holland and "which aimed to take stock of

---

121 Van den Berg, "De kunst van het weglaten," 71.

122 Faber, "25 mei 1991," 172.

123 Ibid.

124 Ibid.

125 "Els van der Plas," *Nationale Opera en Ballet,* https://www.operaballet.nl/nl/het-instituut/organisatie/directie/els-van-der-plas.

126 Faber, "25 mei 1991," 175. Note the explicit distinction between Japanese, who were considered "Western allochthonous," and the other "Asians."

127 Ibid.

128 Judith Koelemeijer, "Grachtenpand inspireert niet-westerse kunstenaars," *De Volkskrant,* September 10, 1996, https://www.volkskrant.nl/nieuws-achtergrond/grachtenpand-inspireert-niet-westerse-kunstenaars~bbc50c6d/.

129 Ibid.

the 'foreign' artists who lived and worked in the Netherlands and involved seventy artists."[130]

In a 1996 interview, Van der Plas explained that one of the reasons she started the Gate Foundation was that she wanted to show the modern art that she encountered on her travels but was not being showed in Dutch museums: "If there was talk about non-Western art, the conversation quickly turned to primitive art."[131] Moreover, back then a Thai artist from New York was considered to be more interesting than a Thai artist from Thailand.[132] She noted the fact that modern art museums continue to put up barriers to entry: "When you want to do something for or with non-Western artists, you quickly end up in the murky circuit of community centers or other institutions filled with good intentions."[133] This is shown precisely by other exhibitions in this period such as *Schakels* (*Links*) (Museum voor Volkenkunde, Rotterdam, 1988), *De stad, een wereld* (*The City, a World*) (Artoteek Zuidoost, Amsterdam, 1989–1990), and the much praised exhibition *Double Dutch* (Tilburg, 1991/ Ministry for Foreign Affairs Den Haag, 1992), which presented a high point in this overall development.[134]

Double Dutch: Transcultural Influence in the Visual Arts was initiated by the Stichting Kunst Mondiaal (Mondiaal Art Foundation) whose goal was to organize easily accessible and multidisciplinary art projects in public space such as schools, parks, and government buildings. The positive reviews of the show expressed appreciation of the idea, execution, and consultation that created a contextualization through the notion of world art that was much better than found in many museums.[135] Faber stated that the combination of "artists" with a partner

---

130 Faber, "25 mei 1991," 172.

131 Koelemeijer, "Grachtenpand inspireert niet-westerse kunstenaars."

132 Ibid.

133 Ibid.

134 Ulco Mes, "Golf van veranderingen," in *Double Dutch* (Stichting Kunst Mondiaal, 1991), 16.

135 Paul Faber, "Double Dutch: Tilburg en de rest van de wereld," *Kunstbeeld* 15, nos. 7–8 (1991): 23.

who was based in the Netherlands but came from a different culture was not based on "the geographical origin of the artists but rather their cultural baggage, curiosity, and the artistic will to cross cultural borders."[136] Out of 180 applicants the organizing committee chose nine artists based on their oeuvre and their proposals,[137] with the intention of producing an artistic experiment that could also be seen as a metaphor for social encounters in a multicultural society.[138] The couples consisted of a "Dutch artist who uses other cultures as a source of inspiration, and an artist from another cultural domain but who work in the Dutch art environment."[139] Because of the quality of the work, "one-dimensional travel impressions or a socially motivated presentation by 'allochthonous artists,' was avoided."[140]

In the *Double Dutch* catalog J. Mensink states the developments that took place in this time frame can be interpreted as "speaking with a forked tongue. A confusion of tongues that may lead to extremes, cross-pollination, or self-pollination, incomprehension or curiosity, dangerous prejudices or exciting new art."[141] Art historian Ulco Mes proposes "asking in which way mutual cultural influence becomes visible in the works made by the artists."[142] Expanding on these notions, Ad van Rosmalen introduces the idea of the *daardroom* (there-dream). He argues that the use of motives that are not so-called culturally native give the imagination an extra dimension:[143]

If one could speak about cultural influence it could be an influence that is not so easily characterized as "here and there." Both [artists] are "here" while "there" roughly plays an equal part in the daily experience. It is pointless to make

---

136 Faber, "25 mei 1991," 171.
137 Ibid.
138 Ibid.
139 Faber, "Double Dutch," 22.
140 Ibid.
141 J. Mensink, "Double Dutch," in *Double Dutch*, 8.
142 Mes, "Golf van veranderingen," 19.
143 Ad van Rosmalen, "Een wederkerige droom," in *Double Dutch*, 25.

distinctions in degrees of origin of who is more from "there" and who lives more "here." What one could say is that just the fact that the artists see each other as from "there" is of greater importance than the fact that they both maybe only have second-hand experiences located in the country of origin. The question becomes topical as to what the nature is of that "there." Possibly these artists are each other's *daardroom* [there-dream] and there is less a question of cultural influence but rather personal and reciprocal influence that is common to artists.[144]

Following the conventional systems of cultural histories and assumptions, Ulco Mes states in the *Double Dutch* catalog that "the organizations, often tacitly, assume that cultural elements, in one way or another, are visible in the artworks and that information about cultural backgrounds increases insight into the artworks."[145] Presumably there is a relation between the artist's cultural identity and style: "In all cases cultural identity is determined by geographical information: country of birth, work, and city of residence of the artist."[146]

The preface to the educational project's didactic workbook accompanying the catalog and exhibition remarks that this period makes clear that "more and more often transcultural influences in contemporary art are being recognized"[147] and that there is a lack of present-day (1991) material that can be used as guidance to deal with this "new attitude."[148] In the introductory chapter of the workbook F.J. Witteveen puts forward the culturally relativist idea that there is no difference between Western and non-Western art "because it becomes ever clearer that

---

144 Ibid., 21.

145 Mes, "Golf van veranderingen," 16.

146 Ibid.

147 Theo Andriessen and Sirano Zalman, "Voorwoord," in *Double Dutch Educatief Project: Inleiding bij het didactisch werkboek* (Stichting Kunst Mondiaal, 1991), 4.

148 Ibid.

a sort of formal iconographic globalization is taking shape."[149] He argues that terms such as "intensity" and "vehemence" in arguments about quality of the work are disastrous to developing a nuanced view.[150] He calls for a rejection of formal Greenbergian paradigms and iconology, which have the tendency to sidetrack the viewer if not applied correctly and, more importantly, when inspired by preconceived opinions about the artist's cultural background. Witteveen proposes instead abandoning regional thinking and approaching the works as art and as an "artistic achievement"[151] while avoiding terms such as "cultural identity and multicultural pluriformity."[152] All of this is an effort to prevent the emergence of what he calls an "art geography" that would be comparable to nineteenth-century ethnographic museum discourse.[153] In this way, the Dutch art scene construed an understanding of the art world through transcultural mixing of foreign and native artists

In addition to the above-mentioned exhibitions the exhibition *Zo ver het oog reikt: Trans-culturele invloeden in het werk van zes Brabantse en zes van oorsprong niet-westerse kunstenaars* (*As Far as the Eye Can See: Transcultural Influences in the Work of Six Brabantian and Six Originally Non-Western Artists*) (1988–1989) was mounted in Den Bosch. According to the exhibition catalog, it was based on the idea that "with art one can experience the richness of cultures as well. After all, people from other countries are more than just unemployment percentages. Good quality art with an ethnic tinge also gives the unemployed foreigner something to be proud of and to recognize themself in."[154] Because "problems too often obstruct the positive sides of

---

149 Frans J. Witteveen, *Double Dutch Educatief Project: Inleiding bij het didactisch werkboek* (Stichting Kunst Mondiaal, 1991), 16.

150 Ibid., 17.

151 Ibid., 27.

152 Ibid.

153 Ibid., 16.

154 J. Mensink, "Steunfunctie-instellingen en kunst," in *Zover het oog reikt: trans-culturele invloeden in het werk van zes Brabantse en zes van oorsprong niet-westerse kunstenaars* (Provincie Noord-Brabant, 1988), 4.

a multicultural society. Positive really means: getting acquainted with each other's culture."[155] This goes beyond

> the field of food, drinks, and sport [where] the inherent qualities of migrants have long been recognized. [… R]ecognizing [and acknowledging] idiosyncratic artistic qualities in the area of visual arts is still a cumbersome process. Separate exhibitions of allochthonous artists are therefore the safest way. With that, benevolence is demonstrated and the issue itself is circumvented.[156]

With this in mind, looking at Turkish, Moroccan, Yugoslav, Spanish, Greek, Surinamese, Antillean, and Aruban immigration to the Netherlands, *Zo ver het oog reikt* focused on exhibiting (originally) "non-Western professional artists together with Dutch professional visual artists."[157]

This is also the period when the first notable contemporary exhibition taking steps to curate and perceive from a Black perspective in the Netherlands was mounted: *Wit over Zwart* (*White about/over Black*), with the English subtitle *Images of Blacks in Western Popular Culture* (Tropenmuseum, Amsterdam, 1989). The exhibition was conceived by the artist, curator, film director, and founder of the intercultural multidisciplinary artist collective foundation Cosmic Illusion Productions Felix de Rooy (b. 1952) and comprised his collection of so-called Negrophilia items.[158] In the Netherlands this exhibition had more impact than *Magiciens de la Terre*, which was taking place around the same time.[159] It was an exhibition about *beeldvorming* (forming of a [mental] image) in the past two centuries based on the

---

155 Joep (Johanna) Baartmans-van den Boogaart, *Zover het oog reikt: transculturele invloeden in het werk van zes Brabantse en zes van oorsprong niet-westerse kunstenaars* (Provincie Noord-Brabant, 1988), 3.

156 H. Egbers, "Kleuren verschieten," in *Zover het oog reikt*, 34.

157 Mensink, "Steunfunctie-instellingen en kunst," 5.

158 *Theaterencyclopedie*, s.v. "Cosmic Illusion (1983–2009)," http://theaterencyclopedie.nl/wiki/Cosmic_Illusion_(1983-_2009).

159 Extensively discussed in Chapter Four.

4,000 mass-culture images that Cosmic Illusion had collected, which propagated the image of the *Blanke* (white with a capital B) superiority against Black humiliation.[160] The makers of the exhibition expressed hope for a "collective consciousness in which there is space to undo ingrained [negative] stereotypes."[161] In nine chapters the exhibition and accompanying brochure covered world images; the European self-image; slavery and the absence of images; race-science — *beeldvorming* by scientists; Africa as idealized décor; South Africa — rigid images about culture and identity; from slave to servant; Black entertainers; stereotyping and beeldvorming, including in advertising and in the world of children.

For the next generation of Dutch Afro artists it is apparent that they are assessed based on their capability of abstracting the particularities of their cultural background into a (recognizable) Western idiom. How this works is demonstrated in Dutch world art patronage, which is tightly intertwined with discovering and encouraging talented non-Western individuals. An example is Houcine Bouchiba (b. 1956) who lived in the Netherlands for twenty years, was noticed at Ateliers 63 in Haarlem and encouraged to shape his ideas, which led to his works eventually being bought by the Stedelijk Museum (2001).[162] Another example is Egyptian-born artist Achnaton Nassar (b. 1952), who studied in Egypt and at the Rijksacademie in Amsterdam and lives in the Netherlands, and who was framed as someone who sees freedom as "choosing the unknown over the known and security."[163] Nassar's background in folk culture were "riches of the most colorful kind, full of atmosphere and surprise and like a many-layered jumble also still harmonious."[164] Compared to

---

160 Jesse Bos and Hester Poppinga, *Wit over Zwart: Beelden van zwarten in de westerse populaire cultuur* (Koninklijk Instituut voor de Tropen, 1989), 4.

161 Ibid.

162 Willem van Beek, "De gelukkige familie van Houcine Bouchiba: Onder de Afrikaanse zon," *Kunstbeeld* 25, no. 3 (2001): 20.

163 Hans Sizoo, "De vrijheid van Nassar," *Kunstbeeld* 26, no. 2 (2002): 22.

164 Ibid.

this description of Egypt, the Netherlands is a young fresh culture, which also has its advantages for an artist.[165]

"Suriname is Mud": The Racialization of Afro-Dutch artists in the Noughties

As I argued before, the answer to how and where to locate the Dutch Afro artists was refracted through African American artistic discourse. This ethno-political cultural framework around Blackness is different from the Dutch situation, because, in the Dutch discussion, race does not openly play a role in artistic appreciation. Nevertheless, a key understanding in this process of influence is the way in which US and Dutch Afro-ness are aligned as racially similar and therefore comparable.

Such awareness sets up African Americans as a separate cultural nation whose artistic production is informed by and needs to be confirmed through European Americans first. Once this is done, their influence on the world stage is presented as that of ethnic and cultural difference in a multicultural society. The issue of Black identity seems central to the discussion of the work and it has to be restated that it is white American appreciation that acts as its filter. The way the filter works is by locating the way in which the artists occupy the place of Blackness in the general artistic and racial discourse of the United States.

Briefly summarizing the African American development that influenced Dutch thinking, Perrée writes that in the 1980s there was a rise in popularity of artists of color. During this development the galleries embraced artists that "acted Black," because "obviously they had to fit into the politically correct trend" of the time.[166] He argues that "[m]ulticultural art threatened to be absorbed by the *blanke* [white] Walhalla,"[167] and it was a "sophisticated variety of the old master–slave relation."[168]

---

165 Ibid.
166 Rob Perrée, "Nieuwe stroming in de Afrikaans-Amerikaanse kunst: Vertegenwoordigers van Post-Black," *Kunstbeeld* 25, no. 11 (2001): 16.
167 Ibid.
168 Ibid.

The ideas about the quality and white American appreciation filter are echoed by the African American artist Martin Puryear in the catalog for the exhibition *Black USA*, held at the Overholland museum. He states that the consciousness about his Blackness appears to stand in the way of critiquing the work on its own merits: "Black artists are still not accepted in a matter-of-fact way. [...] But once you get some attention, it's the reverse. Then you're more special, because you're Black."[169]

But while doing so, it was essential for both artist and critic to circumvent the quality argument. In the Dutch context, this was accomplished by framing African American art developments as being under European and Dutch influence, as is proposed with regard to Romare Bearden in the *Black USA* catalog. He is portrayed as an artist who was inspired by his European avant-garde contemporaries and the Dutch painting masters of the Golden Age. Concerning the role of art, he and other artists asked the question: "what role should be fulfilled by a Black artist in this day and age?"[170] According to the text, the answer to this question is that the creation of art is a necessity for survival in an environment of segregation, humiliation, and lack of food.[171] Simultaneously, it offers an investigation into the dominance of white culture over Black hidden histories. Therefore, inserting Blackness into white visual narratives interrogates the role of Black people in society and the relationship between Black and white.[172] The text continues by saying that thinking about "the social position of Black artists in the United States, it is a way of applying medicine to race and racism in the USA."[173] With this narrative, the whole discussion on race and its consequences is safely placed within the context of the USA while appreciation of the artists is secured through well-intended sympathy for their struggle. Because the Dutch do not

---

169 Beek, *Black USA*, 79.
170 Ibid., 27.
171 Ibid., 55.
172 Ibid., 47.
173 Ibid., 61.

"do race" and policy is geared toward welfare, the narrative of Dutch Afro racial or ethnic plight cannot be maintained in the local art environment.

Focusing on an artist's training is another way of circumventing the quality argument that emerges from the *Black USA* catalog. When sculptor Puryear speaks about his global training and the origins of his knowledge, the Dutch difference in terms of cultural appreciation for other cultures becomes even more apparent. In the English text about his global education Puryear says that, during his time in Sierra Leone, "He became fascinated by the craftsmanship and feeling for materials possessed by the local woodworkers."[174] The Dutch text adds the relative clause *die met primitief gereedschap gebruiksvoorwerpen maakten* (who produced utensils with primitive tools).[175] This is contrasted to his time in Sweden where he learned the "subtleties of cabinet making."[176] In Sierra Leone people put "things together in a way that is not as neat as when white people do it."[177] This exemplifies that, even when being from a different cultural background, it is possible to master the Western art idiom when trained in the Western (Dutch) system.

According to Perrée, by the end of the 1990s, many American artists no longer wanted to be shown in the kind of "Black History Month"-type exhibitions and demanded a more equal treatment from the galleries.[178] He insists that, effectively, a new generation that had the same education as their white counterparts knocked on the doors and "undoubtedly took advantage of the emancipatory prep work of their older colleagues."[179] They continually considered new terms. Perrée finds Thelma Golden's (and Glen Ligon's) "post-Black" to be the most notable of all these terms.[180] This term backgrounds Blackness with-

---

174 Ibid., 73.
175 Ibid., 72.
176 Ibid., 73.
177 Ibid., 95.
178 Perrée, "Nieuwe stroming in de Afrikaans-Amerikaanse kunst," 16–17.
179 Ibid., 19.
180 Ibid., 16.

out suggesting "that the previous generation is dated and the problematic of racism belongs to the past."[181] According to Perrée, post-Black is "more often than not a crude generalization, a stigmatizing disguised form of paternalism" in the hands of curators,[182] because the term can be used to mitigate the effects of racism on the artists and their practice. In the Netherlands this meant that, taking a cue from the Americans, works that explicitly dealt with Dutch Afro-ness as an identity question could be relegated to the sidelines through a version of the quality argument construed through the concept of post-Black.

In the Netherlands we encounter the idea that, on the one hand, art is art and its rules are equal for everybody, such that there should be no need to separate a group, while, on the other, artistic and qualitative relevance comes from the ability of the work to participate in the existing discourse and not from the ethnic background of the maker. With this in mind, ideas about the validity of African American and Dutch Afro cultural backgrounds in art are conflated. The difference between the two seemingly similar (because Afro) backgrounds is based on their respective trajectories and ultimately on who decides what is relevant and in what context. African American relevance was established in the United States through literary, musical, and visual Modernism and therefore has authority (in the Netherlands). As a consequence, African American culture is perceived as distinct from Euro-American culture and in fact approached as non-Western artistic expression. This argument is supported by the observation of curator, museum director, and art historian Simon Levie that, irrespective of cultural background and geographic location, non-Western artistic expressions and ancient art traditions presented as contemporary art exist as Art and only become *museum-fähig* (museum-worthy) when they are on a carrier approved by the West and can be judged by Western standards, such as "composition, use of

---

181 Ibid., 19.
182 Ibid.

color, painting technique [...] and not in the first place what the image means."[183]

With their critique of contemporary African American (non-Western) artistic expression, New York art criticism is set up as paramount in articulating the difference in cultural background and methods of expression in the arts. This dominance is underlined by the fact that, according to Perrée, even though

> Paris has been it for decades, Cologne made a failed attempt in the 1980s to become it, London has the artistic potential and is getting the infrastructure to possibly become it, Berlin thinks it can be realized from behind the drawing board, but New York has been it for fifty years already: the capital of contemporary art.[184]

US criticism is part of an environment that makes engagement inevitable, which is expressed through a diversity of methods and has the potential to somewhat adjust what Perrée calls Dutch "naïve ideas about minority culture."[185] In the Netherlands, the Dutch are in control of deciding whether or not other narratives are relevant to the local art discourse. Considering the initial cultural policies of integrating with preservation of the native culture that developed into an understanding of assimilation in the guise of integration, appreciation of artistic expression that does not pass the cultural standard in the Netherlands was out of reach for Dutch Afro artists. This is exemplified by a personal interview about a month before the opening of the exhibition *Twintig Jaar Beeldende Kunst in Suriname, 1975–1995* (*Twenty Years of Visual Arts in Suriname, 1975–1995*) (1996), curated by Paul Faber and Chandra van Binnendijk, when then director of the Stedelijk Museum Amsterdam, Rudi Fuchs, remarked:

---

183 Simon Levie, quoted in Welling, "Het Aboriginal Art Museum," 23.
184 Rob Perrée, "Een trip door de hoofdstad van de hedendaagse kunst: New York, A Nuthouse," *Kunstbeeld* 24, nos. 7–8 (2000): 56.
185 Rob Perrée, "Brooklyn Museum toont Hip-Hop Nation: Kunst van de straat," *Kunstbeeld* 24, no. 11 (2000): 28.

I am putting together an exhibition of Surinamese artists. It does not include a single really good one, but I find it an intriguing phenomenon. Suriname is mud, a tropical kind of Zeeland.[186] What will be shown in the Stedelijk later on is a sluggish stuck-in-the-mud variety of Dutch painting. I have respect for that struggle: I admire the courage it takes. *Dat mag gezien worden* [It deserves to be seen].[187]

In Fuchs's comment we can see the widely accepted Dutch colonial superiority at work with regard to a former colony. What is reiterated in this comment is the premise of cultural inferiority while maintaining the possibility of rising to the Dutch (visual) cultural standard, in line with the ideas about art coming from the African continent. At the same time, entangled in the double bind of local authenticity and Dutch artistic doctrines, there is a hint of the leeway given to art coming from Latin America, as Suriname's acknowledged cultural life was modeled by white patrons, comparable to the situation in Haiti. In Fuchs's remark the works are appreciated for their "exotic" variety albeit without contextualization through the Dutch colonial project or recognition as an idiosyncratic artistic development. Fuchs's remark started living a life of its own and cast him and the exhibition in an unfavorable light. As a critic of Fuchs noted, if Suriname was an "intriguing phenomenon" it had to do with the history of the Dutch (colonial) cultural policy in the Netherlands. Even though the anthropologists Richard Price and Sally Price "spent a few years in Suriname and produced a book and an exhibition *Afro-American Arts of the Suriname Rain Forest* (1980) [...]. This exhibition was offered to the Netherlands twice but was turned

---

186 Zeeland is a province of the Netherlands.

187 Frénk van der Linden, "Museumdirecteur Fuchs: 'Het ergste van vreemdgaan is de ontrouw aan jezelf,'" *NRC Handelsblad,* November 2, 1996, http://www.nrc.nl/handelsblad/1996/11/02/museumdirecteur-rudi-fuchs-het-ergste-van-vreemdgaan-7330346. The final sentence in Dutch has a clearly patronizing tinge to it.

down."[188] The exhibition looked at Suriname's Maroon art and recognized it as an idiosyncratic visual form of abstraction coming from people of African descent.

What this means is that Dutch cultural "common sense" and policy changes that influenced exhibitions also changed expected outcomes and artists' reaction to them. The Dutch Afro artistic presence must be understood in tandem with and in relation to how African and diaspora artists were being perceived at that time. Contemporary Dutch Afro artists, just like the African Americans in the United States and the Black British, were caught between being considered as belonging to a different culture from the West and their mastery of the Western idiom — in other words, how encultured they were.[189]

The difference between how local artists with a migrant background and foreign non-Western artists were treated and perceived prompted elements in the *Pantser of ruggengraat: Cultuurnota 1997–2000* (*Armor or Backbone: Cultural Policy Paper 1997–2000*) by the Ministry of Education, Culture, and Science under deputy minister Aad Nuis (r. 1994–1998).[190] The policy paper spoke about correcting the lack of attention given to art from other parts of the world, coining the idea of "diversity art." This move proved to be the catalyst that would change the artistic output emerging from the Dutch Afro condition, how it was discussed, and how its second generation of artists was curated.

---

188 Lucien Lafour, "Fuchs (1)," *NRC Handelsblad,* November 9, 1996, http://www.nrc.nl/handelsblad/1996/11/09/fuchs-1-7331354.

189 A shining example of the 1990s is Avery Preesman (b. 1968), who was brought up (second generation) in the Netherlands and for whom the "formal aspects are subordinate. His canvasses are more than abstract expressions of emotions, they are contained emotions, emotions that are visible, without showing themselves." Rob Perrée, "Emoties die schuilgaan," *Kunstbeeld* 25, no. 3 (2001): 13. The artist is looking for the "hardest option," which is described as "the space" on the canvas. He "absorbs the environment, turns the environment into the self, without making explicit what this environment is exactly" (12).

190 Aad Nuis, *Pantser of ruggengraat: Cultuurnota 1997–2000* (Ministerie van Onderwijs, Cultuur en Wetenschap, 1997), http://catalogus.boekman.nl/pub/96-550A.pdf.

The 1999 government policy paper *Cultuur door confrontatie* (*Culture through Confrontation*) introduced by the new deputy minister Rick van der Ploeg (r. 1998–2002) explicitly introduced the term "allochthonous" in relation to artists,[191] based on the patronizing idea of distinguishing (and separating) non-white artists as a group that needed additional support, arguing for the integration of artists with a migrant background into the existing art funding system. In doing so, it framed the second generation of non-Western artists, which had been brought up in the Dutch system and were working within the Western idiom, as allochthonous.

Toward the end of his tenure in 2000, this policy became increasingly criticized for leaning toward welfare policies before 1987. Artist Gillion Grantsaan (b. 1968) declared: "So what? In the beginning they did nothing at all. Maybe this will support Black people."[192] However, rather than focusing on including artists, Sandra Jongenelen argued that it caused cultural institutions to compulsively seek out allochthonous audiences.[193] Eltje Bos commented that "realizing the intent to promote intercultural expressions through regular facilities"[194] didn't work out well. "The cause of this is that the deputy minister did not take measures to ensure that this intention could be realized. In the execution this leads to the decision to end the specific policies and to establish a separate arrangement circumventing the official circuit."[195] She added that " the specific policy impedes the realization of its own objectives."[196]

At the same time, Van der Ploeg's policy failed to account for strategies of an artist such as Remy Jungerman (b. 1959) who rose to prominence because of his identification as Surinamese,

---

191 Rick van der Ploeg, *Cultuur als confrontatie* (Ministerie van Onderwijs, Cultuur en Wetenschap, 1999).

192 Sandra Jongenelen, "Kunstenaars tussen twee culturen," *Kunstbeeld* 24, nos. 7–8, (2000): 14.

193 Ibid.

194 Bos, "Beleid voor cultuur en migranten," 72.

195 Ibid.

196 Ibid.

creating installations that deviated from what was known from Surinamese artists up until that time. But when he, in response to being otherized, started making works in an international formal language in an effort to culturally pass as Dutch, he was no longer recognizable as a Surinamese. He says: "'The images I was producing at that time were almost a reaction to be understood. It's like — I can also create an image that you can comprehend. An image that you literally understand. An image about current affairs."[197]

This strategy worked well outside of the Netherlands but did not change his position inside the country as much. Jungerman's newly found culturally passing position confused curators who were grappling with the new environment of world art and the state policies. As a result, invitations to participate in exhibitions stopped arriving. The underlying contradictory rationale was that the Afro artists were good *because* of the preferential treatment they received from the state. But as a consequence, the quality of the work itself was put in question. While Jungerman's work no longer fit the mold of difference, he was still from elsewhere — the former colonies.

> People forgot that you were already acquired by the Stedelijk Museum and had quite a few exhibitions to your name [...]. However, in their experience you were acquired because you were allochthonous.[198]

> We were stunned because we were already in the picture. We were already taking part in Europe and had exhibitions in the Stedelijk Museum and suddenly you noticed that all of a sudden you had nothing left.[199]

---

197 Interview with Remy Jungerman in his studio, Amsterdam, March 15, 2016.
198 Ibid.
199 Ibid.

Although this Van der Ploeg's policy and terminological shift were geared toward advancing the position of "allochthonous" artists, it thus had an adverse effect on those who were already participating in the general art scene. They now found themselves in a racialized position, which rendered their work secondary to their ethnicity. Even though previously their ethnicity had played a role in regard to what was expected of them as artists, this new framing became an additional obstacle, causing visual language that had been successful up to that point to become scrutinized. References to personal cultural background now suddenly became suspect as levers to gain public financial support, raising the suspicion that the artist just wasn't good enough to participate in the general art discourse. Conversely, once Jungerman returned to using his Surinamese background in his work, he regained attention within the Dutch niche of "diverse" art.

The shift in government policy thus forced Jungerman and his colleagues into a position where they had to fight the (stereo)type created by affirmative action, leading them to second-guess their own work. Jungerman concluded that although they had arrived, having developed a personal visual language, the referentiality of that visual language prevented their connection to the broader art world or that at least that connection had been severed through the new policy. At the same time, due to their increased separation, the broader art world in the Netherlands did not understand aspects of their visual language as a personal contribution but rather as a different language altogether that they did not understand and did not sufficiently investigate and invest in. As a result, a new visual language had to be construed that was in sync with US-centric discourse in order for Dutch Afro artistic production to rearticulate itself and place it within the newly shaped context of allochthonous diaspora. Jungerman concludes that the ethnically based stage that was offered after this policy change was nevertheless too small.

Whether (local) non-Western Dutch artists fit into or by exception master the Western artistic idiom or not, their positioning on the Dutch stage is strongly determined by the quality argument. Art critic Sebastian Lopez observed this inequality as the phenomenon of "cultural, social, and intellectual discrimination, which for the migrant, in finding a new homeland and also when making autonomous art, can hinder and even lead to a new flight, this time as far away as possible from patronizing Europe."[200] Consequently, Dutch Afro artists' awareness of the role that their skin color plays with regard to their position on the Dutch art stage results in a critical stance:

> The Netherlands is a racist or Eurocentric country. The European culture is everything to them, the rest is less. The Dutch are also bad at imagining through the other. I am not saying this out of rancor, but Dutch society has given me nothing that shows that I belong.[201]

Artist, writer, and curator Michael Tedja (b. 1971) argues that, apart from handling changing cultural policies, dealing with the quality argument means understanding that "the consciousness of a young Black artist in Europe cannot be compared to that of others."[202] They "cannot afford the luxury of producing images that have minimal or no history,"[203] as these young artists try to create a space from which to operate. For Tedja this space of operation emerges when literally placing the drawing behind the painted image. He calls this the narrow escape.[204]

Tedja's colleague and friend artist Gillion Grantsaan (b. 1968) "tries to develop a self-acquired art form, next to the ruling art, that can be judged on its own merits."[205] He looks

> at the gaps in art history that may lead to new cross-cutting relationships. As Martin Kippenberger has said, "Only real

---

200 "Vanwaar je dacht te vertrekken sta je geplant," 35.

201 Gillion Grantsaan, cited in Jongenelen, "Kunstenaars tussen twee culturen," 13.

202 Michael Tedja, "Narrow Escape," *Kunstbeeld* 26, nos. 7–8 (2002): 12.

203 Ibid.

204 Ibid., 10.

205 Ibid., 12.

negroes know insult." Jeff Koons says: "Exploit the masses." Gerhard Richter says: "Politics is impotent." And Basquiat said: "I use a lot of colors, not only black!" You could say that all my work is already there, but its independence is not yet visible. "Light only penetrates the darkness that's already there, I am already there."[206]

Grantsaan speaks about how his engagement changed over the years. Starting with issues around consumption in the 1980s, he progressed to "nullifying our invisibility, to a place in history that I am here. I wanted to portray that, also for others. If you do that, you are legitimized and become more than a side-table."[207] What these artists show is that they are well versed in the Western idiom and theory and are grappling with the position they are maneuvered into because of their ethnicity, in other words, being made allochthonous.

To exemplify how the quality argument functions with regard to an artist of migrant background but who is not considered allochthonous, we may look at the positioning of Fiona Tan (b. 1966).[208] Born in Indonesia from a Chinese father and a Scottish mother, Tan's practice is not discussed in terms of heritage.[209] In contrast to the artists discussed above, she is granted personal autonomy that is not connected to her background. Saskia Monshouwer, who reviewed her work, writes:

She asks questions in her work, that is her perspective. Because in the form of a question it is possible to merge ratio and emotion. It is a form in which analysis and experience

---

206 Ibid.

207 Jongenelen, "Kunstenaars tussen twee culturen," 16.

208 I am not arguing here that she does not face the same or similar intellectual and ethnic dilemmas, but rather how her work is discussed in Dutch art discourse.

209 Saskia Monshouwer, "Een kinderdroom: Tijdloze beelden en existentiële inzichten," *Kunstbeeld* 24, no. 9 (2000): 16–17.

are woven into one another. It leads to timeless images and existential insights.[210]

With this kinds of interpretation, which only hint at her background, Tan is granted the allure of the artist without the explicitly racialized mechanisms.

Even though some, such as Dutch newspaper opinionist of Surinamese descent Anil Ramdas, opine that "Allochthonous artists are more easily celebrated for their heritage than for their talent,"[211] Grantsaan, who, considering the negative comments of visitors, experiences his non-Dutchness as a handicap, fails to agree. He says he did not experience affirmative action even in the academy.[212] The same appears to hold for artist Iris Kensmil (b. 1970): "Never have I noticed any of this. Not even during openings. In those cases, it is always about the quality of my work. That is what is being talked about."[213] Saskia Monshouwer notes that in the first encounter with Kensmil's work she did not know quite what to make of it. She wonders whether the words she read were a political statement: "Is it about text or painting?"[214] When she sees more of the works together she realizes that the works "are making a promise. They are radical" and a relation to previous works can be made.[215] Kensmil deliberately plays with letters as painterly forms and seduces the viewer to extract meaning from them. Monshouwer concludes that we also "dispense meaning to a painting which goes beyond iconography and the way we understand the meaning of a painting is undoubtedly structured differently from the way we understand language."[216]

---

210 Ibid., 17.

211 Jongenelen, "Kunstenaars tussen twee culturen," 13. Notably, the article describes Ramdas as a "Surinamese newspaper opinionist."

212 Ibid.

213 Ibid. Please note that Grantsaan is dark-skinned while Kensmil is light-skinned. Colorism may have an influence on perception.

214 Saskia Monshouwer, "Iris Kensmil," *Kunstbeeld* 25, no. 11 (2001): 44.

215 Ibid., 45.

216 Ibid.

The curatorial decisions and strategies in Dutch museums are tied up with state cultural policies and how art from other parts of the world is appreciated. Integrating foreign non-Western art proved to be a lengthy process, because the space that was given to non-Western art in contemporary art museums around 1998 was limited. The incidental acquisitions were mostly of artists who were recognized on the international art market and these acquisitions seemed to be of a fashionable nature. Developments "elsewhere" were the territory of ethnographic museums and, as Welling stated in 1998, it

> testifies to the one-sided focus on Europe and (North) America. In a multicultural world this [attitude] is no longer of this time, but it also bears witness to the arrogant denial of the high artistic level of much non-Western art.[217]

> The ethnographic museums are doing their best, from time to time, to exhibit contemporary art, as far as their limited budget allows.[218]

Underscoring the diversity, internationalism, and world art influence on the Dutch art environment and what this meant for Dutch Afro artists, Jungerman called the Dutch pavilion at the 2003 Venice Biennial into question. Rein Wolfs, at that time the head of presentations at the Rotterdam museum Boymans van Beuningen, was its curator. The Dutch contribution to the Venice Biennial with the title *We Are the World* included the artists Carlos Amorales (b. 1970), Alicia Framis (b. 1967), Meschac Gaba (b. 1961), Jeanne van Heeswijk (b. 1965), and Erik van Lieshout (b. 1968). Jungerman stated: "The image is so politically correct," reflecting how "colourful, mixed and good Dutch society is."[219] Had they given space to one or two artists, the statement would have been "Look, the Netherlands can also

---

217 Welling, "De vitale traditie van Benin," 49.
218 Ibid.
219 Ibid., 61.

be represented by an African-born Black man [Meschac Gaba], a Mexican [Carlos Amorales] or whatever. This is acceptance in its full glory. The Netherlands has a strong group mentality which levels out everything."[220] The interviewer asked whether there might come a policy that declares that you can no longer receive government support because you are no longer a foreigner. Jungerman replied that this question reached the core of the problem:

> Foreigner, native, what does that mean? The development has already taken place, "We are here to stay." This is what the policy has been aiming to do for centuries. There is no way back. I think that the insight has to develop in the Netherlands that you participate if you are good, whether you are a foreigner or not.[221]

I agree with Jungerman's critique, as the contribution to the 2003 Venice Biennale was an example of Dutch internationalism combined with a compliance with a world art logic that shunned the local non-Western artists dealing with the same issues. Because the latter are subjected to the logic of the Dutch quality argument, which implies a denial of the plight of the Dutch Afro condition while being subject to the double-bind of local authenticity and fitting into Western artistic doctrines, questions in the world art debate around the location of the art and the artists are reiterated in the local Dutch context. Effectively, asking whether non-Western art can be located as native to the global art world is like asking whether Dutch Afro artists can be located as native to the Dutch art world.

> Would they think my work is better because I have a foreign background? It is more likely to have a negative effect. You see them thinking: "This smells like ethno" or "oh no, … it is multicultural. A little bit exhausting …" "Are you still work-

---

220 Ibid.
221 Ibid.

ing on that?" or "You should be over it by now" or smoothed over "You can't hear you are from Suriname at all."[222]

Visibility on One's Own Terms

One way of escaping this predicament is by altering the scale of operation and establishing visibility on one's own terms through international connections. Our discussion of articles, reviews, and interviews from Dutch art magazine *Kunstbeeld* shows that, from the exotic to the postcolonial label, the indication of an idiosyncratic visual language in the arts is not equally distributed among the different areas in the world. Different regions are appreciated differently and Dutch discourse dealing with art emerging from the former colonies makes a distinction between Indonesian art and art from Suriname and the Dutch Antilles. In the Netherlands itself, the lack of a coalesced Dutch Afro identity has prompted policymakers, curators, and critics looking for examples of how to deal with and relate to this new subjectivity in other diaspora places. As a consequence, contemporary Dutch Afro artists deal with the inheritance of a local art world that moved from a transcultural understanding of their practices (1980s) to one where diversity (1996) became the key word and they were rendered allochthonous (1997). Despite the Dutch culture and education that coconstituted their (artistic) subjectivity, the cultural background of the second generation (born c. 1970 and later) came to be understood as distinctively different. In other words, their artistic output was perceived as, and placed in, a different cultural area, located within non-Western artistic expressions. This last phase occurred in an environment where, on the international stage, ethnicity no longer was a driving concept. While they were at the beginning of trying to grapple with their ethnic background, which was made explicit through state policy, they were at the same time

---

222 Gillion Grantsaan, cited in Jongenelen, "Kunstenaars tussen twee culturen," 13.

in a straight "competition" with artists operating in the area of world art whose works were described as *eigen-aardig.*

The critical combination of being rooted in the immigration wave that started in the late 1960s while growing up to coincide with the contemporary period of the emergence of world art constitutes the Dutch Afro artistic problem space of the late twentieth century. In this space several forms of curatorial and critical knowledge as to how to deal with the diaspora come together in considering political, artistic, and curatorial questions from a majority group perspective.

The problem with this international orientation (which leads to cultural policy) was that it failed to work, because of the basic Dutch premise of gradual cultural assimilation in the guise of integration. Here internationalism failed to not land, as it couldn't be applied to a group that was set up to integrate while keeping its own culture through *welzijnswerk* (welfare work). The system assumed that artists were not getting into the arts system because they were not taking the *welzijnswerk* route that had been set up. In other words, though integration was happening it was effectively being halted by cultural policies intended to support assimilation processes. Effectively, non-Western foreign artists were being instrumentalized by the system as an ideological tool to produce a particular international-looking discourse.

Dutch Afro artists continue to struggle to formulate a reply to this development that, in the words of Alain Locke's *Enter the New Negro* (1925), would "'smash' all of the racial, social, and psychological impediments"[223] that construe them as different. It is in an effort to move away from the implicitly racialized space that is reserved for them through state cultural policies and to imagine a different horizon for the future. One way of escaping this predicament is by altering the scale of operation and establishing visibility on one's own terms through international connections. Alternatively, local curators can formulate a political

---

223 Richard J. Powell, "Re/Birth of a Nation." In *Rhapsodies in Black: Art of the Harlem Renaissance,* exh. cat. (University of California Press, 1997), 18.

position with a broader range within the Dutch environment. The opportunity was seized when consecutive cultural policies led to a well-funded, defining moment, when the Mondriaan Fund initiated the *Intendant Culturele Diversiteit* (*Cultural Diversity Administrator*) in 2006, a Development Prize for Cultural Diversity that produced the two distinctive curatorial projects: *Be(com)ing Dutch* by the Van Abbemuseum discussed in Chapter Three and the *Wakaman* project by Dutch Afro artists discussed in Chapter Four.

3

Be(com)ing Dutch: Between Institutional Desire and Exclusion

Museum Time: Looking for a New Language

In 2005, the launch of the Stimuleringsprijs voor Culturele Diversiteit (Development prize for Cultural Diversity) for Dutch contemporary art museums marks a defining moment in the cultural politics of the Netherlands. Taking an example from art events such as *Africa Remix* (London, 2005) and *Short Century* (Berlin, 2001), where "diversity was the point of departure rather than just showing African art," the prize was created by the Mondriaan Fund and the Netherlands Foundation for Visual Arts, Design and Architecture "aiming for an increase in cultural participation of allochthonous people."[1] In this chapter I will explore this moment through the institutional lens of the Van Abbemuseum, which was the recipient of the €500,000 grant. The jury for the prize comprised Salah Hassan (Cornell

---

1   Gitta Luiten cited in Joost Ramaer, "Prijs voor culturele diversiteit musea," *De Volkskrant*, October 27, 2005, https://www.volkskrant.nl/cultuur-media/prijs-voor-culturele-diversiteit-musea~bf660f77/. In my discussion below I will focus mainly on the role of the Mondriaan Fund, being the organization that used to be oriented toward institutions.

University, USA), Rose Issa (independent curator, UK), writer Abdelkader Benali (Netherlands), and world art studies professor Kitty Zijlmans (Leiden University, Netherlands). The Van Abbemuseum won the prize for its curatorial and discursive two-year project *Be(com)ing Dutch* (2006–2008).

Their experience of this process and being an agent in and of this assignment toward "cultural diversity" in the museum offers us a way of investigating diversity along the axis of culture in the Dutch landscape. Through the exhibition archive and interviews with the director and curators, an image emerges of an institute that is grappling with an internal desire to be inclusive and the external forces that place non-Western (i.e., non-white) art outside of the existing art canon, showing that, even though hindered by their own cultural limitations, deriving from their lack of knowledge of Dutch sensibilities at that time, the director and chief curator explore the edges of what it is acceptable to speak about in the Dutch art context with the *Be(com)ing Dutch* program.

In tandem with the developments in art of the late 1980s and 1990s, the Van Abbemuseum was no stranger to the discussion around world art and its consequences for curatorial practices. Having worked at the museum in this position since 1997, Christiane Berndes, curator and head of collections, recalls that the question about how to deal with global changes while having the ambition to work globally was alive and well.[2] She notes that, with only four staff members, they wondered how they could expand the collection and produce a strategy for these issues. She also notes that these questions emerged but were not really discussed in detail before the departure of the museum's director Jan Debbaut (1988–2003), who had also been part of the *Magiciens de la Terre* advisory team. In the final years of Debbaut's tenure the museum was renovated, and the completion of the newly added space in 2003 coincided with the moment when the curatorial staff started questioning how to react to the

---

2   Christiane Berndes, interview with author, Van Abbemuseum, Eindhoven, December 8, 2016. Citations below are from this interview.

changes in the world with a collection that was rooted in Dutch art and was mainly focused on Western Europe and North America: the post-war canonical collection established by Edy de Wilde (1946–1963), which focused on classical Modernists such as Picasso. Focusing on collective and individual creativity, it was expanded during Jean Leering's tenure (1964–1973). Through the inclusion of conceptual work from the United States and German painting, Rudi Fuchs added a third layer (1975–1987), while Debbaut contributed art at the intersection of Modernism and Postmodernism and later moved toward audiovisual and process-based work.

As a result of his background as a director at the Rooseum Center for Contemporary Art in Malmö (2001–2004) and Tramway in Glasgow (1992–1997), the appointment of Charles Esche as the new director of the Van Abbemuseum in 2004 brought an international network, experience, and a clear position with regard to the future of the collection. According to Esche, his appointment had to do with the idea that the fragmented collection policy had to come to an end and that something needed to change, even though the administrators did not know quite what. Berndes observes that, with his appointment, Esche brought the museum to the center of the larger discussions.

Interviewing Charles Esche ten years after the *Be(com)ing Dutch* programme in 2016, I wanted to understand the motivation behind the project and asked him about his personal history with regard to "becoming Dutch." Esche grew up as a migrant in the mid-1960s, coming from a German family born in England, and later moving to Scotland as an adult. He frames his drive around *Be(com)ing Dutch* in terms of a European identity, as someone for whom the "question of identity, of who you were and what you were allowed to be, was very much part of his daily experience where you had this experience of not being English."[3] He describes how, in his experience, "the hatred of

---

3 Charles Esche, interview with the author, Van Abbemuseum, Eindhoven, November 21, 2016. Citations below are from this interview.

Germany was still quite common in England. So, you had a certain question about who you were and how you would identify with the place that you were living in, and have a certain distance from it." As a result of this background, the idea of how to build an (imagined) community such as the nation as a form of collective became a strong influence on his thinking. This also informed his own way of belonging to such a community and became part of his personal approach. This is exemplified in his decision to become and self-identify as Scottish, even though that identification has its own problematics.

Secondly, and in the same line, Esche was informed by the Swedish project he had worked on, called *In 2052 Malmö Will No Longer Be Swedish* (2002). This project explored whether the country's second largest city had a reason to exist independently of its relation to the capital. In his words, the question thus became "what if Malmö in the future no longer identified with Stockholm and with Swedish-ness but created some kind of alternative identity maybe in relation to Denmark?" Esche describes how "in *Be(com)ing Dutch* it was this idea of this construction of a European identity. How does that match with these national identities, which are sort of leftovers but are still incredibly important?" Discussing the fact that education is controlled by the nation state, he argues that it is hard to imagine a community of Europe if Dutchness continues to be imposed by the state and reiterated through right-wing politicians such as Rita Verdonk, Pim Fortuyn, and Geert Wilders. With this history it was obvious to Esche that the Van Abbemuseum should apply for the Stimuleringsprijs voor Culturele Diversiteit.

Through his appointment as director of the Van Abbemuseum, Esche became part of the mini-convent, an informal gathering of Dutch museum directors. In 2004, with Esche being the only foreign museum director at that time, he already knew that his colleagues thought that countries such as Morocco were no place to find art. The white middle-class cis-gendered heterosexual view embodied by these directors dictated that Jörg Immendorf and Martin Kippenberg were genuine artists, and there was antagonism toward Esche's ideas at the time. Esche was considered political, didactic, and pedantic, and he points out that his colleagues insisted that "they were into pleasure and art as beauty." When the Mondriaan Fund indicated that they wanted to invest in cultural diversity, Esche describes how "all these people stood up and said it's outrageous that the Mondriaan Fund should want to prescribe museum policy: 'And why should I want to go to Morocco because it's full of, you know, Islamic peasants or whatever?'" Charles notes that all these very reactionary attitudes suddenly got expressed and that the directors complained about the Mondriaan Fund in the media. Despite all this, Esche comments that several of the institutes that complained nevertheless applied for the prize, while some changed their position and eventually became quite supportive. For him the title *Be(com)ing Dutch* was "a personal and professional interest played out in the museum in real time."

With hindsight he thinks that what was being defended by the majority of the directors around that time "was still the old Modernist card, the square, the grid, Sol LeWitt." Esche points out that the art world as it was understood before then extended from New York, maybe Los Angeles, to Vienna and from Stockholm to Naples. Within this art world, he observes a construct that was overwhelmingly white, heterosexual, and male, with "some allowance for gay men of the right class and the right ethnicity, but that was it, that was the art world." He goes on to point out that this meant that the Van Abbemuseum, up until then, had not collected any work from, for instance, the Middle East or Turkey. Effectively, the majority of the Dutch art world was still working within the context of 1968 and the revolution against the establishment, while 1989, when walls fell and the world opened up, had already happened.

When Charles Esche came to the Netherlands and became the director of the Van Abbemuseum he also did not find a Black movement such as he had seen in the United Kingdom in the 1980s and '90s and assumed it was simply not there. He further remarks that there was a "reliance on the art world and the art world systems of reference to produce subjects for dialogue," describing how they "still relied on the Modernist idea of art having a particular place in the world." His perspective was very different:

> I was thinking about stanley brouwn at the time, thinking about why he doesn't have any pictures of himself taken. And [...] someone like [artist of Surinamese descent] Melvin Motti, who we asked to participate in [*Be(com)ing Dutch*] but didn't want to participate because he didn't want to be Black in that context or didn't want to be dealing with identity issues. [...] I think at that time we just thought OK, it is not really in Dutch society, we cannot really deal with this Black issue.

Esche remarks that "it wasn't ripe for the picking; you just had to really dig." What was missed here, the so-called blind spot, was the resistance of "Black" artists against labeling, while the curatorial team was looking for "a sort of British militant Black." Simultaneously, "successful" second-generation Dutch Afro artists were working inside of the existing art paradigms in an environment where their "difference" had only recently come into focus with the late-1990s shift in cultural policy. To conclude, what "was ripe for the picking was of course Rita Verdonk, the growing Islamophobia, and the question of identity."

At the same time, changes in cultural policy caused the closure of the Gate Foundation, which also sent the political message that that particular version of diversity politics was no longer of interest. Esche relates that "it was very double because on one hand they were funding *Be(com)ing Dutch* and on the other hand they were closing the Gate Foundation archive more or less at the same time. So there was this sort of push/pull of how you would deal with diversity." In addition to the disinterest of the mini-convent of museum directors, public letters attacking director of the Mondriaan Fund Gitta Luiten and the Van Abbemuseum for accepting the prize placed severe constrainst on expanding the idea of *Be(com)ing Dutch*. As Esche recalls, "there was no reason for this nonsense about cultural diversity to affect museums, which are autonomous."

Esche's account of that period provides us with a glimpse of the attitudes of modern and contemporary art museums toward art made by ethnic minorities in the Netherlands and world art. A strict divide between the Western axis of art and "others" was fiercely defended, and directors like Debbaut were more concerned with finding the links between these two, rather than exploring the qualities of the latter.

Esche's approach toward the museum was founded on the exploration of issues of belonging within the European environment. This included art spaces that, from a previous Dutch perspective, were not considered a constitutive part of the art world. Even though they existed, as the next chapter will show, the Dutch art world system did not wholeheartedly include obviously migrant subjects that specifically discussed the particularities of belonging in the (Dutch) visual arts. Esche and his team failed to locate these places because they were looking at "the art world systems of reference to produce subjects for dialogue." Esche comments that, in the Dutch art world of that time, this sort of cultural diversity politics did not belong in autonomous (i.e., modern and contemporary art) museums that were supposedly concerned with "art as beauty." At the same time, public cultural policy was concerned with diversity, and organizations such as Rijksmuseum voor Volkenkunde (State Museum for Ethnography) in Leiden were inviting Okwui Enwezor to conduct a symposium (2001) on non-Western contemporary art in ethnographic museums. I suggest that cultural policy and ethnographic museums were looking for language that could, in their terms, undo the quality argument in an effort to integrate minorities into the existing modern and contemporary museums as "art as beauty." The museums, conversely, had to develop a language rooted in artistic quality based on a level playing field of cultural and aesthetic appreciation.

Esche considers the supposed autonomy claimed by the Dutch modern and contemporary art museums vis-à-vis cultural policy and their reaction to it a misunderstanding: "I can't even begin to understand the mentality that we claim autonomy and meanwhile you just take money from the state." Arguably, due to the funding system in the Netherlands, a large amount of the art and institutions are a form of "state art," and in the case of the Van Abbemuseum, which functions under the supervision of the city council, the alderman of culture together with the council effectively function as the board of governors. This means that the policy of the museum directly reflects on the city council, which approves the museum's policy plan every four to five years. Esche points out that this can become tricky, as was exemplified in 2011 when the social-democratic PvdA (Labor Party), which was part of the ruling coalition in the city council and politically catered to white middle-class voters, wanted to get rid of Esche as a director. They wanted a more "populist" policy that would bring in large numbers of visitors, as had been implemented earlier successfully at the Groninger Museum. The attempt failed, but it showed the direct political influence on the museum. New city elections therefore may, but not always do, have a direct impact on the museum's direction.

When former acting head of exhibitions at the Irish Museum of Modern Art (2001–2002) and co-founder of If I Can't Dance, I Don't Want To Be Part Of Your Revolution (2005) Annie Fletcher joined the Van Abbemuseum in 2005 as chief curator, the museum still had the nature of a regional museum with a history of transnationalism that was supposed to buy international art, while paying due concern to its "national role, because everything financially is structured in relation to that."[4] Museums received earmarked state funding to acquire Dutch artists or represent the Netherlands abroad. As a municipal museum, this dictated what Fletcher calls the "local and national social contract." But with the many museums in the country, the Van Abbe could navigate its own, deviant path, as they did not have a representative function on the national level like institutions such as the Rijksmuseum or the Stedelijk Museum in Amsterdam.

---

4   Annie Fletcher, interview with the author, Van Abbemuseum, Eindhoven, October 28, 2016. Citations below are from this interview.

Nevertheless, the autonomy of all Dutch art institutions is bound to their acquisition policy. Esche explains that one of the conditions was that the work acquired is indeed *recognized as art*. The assignment of this recognition was left to the market, which implied that for the museum it was difficult to buy a work from an artist who was not represented by a gallery or — the less convincing route — acknowledged by other public institutions. It was equally difficult to buy a work that did not have an official author, or was by someone who did not self-identify as an artist. He points out that the museum could only buy objects made by humans who call themselves artists, which, as a result, also impacted collecting in the realm of cultural heritage. Esche describes how, with state regulations on what art is, the intention with the *Be(com)ing Dutch* project — "struggling with an idea of the postmodern" — was to enlarge the grid of possibilities:

I think at that time I was still struggling with an idea of the postmodern, which I was discarding but I didn't really have very much else to do [...] as a way of trying to continue the traditions of emancipation, traditions which I would see in modernity which I no longer see. I don't see anything emancipatory in modernity anymore in the way that it works. It is basically colonialism under another name. And there isn't anything emancipatory about colonialism. But at the time I would still keep those two apart. I would have kept colonialism and modernity or Modernism apart. And I would have seen Modernism as being this sort of avant-garde and communism and these things, which I still felt to be emancipatory at that moment. And so, I was trying to rescue that bit. And I suppose continue it, while discarding this part, discarding the colonial racist heritage. And I think I saw that as being possible. I would now say that's ridiculous [...] I think it was about pluralising modernity [...] I wouldn't have understood that it's necessary to put modernity in its box.

Fletcher adds that, as a result, *Be(com)ing Dutch* led to a rethinking of the museum's curatorial practices. She realized that, if they were to do a project like *Be(com)ing Dutch,* it needed to directly impact their collection policy, considering the potential role of the museum as a public space, what they were collecting, and how this connected to the public. Fletcher describes how they started to understand that all their programming would need to reconsider the infrastructure of the museum in different ways. Rather than simply traversing the museum and absorbing history, they envisioned another way of engagement. Fletcher emphasizes the tension between the *autonomous object* and the *autonomous experience* within a museum environment, the cathedral of autonomous art, where according to the prevalent morality politics had no place.

This tension is exemplified in the *Read the Masks: Tradition Is Not Given* (2008) project by artists Annette Krauss and Petra Bauer, developed as part of *Be(com)ing Dutch,* which questioned the social and political implications of the Dutch tradition of Zwarte Piet (Black Pete). Here, an art project questioning a racist Dutch cultural tradition exploded in the political sphere, with politics in turn catapulting itself into the museum on the basis of parliamentary questions asked about the work. In one of those questions, Freedom Party members of parliament asked Minister of Education, Culture, and Science Ronald Plasterk whether he was "willing to personally educate the two German ladies about our Dutch culture in order to help them overcome their adjustment issues."[5]

Fletcher observes that "there's this lag, the normal common sense of how the museum operates in terms of how it governs time, versus urgent political time that smashed into the museum." Or, in other words, how everyday time intervenes in the space of what she calls "museum time." She notes how museum time and the white cube have their own coding sys-

---

5   Tweede Kamer der Staten-Generaal, *Aanhangsel van de handelingen* 627, November 27, 2008, https://zoek.officielebekendmakingen.nl/ah-tk-20082009-627.html.

tem that differs from the black box, the cinema box, political activism, and popular culture. In these spaces, the body acts and understands itself differently. In understanding the workings of the museum and its "autonomous" role, "these big forces are at play and they're not necessarily complementary."

Dutch Deflection: On the *Be(com)ing Dutch* Project

In April 2006 the Van Abbemuseum applied for the Stimuleringsprijs Culturele Diversiteit with the title *Be(com)ing Dutch in the Age of Global Democracy.*[6] The application comprised the core questions, structure and timeframe, curatorial projects, residencies, the so-called "Eindhoven Caucus," and the *Be(com)ing Dutch* exhibition,[7] situating the museum at a point where "[a]s the question of cultural identity becomes ever more of an issue in political and cultural debate [… it] seeks to renew the mission of the museum in the light of the enormous political and economic changes since 1989."[8] The Van Abbemuseum proposed a consistent and prolonged attempt to build a diverse, geographically concentrated public that was engaged as producers, speakers, viewers, and networkers.[9] The main question concerned national identity and whether nationality was imposed by birth or was something that we can become.[10]

The application articulated the urgency of the project in relation to the fact that "our collective response is still up for grabs,"[11] aiming "to propel the agenda of multiculturalism from notions of tolerance and difference toward building a shared but agonistic democracy on the cultural level through the use of one of the few remaining public sphere institutions left to us — the

---

6   Van Abbemuseum, "The Van Abbemuseum Proposal for 'Stimuleringsprijs Culturele Diversiteit,'" April 19, 2006, Van Abbemuseum Archive, Symposia; Be(com)ing Dutch, Voorbereidingen, Algemeen, 2007, 1.

7   Ibid., 2.

8   Ibid., 3.

9   Ibid.

10 Ibid.

11 Ibid.

museum."[12] Multiculturalism in the Dutch context should be understood as integration while at the same time maintaining one's own culture. This definition matches the Dutch twentieth-century class system known as *verzuiling* (lit., "pillarization"), where groups are separated vertically in "pillars" on the basis of ideology and religion and stratified horizontally on the basis of socio-economics, with democratic elites facilitating communication across pillars and the maintenance of broad cross-pillar political coalitions. This class system produced the famous Dutch notion of tolerance, that is, mutual tolerance between the different "pillars." The Van Abbemuseum proposed to "connect the more abstract discourse to specific local phenomena" by "including the history of Dutch colonialism" as well as the presence of people with a migration background from other regions and "the indigenous Dutch communities."[13] Two years later, "Esche claimed that discursive practices would always require a kind of non-metaphysical 'leap-of-faith' — a secular belief that they will change our imaginations — and subsequently the way we look at the world and interact with other people. Furthermore, this leap of faith must be taken by artists, curators and public alike."[14]

The Van Abbemuseum identified six sets of core questions, from which I would like to highlight three:

1. How can the policy of cultural multiculturalism be redefined as one that addresses the singularity of the public — the fact that two Turkish people may have less in common with each other than any other randomly chosen inhabitant of Eindhoven with any other random chosen inhabitant of the city?[15];

---

12 Ibid., 3–4.

13 Ibid., 4.

14 John Byrne, "Be(com)ing Dutch: From Autonomy to Caucus & Back Again, International Contexts," *The Visual Artists' News Sheet* (September/October 2008): 24.

15 Van Abbemuseum, "The Van Abbemuseum Proposal for 'Stimuleringsprijs Culturele Diversiteit,'" 5.

2. What is the role and expectations of artists in a global discussion? How is the intimate encounter of a viewer and an artwork sustained and given authority? Does art speak across boundaries of space and national culture? How is it effected or made possible by historical colonial relationships or a complete sense of otherness?[16]; and
3. How can artworks and/or exhibitions function as sites of discourse, education, and the expression of alternative models of social change?[17]

While the museum acknowledged in their proposal that these questions could only be answered provisionally, they would continue to inform research in the future.[18]

The project had three phases planned between May 2006 and September 2008:

1. Research and a series of collaborations (Plug-Ins), residencies, and commissions (May 2006–March 2007);
2. The Eindhoven Caucus (January 2008–April 2008); and
3. The exhibition, including a reader (May 2008) and the book *Becoming Dutch in the Age of Global Democracy* (September 2008, not materialized).[19]

The first phase of the project further included visits to Istanbul, Diyarbakır, Izmir, Cairo, Beirut, Ramallah, Tel Aviv, Jakarta, Yogyakarta, North Africa, and Suriname "to connect to both artists and writers who may be appropriate for one or more elements of the project."[20] Among other things, the curatorial team hoped to find partners in these places that could be part of the residency program and contribute to the exhibition.[21] These visits would be followed by a three-day gathering "of curators,

---

16 Ibid.
17 Ibid.
18 Ibid.
19 Ibid., 6–7.
20 Ibid., 10.
21 Ibid., 14.

organisers, artists, and thinkers to share models, examples, and experiences" reflecting on the city, cultural identity, and agonistic democracy in the age of globalization and the museum as a public forum, called a "caucus."[22]

According to the proposal, the museum would use the caucus as a tool to navigate through the years 2009–2011 after the project was finished. At the time of writing, they were putting all their resources, including "the collection, library, and the knowledge of the workers," at the service of the project.[23] The team proposed individuals within the museum as well as partners[24] such as BAK (Maria Hlavajova), InterArt (Soheila Najand), and the Gate Foundation (Sebastian Lopez) to serve in advisory roles and take up the proposed themes in parallel.[25] Others such as philosopher Gayatri Spivak and conservator Tirdad Zolghadr, among others, were listed to be invited as advisors. Curators from Seoul, Warsaw, Almaty, and Istanbul were invited to do research and curate.[26] Between the arrival of Charles Esche and Annie Fletcher, this proposal, and its eventual implementation, the museum shifted from a collections- and object-based approach to one in which discourse and programming took a central place.

On January 26, 2007, during the opening of the three-day event *Gatherings,* Mondriaan Fund director Luiten explained the rationale behind supporting *Be(com)ing Dutch.* Each year €26 million is spent on cultural projects within and outside the Netherlands while "the subject of cultural diversity was pretty much absent from the debate in the modern art world."[27] Large institutions did not propose this subject and the Mondriaan

---

22 Ibid., 10.

23 Ibid., 8.

24 Full list of partners is available at "Introduction," *Becoming Dutch,* http://becomingdutch.com/introduction/.

25 Van Abbemuseum, "The Van Abbemuseum Proposal for 'Stimuleringsprijs Culturele Diversiteit,'" 9.

26 Ibid., 8.

27 Gitta Luiten, "Gathering," January 26, 2007, Van Abbemuseum Archive, Symposia; Be(com)ing Dutch: The Gatherings, Algemeen, 2007.

Fund wanted to make it visible on a larger scale by spending money on a single large-scale project,[28] which would get the attention of large institutions. Luiten noted the criticism that "it was too much money for a single project, but these same museums don't have any problem asking us for €2 million to buy a Rembrandt,"[29] while this particular project only represented a small part of the foundation's overall budget. Furthermore, these institutions have not "been inspired by the top intellectuals of especially Dutch emigrate [*sic*] countries. Because of this it's difficult to address issues that affect Dutch minorities. The means of expression are Western, the concerns Eastern, and the aesthetics are a mix of both."[30] She continues:

> The lack of diversity in mainstream institutions is the result of institutionalized mechanisms of exclusion[-]specific history in addition to the intellectual and ideological orientation of the institution in question. It's therefore critical to conduct a rigorous self-examination to understand the lack of diversity in one's own backyard before embarking on diversifying programs or conducting experiments on how to enhance cultural diversity. Examine the composition of the administrative curatorial staff and board and its ethnic or gender background. Examine the nature of the collection and whether it's reflective of the surrounding communities or the nation or the global art scene. Examine the ethnic or gender composition of the public. Examine the museum's acquisition policy and whether it allows for serious revision in order to reflect diversity or [...] the art and artistic orientation of its direct communities, the nation at large, or the global art scene. I would say you still have things to do.[31]

---

28 Ibid.
29 Ibid.
30 Ibid.
31 Ibid.

Luiten made it clear that the danger of large institutions engaging in cultural diversity was that museum directors would consider the prize merely a tool to increase the engagement of allochthonous people in the museum. However, "The prize is not a tool for that, the interest in public should be there anyway."[32]

When they were awarded the prize, Esche and Fletcher already knew they wanted to hold a caucus in Eindhoven and call the exhibition *Be(com)ing Dutch,* responding to their own European question of "what it was to try and take on this identity of being Dutch as a non-Dutch European," which could easily be framed in relation to the issue of diversity. Fletcher thinks that even though the public understood *Be(com)ing Dutch* as a question of diversity, following the murder of right-wing politician Pim Fortuyn in 2002 and the "first expressions of national essentialism," "diversity was part of what was on offer with globalization if we understand it in that way."

Both original archival material and interviews showed that in the *Be(com)ing Dutch* programme diversity was understood in the context of understanding European culture. Effectively, it meant "mainly Europeans from different locations." In other words, diversity and globalization were understood in "super-white terms." The program reiterated the Western art axis but expanded it to include artists who racially belonged to the same group while living in one of the world art areas. Fletcher remembers this being problematic but also being "told to shut up a lot about it, not aggressively but it was like race is not the issue."

This European cultural modality of diversity was confused with racial/allochthonous diversity. Fletcher believes that deliberate obfuscation might be at play here while Esche suggests that it was not that Blackness was not talked about, "but it wasn't framed in terms of a Dutch Afro consciousness. It was much more an Anglo or maybe an Anglo-American consciousness, directed at how it can inform what it means to build a society that is multicultural." He explains that *Be(com)ing Dutch* was construed against the norms of European modernity and not

---

32 Ibid.

from an "imperial or colonial legacy in the Netherlands." The program was looking at art from "a tradition related to conceptual art, a tradition related to a set of Modernist protocols." In other words, *Be(com)ing Dutch* operated from the previously described space where the Western art idiom decides what is valuable in the Dutch art world. Even though Esche would now describe his project as a spatial zone of colonialism, this was — paradoxically — one of the defense strategies against the backlash and the criticism.

This situation plays directly into the rules that dictate the Dutch art-for-art's-sake principle, using the strategy of trying to avoid the quality argument by expanding the axis of modern art through whiteness, allowing these issues to be highlighted while maintaining an aura of autonomy. What is also relevant is that the terms of diversity changed in the period post-9/11 (2001) and specifically after the murder of Fortuyn in 2002. The cultural focus on people of African descent and other migrant groups in the Netherlands shifted toward a religious focus, in the guise of a cultural one, on people with a Muslim background. Henceforth, Turkish and specifically Moroccan people and those from the Maghreb were culturally targeted. This shift focused on this particular "problem group" and its process of integration and assimilation into the perceived qualities of Dutchness, confirming former colonial subjects, who were mostly brought up with Christianity, as more integrated. As a result, Dutch Afro subjects found more breathing space, which would eventually support a growing Afro awareness as expressed, for example, in Quinsy Gario's art project *Zwarte Piet is racisme* (2011) in which he stated that "Black Pete," the companion of Sinterklaas (Saint Nicholas), is racist, printed the slogan on a t-shirt, and peacefully protested during the annual "arrival" of Sinterklaas early in the holiday season. Nevertheless, the *Be(com)ing Dutch* project prioritized this issue of an Islamic background in tandem with the Dutch and European nationalist developments, particularly due to the perceived absence of a Dutch tradition of Black radical visual arts.

Considering the underdeveloped Dutch internal discourse on the relation between Dutchness and visual culture, it is understandable that the Van Abbemuseum took a different route toward changing institutional policy, along the axis of gender. In the case of the *Plug-In* component, this was achieved through the inclusion of Lily van der Stokker who researched the presence of women in the collection. From this collaboration emerged the idea of starting to collect, in Fletcher's words, "some good feminist practices from the 1960s" — of women artists on a par with the "big male artists" of the 1960s and '70s. This was a way of countering eighty years of collecting that had resulted in what Berndes calls a "bleak amount of female artists" in the collection.[33] This example shows how, in the Dutch context, speaking of the issue of gender in the arts is a very accepted and valued way of showing criticality. Even though the implementation encountered its own difficulties, going through this step in the first years of the project was necessary for the museum to eventually be able to tackle the issue of race in the museum years later.

In the light of the then "current artistic and museum practices," the Van Abbemuseum reflected on its history and policies of the past through the curatorial project *The Living Archive,* which started in October 2005.[34] The project as managed by Diana Franssen, who has worked with the museum for over thirty years. She used the archive (letters, images, and artworks) and her memory of the museum's history as a critical "virus" in the museum, with the aim of using the history buried in the archive as a tool to comment on the big statements made by the museum. Franssen did this through small interventions and by showing art, letters, archives, and artworks together. This curatorial strategy was perceived as anarchist because up until then the archive had not been treated as part of the collection but

---

33 Christiane Berndes, interview with the author, Van Abbemuseum, Eindhoven, December 8, 2016. Citations below are from this interview.

34 Van Abbemuseum, "The Van Abbemuseum Proposal for 'Stimuleringsprijs Culturele Diversiteit,'" 13.

merely as a point of reference or research. According to Fletcher, Franssen argued that the artwork is simply part of the archive, which proved an exciting challenge for the rest of the curatorial team. Fletcher notes that using this assertion as a basis also meant opening up possibilities beyond the "holier-than-thou fetishization" of the artwork and abandoning the observance of a "pure relationship" to it. Berndes remarks that this approach would eventually have an effect on questions about the collection and acquisition, such as: "What is more important, the object or the context of the object? Can the object exist without the context and vice versa? The curatorial team concluded that it had to be seen as a whole. A thought they tried to disseminate." The *Living Archive* was executed by placing a crucial item such as a file, which was not supposed to be public, alongside the work, thus rendering collection part of the archive with individual artworks being provided a personal biography connected to the museum. Berndes argues that this in effect reversed the ideas of universal man, pure experience, and the contextless existence of the artwork, or, within the context of Dutch art discourse, the idea that the art is just the art.

The *Eindhoven Caucus* — "literally [...] a gathering together in order to make a decision on something" — embodied the methodology and central principle of *Be(com)ing Dutch*.[35] The supplement to the proposal, headed by a quote attributed to Irit Rogoff — "You can't have a position without a location."[36] — described it as a "visual art project [...] which consisted of debates, workshops, artists' projects and other forms of collective participation" taking place between September 2007 and March 2008.[37] The proposal described the caucus as "preoccupied with questioning the extent to which cultural

---

35 Ibid., 15.

36 Van Abbemuseum, "The Van Abbemuseum Proposal for 'Stimuleringsprijs Culturele Diversiteit,'" 15. I cannot find the original and context of this quote.

37 M. Vossen, "Toelichting Caucus Stichting Doen," August 22, 2007, Van Abbemuseum Archive, Symposia; Be(com)ing Dutch, Voorbereidingen, Algemeen, 2007.

and intellectual life can contribute to society and is based on the premise that significant art proceeds from a discursive and critical culture."[38]

The *Eindhoven Caucus* was prepared through the activities in phase one and originated in workshops developed by Esche and local partners in South Korea (2002), Indonesia (2003), and during the Cork Caucus with Annie Fletcher in Cork, Ireland (2005).[39] With regard to potential speakers, the application contained the disclaimer that "[g]iven the team's experience of working on this subject and in the areas of origin of the majority of Dutch immigrants in particular, we hope that it is reasonable to trust us as a group to make the final decisions based on the first five months of information gathering."[40] The initial proposal suggested eighteen speakers, nine of whom were based in the Netherlands with six having an immigrant background. One dealt with the relation between Indonesia and the Netherlands (Delphine Bedel) and there was one speaker of Surinamese descent (Gillion Grantsaan). The other four invitees related to Türkiye, the Maghreb, and the so-called Middle East.[41] Additional documents mentioned artists and sharing networks, including participants from Turkey, the Basque Country, Thailand, Italy, Croatia, Estonia, and Morocco.[42] The supplement to the proposal further elucidated that "[t]he specific aim of the Caucus is to position creative artistic thinkers as political thinkers — to mark the space of art as a space of political imagination and to suggest that art might be useful in suggesting future ways in which we can understand our increasingly diverse societies and to formulate a way in which we can live together better."[43] In the attached dissemination plan, the museum proposed to organize "multicultural museum nights" specifically aimed "at those people living in the Netherlands but originating from

---

38 Ibid.
39 Ibid.
40 Ibid.
41 Ibid., 16.
42 Vossen, "Toelichting Caucus Stichting Doen."
43 Ibid.

other countries such as Türkiye and Morocco."[44] While there was a focus on integrating people with a Muslim background, the plan failed to address Dutch Afro-ness.

The caucus centered the question about diversity. Fletcher states that in order to understand what diversity was, it was important to investigate what sort of subjectivities "were left in and what's left out," such as undocumented people. She further points out that they were thinking about the idea of citizenship as an "implicit social contract describing our subjectivity in the state."

The caucus intended to "use that term [caucus] in its contemporary form as well as bringing people together to enact a political representation to suggest that artists and thinkers might be political citizens and political subjects and that they perhaps could talk effectively and propose solutions for the future." Fletcher explains that, in that period, it was uncommon to suggest that an "artist was supposed to be an engaged citizen who could comment on the politics of the day." Even though this had been part and parcel of art production in the past, this connection between artist and engaged citizen had now become enmeshed in questions of race and identity in the Netherlands. The long-term goal of the caucus was "to transform the museum as a catalyst for actively rethinking our contemporary society and its agonisms and diversities."[45] One of the ways of doing so was the development of *Our Dictionary* (2008).[46] The aim of this publication was putting critical pressure on normative terms and definitions.[47]

In the initial proposal, the expected outcomes were the exhibition and the publication. The list of proposed artists emphasized the implicit Islamic relation while including no Dutch Afro

---

44 Ibid.

45 Ibid.

46 Charles Esche, Annie Fletcher, and Ivet R. Maturano, *Be(com)ing Dutch: Our Dictionary* (Van Abbemuseum, 2008).

47 M. Vossen, "Bijlage 2, Aanvraag Stichting Doen — Ref. 07uit16754," July 12, 2007, Van Abbemuseum Archive, Symposia; Be(com)ing Dutch, Voorbereidingen, Algemeen, 2007.

artists, even though the proposal put "the notion of national identity up for question while recognizing its importance to many individuals."[48] For the publication, the philosophers Giorgio Agamben, Jacques Rancière, and Gayatri Spivak were considered "to reflect on Dutch or North-West European cultural politics."[49] Curator Pablo Lafuente, author and journalist Geert Mak (the only Dutch person), and curator Irit Rogoff were considered to look at "the value of artistic production in claiming a multidimensional globalism that is not primarily driven by economic surplus."[50] In effect, the critical analysis of the Dutch situation was put into the hands of non-Dutch thinkers who lacked knowledge of the specific sensibilities at play in the Netherlands. The reliance of Esche and Fletcher on Modernist discourse prevented them from identifying the complexities of Dutch cultural diversity and limited the potential value of their project by framing it in non-Dutch cultural discursive terms. Involuntarily, and as shown earlier in Luiten's comments, the proposal continued the Dutch habit of looking for answers outside of those concerned. In doing so. they underlined not only the lack of confidence in Dutch museums to speak about diversity on its own terms but also more broadly the Dutch deflection of these conversations to a non-Dutch curatorial team.

Eventually, there were thirty-four participants in the *Eindhoven Caucus* of which nineteen hailed from a Dutch city,[51] comprising eleven white Dutch people, seven white people from Italy, Germany, the USA, Chile, Moldava, and Croatia, and one person with a Moroccan background.[52] The exhibition included thirty-eight artists of which twenty-two produced new work.

---

48 Van Abbemuseum, "The Van Abbemuseum Proposal for 'Stimuleringsprijs Culturele Diversiteit,'" 17.

49 Ibid., 18.

50 Ibid.

51 Van Abbemuseum, "Annex 2, Persbericht Stimuleringsprijs voor Culturele Diversiteit Van Abbemuseum Eindhoven & Stichting InterArt Arnhem," Van Abbemuseum Archive, Symposia; Be(com)ing Dutch: The Caucus, Persberichten, 2007.

52 Ibid.

The three guiding themes for the exhibition were "imaginary past," "imaginary present," and "imaginary future."[53]

As part of the caucus, the question concerning the meaning of being Dutch was organized in collaboration with InterArt, directed by Soheila Najand. As a person with an Iranian background, Najand wanted to speak to the entire staff, including the guards and people at the front desk, "to understand what their stakes in new cultural citizenship might be," Fletcher relates. According to the initial proposal, the aim was "to develop a contemporary grammar of communal thinking and the active production of knowledge about new forms of cultural citizenship […while providing] the valuable curatorial insight as a partner in accessing a variety of groups not traditionally involved in the museum and generating new methods of debate and artistic production."[54] InterArt's research aimed at developing "a new grammar for mutual communication and shared solidarity in society."[55] Their aim was to develop theory as a form of action parallel to research, "reflecting on already existing ideas such as democracy, identity shaping, policy and art, interculturality and (post)hybridity."[56] By suggesting *posthybridity*, InterArt shiftted the attention from this cultural identity thinking in the arts to "understanding both the artist and the context as inherently multi-layered contemporary and beyond the inevitable post-colonial discourse on hybridity into a space where they

---

53 Charles Esche and Annie Fletcher, "Welkom bij Be(com)ing Dutch," exhibition guide (Van Abbemuseum, 2008).

54 Van Abbemuseum, "The Van Abbemuseum Proposal for 'Stimuleringsprijs Culturele Diversiteit,'" 11.

55 Van Abbemuseum, "Appendix 3: Re-Imagining the Collection, The Van Abbemuseum Proposal for 'Stimuleringsprijs Culturele Diversiteit,'" April 19, 2006, Van Abbemuseum Archive, Symposia; Be(com)ing Dutch, Voorbereidingen, Algemeen, 2007, 33.

56 Ibid., 34. Joachim Blatter, *Encyclopedia Brittanica*, s.v. "Glocalization," https://www.britannica.com/topic/glocalization: "Most users of the term [glocalising] assume a two-level system (global and local), citing phenomena such as hybridization as the result of growing interconnectedness. Local spaces are shaped and local identities are created by globalized contacts as well as by local circumstances. Thus, globalization entails neither the end of geography nor declining heterogeneity."

are evident to themselves."[57] Yet apart from Soheila Najand, the list of twenty-three proposed artists did not include any visually discernible person of color.[58]

A series of internal seminars, the *Gatherings,* were intended as self-reflective moments. In the first one, three curators were invited to speak about diversity. The Van Abbemuseum also invited Professor at the School of Culture and Communication at the University of Melbourne Nikos Papastergiadis to speak about nationalism and its refusal to die. As Annie Fletcher remarks in our conversation, this was done specifically because "one of the things that people kept telling us at that moment was, why are you talking about nationalism? Why are you talking about becoming Dutch?" She points out that it was understood (also internationally) that the discussion had moved beyond that point and the idea of the nation state was considered "a joke." However, as a key national Dutch museum with a history of promoting Dutch artists in the context of European and American Modernism, one is governed on the basis of these ideas. The (non-native) directors of other Dutch institutions including Nicolaus Schafhausen of Witte de With and Marian Hlavajova of BAK organized several other meetings and talks considering the relation between subjecthood, culture, and nationalism. These directors and curators — German, Slovak, British, and Irish — who were running major cultural spaces in the Netherlands at that moment, provided additional international (curatorial) diversity.

Esche was looking at "how to educate the museum itself [...] bending it into a different shape." He says that this was done by bringing in "people who could talk from different positions" in the seminars. These people were mostly from European practices and it included looking at Nordic colonialism, British postcolonial theories, and Central and Eastern Europe. In an

---

57 Charl Landvreugd, "Notes on a Dictionary: A Polemic Approach," in *Deviant Practice: Research Programme 2016–2017,* ed. Nick Aikens (Van Abbemuseum, 2018), 219.

58 Van Abbemuseum, "Appendix 3," 34–35.

effort to think through the Dutch discourse, the project looked at other European models and discourses rather than internally reformulating it based on the contemporary condition. These gatherings were to introduce different forms of exhibition making, away from solo exhibitions by established artists toward a more political dimension. This convergence moved the conversation from a local to an international perspective that would perpetuate the lack of development of a Dutch discourse on "Blackness."

White Fragility: The Reception of *Be(com)ing Dutch*

For the duration of the project the Van Abbemuseum partnered up with magazine *De Groene Amsterdammer,* which produced a free thematic supplement to their May 2008 issue.[59] This supplement included an interview with Esche and Fletcher, in which the interviewer mentioned the strict demands of the Mondriaan Foundation that the museum submit to rigorous self-evaluation of the "diversity" of its staff, board of directors, and the collection, leading to the following question: "Does *Be(com)ing Dutch* become a test of politically correct thinking because of this?"[60] Esche responded by saying that he is not Dutch and does not understand this criticism of political correctness, as it fundamentally means being aware of the power dynamics within your context, so as to not walk around with blinders while claiming ignorance about your effect on the world.[61]

The November 2007 Van Abbemuseum press release concerning the first weekend of the caucus spoke of "thought-provoking questions and mark[ing] the successful and energetic beginning of a four-week-long debate on cultural difference and the role of

---

59 Koen Kleijn, ed., *Be(com)ing Dutch: Identiteit en nationaliteit in het Van Abbemuseum* (De Groene Amsterdammer, 2008).
60 Koen Kleijn and Stefan Kuiper, "'Musea lopen verschrikkelijk achter': Interview met Charles Esche en Annie Fletcher," in ibid., 4.
61 Ibid., 45.

art by world renowned speakers in Eindhoven."[62] Among high-lights of this first weekend is mentioned Louk Hagendoorn's comment that, "[i]f anyone offends them [the Dutch] or their country, the Dutch are quick to defend it. They do care but don't want to show it [...] the collective urge to conform is greater than people believe. This is one of the explanations of why there was such a dramatic swing of notions of tolerance and multicul-turalism in the Netherlands to a fear of the other and worry that Holland is full."[63] The press release concluded that "*Be(com)ing Dutch* applies to migrants and autochthonous Dutch equally."[64]

At the opening of the *Eindhoven Caucus,* Annie Fletcher defined the research questions that led toward the exhibition as follows: "How does increasing migration relate to the rise of nationalistic feelings, how come that religion is the dominating factor when assessing someone's identity while we have a secu-lar capitalist system, and how does autonomous art relates to socially relevant art?"[65] This line of questioning did not include the idea of race, being in line with the then prevailing focus on Islam. In a 2008 interview Fletcher stated that she had "always been very committed to openly performing research."[66] And that "in general, museums do not openly perform research; that is mainly done in universities or conferences [...]. It would be extraordinarily arrogant to just make a show about such a com-plex subject."[67] Reiterating the November 2007 press release, she stated, "[B]*ecoming* is not just intended for 'minority groups' but

---

62 Van Abbemuseum, "Press Release November 2007," Van Abbemuseum Archive, Symposia; Be(com)ing Dutch: The Caucus, Persberichten, 2007.

63 Ibid.

64 Van Abbemuseum, "Persbericht Stimuleringsprijs voor Culturele Diver-siteit Van Abbemuseum Eindhoven & Stichting InterArt Arnhem," Van Abbemuseum Archive, Symposia; Be(com)ing Dutch: The Caucus, Pers-berichten, 2007.

65 Anneke Stoffelen, "Wij kunnen juist wat meer experimenteren," *De Volks-krant,* November 8, 2007, https://www.volkskrant.nl/beeldende-kunst/-wij-kunnen-juist-wat-meer-experimenteren~a862442/.

66 Arnisa Zeqo, "Dare to Imagine: A Conversation with Annie Fletcher on the Be(com)ing Dutch Project," *Simulacrum* 16, no. 2 (2008): 7–8.

67 Ibid., 9.

for everyone — perhaps especially for those who consider them-selves 'really' Dutch."[68]

The Van Abbemuseum broadcasted its position through curators, speakers, and sometimes through the artists involved, for example through the *Imagined History* part of the *Be(com-)ing Dutch* exhibition. Fletcher specifically looked at artists like Ed van der Elsken (1925–1990) and Johan van der Keuken (1938–1990) who, being white men, were celebrated for their interna-tionalism and cosmopolitanism. In her own words, they acted "as very sophisticated and very tolerant men," fitting perfectly into the myth that defined the 1980s and '90s—right up until it all came crashing down. The seminal and still relevant essay "Het multiculturele drama" (The multicultural drama), pub-lished in 2000 by the political scientist Paul Scheffer described this "crashing down" as the "staying behind of complete genera-tions of allochthonous people and the development of an eth-nic underclass."[69] Esche comments on this "sort of image of this happy hippie community which was somehow multi-ethnic but was entirely dominated by an idea of Dutch tolerance and so its ethnicity was kind of just a decoration."

All the major Dutch newspapers pitched in with their critique. Rob Schoonen of the local *Eindhoven Dagblad* reported on the three-day symposium with "a great many artists, curators, poli-cymakers, and people from the welfare sector," asking whether the *Be(com)ing Dutch Gatherings* were not trying to reinvent the wheel in the wake of the *Actieprogramma Cultuurbereik* (*Action Program Cultural Range*) (1999–2003) of former deputy minis-ter Van der Ploeg,[70] which brought together the state, provinces, and municipalities in an effort to counteract obsolescence and promote *verkleuring* (discoloration).[71] Schoonen commented

---

68 Ibid.

69 Paul Scheffer, "Het multiculturele drama," *NRC Handelsblad*, January 29, 2000, http://retro.nrc.nl/W2/Lab/Multicultureel/scheffer.html.

70 Rob Schoonen, "Cultuur zoekt een weg in veelkleurige wereld," *Eindhovens Dagblad*, Cultuur, January 27, 2007, 9.

71 Frank Huysmans, Olivier van der Vet, and Koen van Eijck, *Het actieplan Cultuurbereik en Cultuurdeelname 1999-2003: Een empirische evaluatie op*

that "even though this plan is on a different playing field," Rotterdam has already been working with culture scouts who instigate projects with allochthonous and autochthonous residents with beautiful results for seven years: "A trip to Rotterdam can clarify a lot."[72] Schoonen further reported on a remarkable question during the event whether "that famed *inburgeringscursus* (civic integration course)" also applied to the "five hundred foreign technicians who work on the High-Tech Campus [in Eindhoven]?"[73] He further remarked that the invited artists would immerse themselves in "strange cultures" in preparation for the 2008 exhibition and that "[t]he expectation is that this art will automatically draw people from other groups than the current white middle class."[74]

Leading Dutch newspaper *NRC Handelsblad* wondered whether one should make place in a museum for work that does not meet a particular aesthetic or production standard,[75] thus shifting the quality argument from the maker to thematics. Taking into account the curatorial developments with *Plug-In* and the *Living Archive,* Esche and Fletcher responded in the same article that the museum was a place where one "should be able to have meetings where everybody walks in and out freely."[76] What they failed to take into account with this position was the invisible threshold of spaces such as the museum that prevented those deemed (lower than) working class from entering—an argument that is nowadays well understood in museology.

Trouw journalist Arend Evenhuis asked why we were still and yet again talking about identity "as though our lives depended on it."[77] He claimed that a better title for the exhibition would

---

    landelijk niveau (Sociaal Cultureel Planbureau, 2009).

72 Schoonen, "Cultuur zoekt een weg in veelkleurige wereld," 9.

73 Ibid.

74 Ibid.

75 Ibid.

76 Ibid.

77 Arend Evenhuis, "Waar waren we ook al weer gebleven," *Trouw,* May 31, 2008, https://www.trouw.nl/nieuws/waar-waren-we-ook-al-weer-gebleven~b4f84e6o/.

have been "Where were we again?"[78] *De Telegraaf* commented that the "gutsy"[79] Esche was preaching from the pulpit. *Het Parool* selected the part where Esche said "I want the museum to be a lively institution, where people talk about contemporary issues,"[80] while *De Volkskrant* quoted Esche saying that "Discussion is important," but discussion in and of itself was not enough: "Something is at stake. This is something that is often forgotten in the Dutch art world."[81] The article further noted that Esche wanted to change something and turn the museum into "an arena for 'conflicting democracy' where political issues are put forward that are not addressed anywhere else."[82] Criticizing all of this, *De Volkskrant* pointed out that "elitist and Western as it is, it is arrogant to think that a museum can make the world a better place [...]. Some modesty [is in place for a museum] concerning the enormous complexity of the social issues and it would be better if it [the museum] concentrated on what it is established for, art itself, whether or not it [art] is socially engaged,"[83] offering the familiar art-for-art's-sake argument with the quality argument hidden behind it.

Art critic Rutger Pontzen provided an analysis of the debate culture in which the caucus was situated:

Where in the 1990s half-lit discussion rooms could hardly be filled with any interest, it has become clear that after years of relative quiet the Dutch art world is not only publishing one volume after another, but also wishes to extensively debate with one another. [...] Because, well, according to the director of the Mondriaan Fund, there was too little debate.

---

78 Ibid.

79 Paola van de Velde, "Kunstenaars over Nederlandse identiteit," *De Telegraaf,* May 23, 2008, 15.

80 Charles Esche cited in Kees Keijer, "Kunst is niet aleen decoratie," *Het Parool,* May 27, 2008, 22.

81 Domeniek Ruyters, "Harteloos Nederland," *De Volkskrant,* May 29, 2008, 15.

82 Ibid., 14.

83 Ibid., 14–15.

The Netherlands did not have a discourse like abroad or an intellectual tradition before that. And if something like a debate emerged, its opinion was that "art museums don't get involved at all."[84]

He continued by saying that the big development funds want the art world to play a more "societal, multicultural role."[85] Pontzen further noted: "Did Luiten not say during the award ceremony of the *Stimuleringsprijs Culturele Diversiteit* to the Van Abbemuseum in 2006 that 'museums must adapt to the fact that the Western world is no longer white [*blank*]'?,"[86] and called her policy a "political agenda in disguise." No wonder that the foreign directors of De Appel (Ann Demeester), BAK (Maria Hlavajova), Witte de With (Nicolaus Schafhausen), and the Van Abbemuseum (Charles Esche) were the ones pushing this agenda forward![87] "These directors are internationally grounded, socially engaged, are not afraid of academic debate, and often possess a messianic missionary drive — exactly the qualities Luiten desperately misses in the Dutch museum directors."[88] Having said all that, Pontzen concluded that all these debates were marked by a high level of consensus and that they were more of a formal exercise rather than an open-ended discussion.[89]

Even before the exhibition opened, *Be(com)ing Dutch* was already located "on a theoretical high ground in the midst of a tough academic discussion."[90] Recurring in several positive reviews was the "intensity, impenetrability, and heaviness"[91] of the exhibition which needed "sympathetic consideration and

---

84 Rutger Pontzen, "Alles en iedereen in debat," *De Volkskrant*, Achtergrond, November 15, 2007, 2.

85 Ibid.

86 Ibid.

87 Ibid., 3.

88 Ibid.

89 Ibid., 2.

90 Ruyters, "Harteloos Nederland," 15.

91 Ilse van Rijn, "Be(com)ing Dutch," *Metropolis M* 29, no. 4 (2008): 86.

patience of the visitor to fathom the underlying histories which are fundamental for a better understanding of the artworks."[92] *Trouw* stated that "*Be(com)ing Dutch* can hardly be condensed into a knacked tulip in a broken wooden shoe with yonder a flying herring."[93] Simultaneously, the use of an English title for the event was criticized in a local newspaper, which remarked: "As if the Dutch language were not adequate to describe the Dutch or Dutchness."[94]

At the same time the question of whether art was supposed to *do* something, a perspective not only held by Esche, reminded Dolf Welling of, "a creepy maxim of years ago, namely that art has to be 'socially relevant.' I think art should only be good. It then automatically becomes of social importance. As soon as it is used for an extra-artistic assertion [...] the quality is less important than the propagandistic output."[95] White fragility also started playing into this, as he claimed the works to be one-sided, showing (only) the "malicious parts of our colonialism."[96] According to *Museumtijdschrift*, the series of Ed van der Elsken's photographic work from the 1950s and '60s showed "dark migrants or visitors," which immediately undermined the idea of an imaginary, pure, white Netherlands of the 1950s that was propagated by right-wing politicians.[97] *NRC Handelsblad* declared that "[v]ital and intuitively working artists such as Erik van Lieshout, Marc Bijl, and Rachid Ben Ali are missing in Eindhoven. Confirmation of old-fashioned leftwing thinking — allochthoneous people and refugees are victims of cold bureaucratic Dutch culture — seems to have been the criterion on which artists were invited. That 'leftwing' crevice not only makes many propositions uninteresting and predictable, it

---

92 Ibid.

93 Evenhuis, "Waar waren we ook al weer gebleven," 60.

94 Mieske van Eck, "Dutch," *Brabants Dagblad*, May 31, 2008, 19.

95 Dolf Welling, "Vechtlustig museum maakt drukte in Eindhoven," *Pulchri* 36, no. 4 (2008): 15.

96 Ibid.

97 Kees Keijer, "Museum in debat," *Museumtijdschrift* (July/August 2008): 27.

also hinders actual deeper perception and analysis."[98] Newspaper *Het Nederlands Dagblad* noted that the exhibition "promises a lot, but is not really exciting. It is too shrouded, too soft, too difficult, too far removed from the questions that are central. [...] There is nothing that knocks you over."[99] *De Volkskrant* concluded that "[n]uance wins from artistic adventure in a stylish presentation which is remarkably determined in its tone [...]. The chosen artists confirm one another in the currently widely prevailing general opinion, which has turned away from the traditional Dutch image as an internationally oriented country which is open to other religions and cultures."[100]

There is a significant number of articles, and together with the *Be(com)ing Dutch* exhibition archives and the interviews a picture emerges of a museum trying to deal with contemporary issues around diversity in art at the beginning of the current century. The appointment of Esche and Fletcher heralded the beginning of a new period dealing with Dutch cultural policy toward diversity in the arts. Looking at the environment in which they landed, it appears that it was precisely because they were foreign and from a different knowledge and curatorial tradition that they we able to explore the reorganization of the museum toward a more inclusive policy on all levels. But in an environment that did not support the idea of art made by artists with a migrant background as native to the Dutch environment, the radical Afro artists of that period did not appear on their radar. Consequently, their thinking about diversity along the axis of whiteness was unknowingly accepting this blind spot while conforming to the critical backlash. In effect, the art world in which the museum was located accepted European diaspora and gendered practices, while failing to view Dutch Afro artists as belonging or contributing to the established Dutch art

---

98 Lucette ter Borg, "Verkrampt door de Nederlandse identiteit," *NRC Handelsblad,* May 31, 2008, https://www.nrc.nl/nieuws/2008/05/31/ver-krampt-door-de-nederlandse-identiteit-11547744-a822169.
99 Maarten Vermeulen, "Onbegrijpelijke nationaliteit," *Nederlands Dagblad,* May 30, 2008, 6.
100 Ruyters, "Harteloos Nederland," 15.

world. Translating this back to Dutch museums that are currently struggling with the *Black* diversity question, this meant that struggling with the white diversity question was actually a relatively easy thing to do. The question then becomes how to diversify the arts with other diasporas?

Thinking Diversity along the Axis of Whiteness

In 2008 Esche stated that it would only be known whether the project was a success in retrospect: "*Be(com)ing Dutch* had annoyed so many people, he hoped that it might mark a shift, and also provide an example of what art could be; an example which he hopes will be subsequently taken up by people who are interested in art having a real social role — 'a discursive role rather than an aesthetic role as such.'"[101]

In July 2009, Van Abbemuseum curator Remco de Blaaij (2006–2011) and Esche wrote a retrospective view on the *Be(com) ing Dutch* project.[102] One of the consequences of the program was that for the first time in the museum's history a direct connection had been made with "young people, local politicians, and economic leaders."[103] The program had also resulted in the museum turning into a place where knowledge was produced, an online platform and catalog, the museum as producer of art through commissions, involvement of artists in the exhibition processes, and gaining a position in reflection on contemporary social developments resulting in *Play Van Abbe*.[104] Through the collaboration with Soheila Nahand of InterArt, they had reached a youthful audience of between fifteen and eighteen years old, from different school types and cultural backgrounds.[105] De Blaaij and Esche's piece offers additional insight into the diver-

---

101 Byrne, "Be(com)ing Dutch," 24.
102 Charles Esche and Remco de Blaaij, "Terugblik Be(com)ing Dutch," July 2009, Van Abbemuseum Archive, Symposia; Be(com)ing Dutch, Voorbereidingen, Algemeen, 2007.
103 Ibid., 1.
104 Ibid., 2.
105 Ibid., 3.

sity reach of the project by recollecting conversations with Kosmose project leader Warner Werkhoven on the meaning of diversity in our society and its use as an instrument.[106] The project also brought together people of fifty different national backgrounds in the gatherings and the caucus. De Blaaij and Esche stated that "cultural, geographical, or societal borders" are not the only bounds of diversity,[107] they looked for a broader view of the diversity construct and consequently "did not only reflect on the construction of the 'other' but included everyone in the development of the program."[108] Public interest in the program varied from judgment "of the removal of the aesthetic position, to complaints about its political prejudice to the appreciation of the integration of a socially relevant debate with the possibilities of visual arts."[109] *Frieze* magazine named *Be(com)ing Dutch* the best exhibition of 2008.[110]

The Mondriaan Fund policy paper 2009–2012 that followed this period expressed the intention to have an annual prize alternating between a heritage institution and an art institution. According to the jury report, "it is certainly challenging to all Dutch museums in the area of modern and contemporary art. It is a call for them to self-reflect and think hard about their institutions vis-à-vis cultural diversity."[111]

The *Be(com)ing Dutch* project called the supposed Western axis of art autonomy of Dutch museums into question, which eventually resulted in *The Autonomy Project* (2010–2011), setting out to understand the actual meaning of that term and whether curators and the public understood how systemic it was in Dutch art education. According to Fletcher, this project investigated what autonomy meant in relation to political engagement. The museum itself, heavily dependent on the market to assign

---

106 Ibid., 4.
107 Ibid., 5.
108 Ibid.
109 Ibid., 6.
110 Ibid.
111 Wouter Welling, "De postkoloniale puzzel," *Kunstbeeld* 32, nos. 12–1 (2008): 60.

value to artworks, was located in the Dutch art world thus interrogating its perceived neutrality and exposing its hidden biases.

In 2016, when I held the interviews for the research that eventually became this book, ideas about the role of the museum had not changed. According to Fletcher, this was because museums are "money-making machines" — meaning that capitalism "is brilliant at consuming political subjects and ideas and converting them, monetizing them, and consuming them, and certainly not changing anything." She notes that the art world and museums did not change because we have never experienced anything since the marketization of art at the current level and scale. She points out that "[t]he art market is extraordinary and dramatic and it is completely invested in the discrete object that has no political implications. It is completely invested in the universe of white men."

By 2017 the Van Abbemuseum's position was that the (ethnically Euro axis) "art market" was no longer leading in their decisions, thus challenging the so-called "autonomous position" of art museums in the Netherlands. What this meant was that over the years the museum had developed into an institution that, owing to state funding, managed to keep a foothold in the "high art" world, while becoming part of different networks that are also frequented by the (Afro) artists whom cultural policy aimed to support. The consequence of the knowledge that was acquired during the Van Abbemuseum's curatorial and discursive programme *Be(com)ing Dutch* was that the curatorial team managed to attract Afro artists' engagement as well as a (diverse) audience participation.

4

He Who Moves in All Spaces: The *Wakaman* Project

Only a curatorial practice that highlights aesthetic articulations rather than ethnic origin or cultural background might resist creating exclusive exhibition spaces and transport artistic positions in a way that reflects our contemporary realities.
— Nana Adusei-Poku, "The Multiplicity of Multiplicities: Post-Black Art and Its Intricacies"[1]

Self-Determining Blackness: The *Wakaman* Context

In Chapter One I referred to my personal subject position, being informed by different cultural backgrounds. Placing this subjectivity within the context of the larger diaspora means accepting that, even though there are similarities, Dutch Afro-ness is differently constituted than African American and Black British discourses would propose. Consequently, I argue that naming

---

1   Nana Adusei-Poku, "The Multiplicity of Multiplicities: Post-Black Art and Its Intricacies," *Darkmatter,* November 29, 2012, http://www.darkmatter101. org/site/2012/11/29/the-multiplicity-of-multiplicities-%E2%80%93-post-black-art-and-its-intricacies/.

this subject "Black" would be presumptuous as regards its social, political, and artistic potential in the Dutch context. Rather, being in a state of "pre-Blackness" opens up the possibility of thinking Dutch Afro-ness along the axis of culture rather than the axis of race.

In tandem with the *Stimuleringsprijs Culturele Diversiteit*, the Mondriaan Fund and Netherlands Foundation for Visual Arts, Design and Architecture also initiated the *Intendant Culturele Diversiteit* (2006–2009) to effectuate affirmative action for minorities in the arts. Through this program, the *Wakaman* project (2005–2008) offered a way for Dutch Afro artists to explore their position in the Dutch artistic landscape in the context of activated cultural policy, demonstrating their actual presence despite the Van Abbemuseum's perceived "absence of Dutch Black radical visual arts."

From explicitly dealing with issues that derive from the Dutch Afro experience to works that reject specific racial, ethnic, and cultural backgrounds, artists employ different strategies to deal with their predicament. Can these Dutch artists claim the title of "artist" in a cultural environment that openly separates natives and immigrants? Whereas the previous chapter showed the perspective of a Dutch museum on questions of diversity through European-inspired models and frameworks of interpretation and discourse, we will now examine the perspective of the Dutch Afro artist in relation to the American artistic post-Black movement as presented in Thelma Golden's catalog *Freestyle*.[2] Whereas post-Black is invested in going beyond the Black label while at the same time inhabiting Blackness, the Dutch subjectivity I will discuss below is invested in both possibly becoming and refusing to be "Black" simultaneously.

Being aware of this apparent paradox produces an understanding of how art production as a language locates the Dutch Afro artist in the Dutch art world. Speaking this language of art production means that artists who never express their Afro heritage or are recognizable as such in their work often find rec-

---

2   Thelma Golden, *Freestyle* (Studio Museum in Harlem, 2001), 14.

ognition and representation with a "good" gallery. The Dutch artist of Surinamese descent stanley brouwn (1935–2017) is an early example of an artist who defied the idea of ethnicity by being absorbed into the prevailing art scene of the moment. As an autodidact he unfailingly fit into the conceptual arts of the Netherlands from the 1960s onward long before the term "allochthonous" was invented to describe non-native Dutch people. He exhibited in *Documenta V* (1972), *Documenta VI* (1977), and *Documenta VII* (1982) and won several Dutch art prizes. Unlike the artists coming out of the Srefidensie gallery that was established in 1971 in Amsterdam, he became successful with the work he made. In his work, the push and pull between making subjectivity subordinate and ethnicity unimportant, while fitting into the themes of the art scene of the time, resulted in appreciation of the work based on its own merits.

brouwn's work fit into the space of *blankness* which, responding to the *Be(com)ing Dutch Dictionary*,[3] I formulated in "Notes on a Dictionary: A Polemic Approach."[4] This term is derived from the Dutch word blank, which comes up in many of the texts and is often casually used by the Dutch-speaking interviewees. Akin to Richard Dyer's "white," *blank* constructs an (artistic) subjectivity "of such a 'natural' transparency that it becomes hardly visible."[5] Understanding the interplay of *blank* and *wit* (white) underscores the potential of local concepts because "white," and not "blank," is used as a racial denominator in Dutch English-language catalogs and reviews. However, these two words neither mean the same thing nor do they have the same emotional charge. In Dutch dictionaries *blank(e)* is defined as "bright white, unsoiled, uncolored: the blank race, submerged under water." For Dutch white people it is the "pre-

---

3   Charles Esche, Annie Fletcher, Ivet R. Maturano, *Be(com)ing Dutch: Our Dictionary* (Van Abbemuseum, 2008).
4   Charl Landvreugd, "Notes on a Dictionary: A Polemic Approach," in *Deviant Practice: Research Programme 2016–2017*, ed. Nick Aikens (Van Abbemuseum, 2018).
5   Ibid., 220.

ferred denomination, one that is continued in the media."[6] *Blank* as unsoiled and objective is a metaphor for *Western* that is a constant in art critique in the Netherlands. The editor in chief of *NRC Handelsblad,* one of the major Dutch newspapers, stated in 2005:

> According to our style guide, when using *blank* [white] or *zwart* [Black] we adhere to general social use. We do not write about *witte* [white] people but about *blanken* [white people]. [...] The style guide associates the term *wit* with the world of welfare in which everybody who is not specifically *blank* is referred to as Black.[7]

In "Notes on a Dictionary" I unpack this idea and the problem of the translatability of concepts further:

> Here it becomes apparent why direct translation from an English-speaking context obscures particularities in the Dutch context and why investigating the Dutch particularities can lead to new insights. Taking the word *blank* out of its native Dutch context to look for meaning in English becomes a tool for unpacking a seemingly harmless way of speaking. With "empty or clear, or containing no information or mark."
>
> Going back and forth between Dutch and English provides the opportunity to give new meanings to words. Due to the social meaning of the word, *blank* can acquire a meaning as an artistic tool in English texts that would be hard to theorise in Dutch.[8]

In English this means releasing *blankness* from the racial connotation it has in the Dutch language. In the visual arts this opens up thinking about a space that is racially and ethnically

---

6   Ibid.

7   Folkert Jensma, "Zwart/wit en de website," *NRC.NL Archief,* September 24, 2005, http://vorige.nrc.nl/opinie/article1638169.ece/Zwart/wit_en_de_website. (This URL is no longer active.)

8   Landvreugd, "Notes on a Dictionary," 221.

decontextualized, a so-called "blank space." The ultimate result is that in this space "white" artists would also have to recognize their ethnicity and not assume the emptiness of *blankness.* Arguably, this blank space, being racially and ethnically decontextualized and functioning as an equal playing field of artistic creation within a Western context, coincides with the imagined normal space I proposed in Chapter One. On this equal playing field every artist would then have to contemplate how blankness relates to ideas of Western-ness.

For Dutch Afro artists such as brouwn, by entering an already established context of Dutch artists on the terms of *blankness,* understood in the context of the Netherlands as white Western-ness, the work is released from the person who made it. *Blankness,* or the absence of *Blackness* in the arts, is then the moment when there is no hint that the work is driven by ethnic concerns and comes from a so-called "neutral" (blank) space. Using this strategy does have a certain agency as it results in critical language about the object and its relation to the prevailing art discourse rather than a focus on its maker's ethnic relation to that discourse.

Alternatively, for the Dutch Afro artist, taking an ethnic position may be a matter of principle based on its usefulness. In relation to access to the market, historically taking an ethnic position meant connecting to a small niche with low visibility on the general local art market and barely any interest coming from the diaspora art world. By way of tackling the niche problem, artists could and can respond by not making "ethnic" art while holding on to the so-called ethnic position. Here, then, the produced language does not "sound" as it is supposed to in the general art discourse, but often results in a perspective that is perceived as "new." The other option is to maintain the ethnic position and foreground the issues connected to the Dutch Afro condition as inherently Dutch.

This latter position is the one occupied by the Wakaman artists. Their efforts bring me to the paradox of the imagined normal space in the Dutch art world, which is to speak Dutch Afro-ness without making a point out of ethnicity. The crux of the problem is not the desire for the work to culturally pass, but rather having the agency to be recognized as native without being limited or directed by the structures of blankness that constitute the existing Dutch art world.

Martin Hewson describes agency as "the condition of activity rather than passivity,"[9] distinguishing three main types of agency: individual agency, agency by proxy (meaning on behalf of another), and collective agency.[10] He also mentions three main bases of human agency: a purposive or intentional basis; one that comes through the power of resources and capabilities; and a basis of rationality which, for it to "act with effect, it is necessary for agents to reflect upon their circumstances and to monitor the on-going consequences of their actions."[11] For the contemporary artist subject to the Dutch Afro condition this means that these different types of agency, explained as activity in relation to the Dutch art world, are inhabited differently depending on the future horizon that currently is the apparent paradox of simultaneously refusing to become and becoming Black.

Before discussing the *Wakaman* project (2005–2008) and its curatorial outcome, it is useful to go back in time once again and look at several contextualizing exhibitions and moments. This history links the artists' practices to curatorial attempts at normalizing Afro-ness in the Dutch art context and underscores the influence of African American-ness on this process. Contemporary Dutch thinking through (visual) language leapt into view with an event that had more impact on the cultural scene in the Netherlands than the often referenced Paris exhibition *Magiciens de la Terre*. The exhibition *Wit over zwart* (*White about/over Black*) by artist–curator and founder of Cosmic Illusion Felix de Rooy in the Tropenmuseum in Amsterdam was

---

9 Martin Hewson, "Agency," in *Encyclopedia of Case Study Research*, ed. Albert J. Mills, Gabrielle Durepos, and Elden Wiebe (SAGE, 2010), 12.
10 Ibid., 12–13.
11 Ibid., 13.

extremely well-visited, with 28,000 people in the first month.[12] The Dutch word *over* in the title has a deliberately double meaning, translating into both "over" and "about." Also, the choice of the then relatively new words *wit* (white) and *zwart* (Black) presents a deliberate attempt to depart from the use of the common racial terms *neger* (negro) and *blank* (white). As Jan Nederveen Pieterse explains in the book *Wit over zwart,* these new terms derived from the exhibition: "Black is relatively neutral [...] it is a political color [...] Because of symmetry the term white is chosen as counterpart to black, instead of the commonly used blank in the Netherlands."[13] The exhibition *Wit over zwart* made a big impression on those who visited it, because it efficiently located the issues of Blackness in the context of the Netherlands. According to Rob Perrée, "This exhibition had a lot of effect, it was kind of revealing because of course you knew this sort of stuff, but he [Felix de Rooy] knew how to illustrate it."[14]

De Rooy's curatorial work in the early 1990s makes him the first contemporary Dutch artist–curator subject to the Dutch Afro condition. By focusing on the relation between white and Black as the topic for the exhibition, he was ahead of the discussions that would only take place in the next century, producing a language that was unfamiliar to the Dutch audience at that time. Famously, then Minister of Culture and prominent feminist Hedy D'Ancona, while being escorted past all the racist images worldwide, exploded, saying, "but this isn't racism," when shown the image of the Dutch blackface figure Zwarte Piet.[15] Her denial of the racial stereotyping and the underlying

---

12 "Aantal bezoekers Nederlandse musea gestegen," *NRC Handelsblad,* January 17, 1990, https://www.nrc.nl/nieuws/1990/01/17/aantal-bezoekers-van-nederlandse-musea-gestege-6921606-a126352.
13 Jan Nederveen Pieterse, *Wit over zwart: Beelden van Afrika en zwarten in de westerse populaire cultuur* (Koninklijk Instituut voor de Tropen, 1990), 8.
14 Rob Perrée, interview with the author, Skype, March 6, 2016.
15 "Het beeld ook als het anders is bedoeld: Stereotypering is racistisch," *NRC Handelsblad,* October 19, 2013, http://www.nrc.nl/handelsblad/2013/10/19/het-beeld-ook-als-het-anders-is-bedoeld-stereotypering-1304504.

racism in Dutch society indicates why, with the policy of assimilation in the guise of integration into the rejected pillarization model of tolerance, this exhibition failed to become an institutional curatorial model in the 1990s.

De Rooy personally received heavy criticism for this exhibition, removing him from the general art discourse in the Netherlands. He followed the fate of cultural anthropologist Philomena Essed, who published the book *Alledaags Racisme*[16] (*Everyday Racism*) in 1984. At that time, she noted that Black researchers choosing racism as their topic were scrutinized on their methodology.[17] When she published her doctoral research in 1991 under the title *Understanding Everyday Racism*[18] she was once again closely examined by the Dutch press and the academic world, which cast doubt on the content of her thesis and its methodology. This refusal to face the fact of racism in the Netherlands, attacking research, and questioning its scientificity continues until today, as witnessed by the vicious attacks on, for instance, Gloria Wekker's 2016 book *White Innocence*.[19] We are dealing here with the quality argument applied to academic research or, as Sebastian Lopez observed in 1996, "intellectual discrimination" expressed from a patronizing Dutch position.[20]

In the Netherlands the idea of racism (in the arts) is always located *outside* the country. To exemplify this, around 1990, when Dutch Afro art was mainly produced by what Stuart Hall named the "last colonials," the Dutch language about Afro art production came into existence by looking at art from outside the Netherlands. Overholland, an exclusive private museum, located in an old villa next to the Stedelijk Museum in Amster-

---

16 Philomena Essed, *Alledaags racisme* (Feministische Uitgeverij Sara, 1984).

17 "Zwarte schrijfster: Prinses Irene is een echte bondgenote," *Het Vrije Volk,* September 19, 1984.

18 Philomena Essed, *Understanding Everyday Racism: An Interdisciplinary Theory* (SAGE, 1991).

19 Gloria Wekker, *White Innocence: Paradoxes of Colonialism and Race* (Duke University Press, 2016).

20 "Vanwaar je dacht te vertrekken sta je geplant," *Kunstbeeld* 30, no. 2 (1996): 35.

dam and owned by the collector Christiaan Braun, opened in 1987. The museum closed its doors in 1990 with the final exhibition, *Black USA*. This exhibition was the first Dutch museum exhibition of African American art. The review in *NRC Handelsblad*, by art critic Janneke Wesseling, starts with a quote by one of the participating artists, Benny Andrews (1930–2006): "I fight against the image of the Black artist because it is too limited. It means that they are only interested in your work because of your race, and not for the quality of your art."[21]

This idea forms the basic assumption about the exhibition throughout the review. The potential visitor was asked the same question, whether they should approach the work on view as art measured by one's own Western standards or whether the theme of racial discrimination and skin color of the artist is more important than the quality of the work.[22] Wesseling goes on to say that measuring by one's own Western (i.e., *blank*) standards is the most objective and fair toward the artists, but wonders whether Western standards are sufficient and whether this is not a different sort of art, "negro art," with its own norms and world of imagination.[23] This quality argument logic and line of thinking not only posits Afro-ness as different from blankness but also places it outside Western standards, validated through a Black authoritative voice by quoting "June Kelly, the only Black gallery owner in five hundred gallery owners in New York, that the 'Black imagination only speaks to Blacks.'"[24] This method of questioning the validity of art made by African Americans is an example of how art made by Afro people concerned with Afro subjectivity was and would be questioned in the coming decades.

---

21 Janneke Wesseling, "'Black USA' laat vragen open over de zwarte identiteit," *NRC Handelsblad*, May 16, 1990, http://www.nrc.nl/handelsblad/1990/05/16/black-usa-laat-vragen-open-over-de-zwarte-identiteit-6930066.
22 Ibid.
23 Ibid.
24 Ibid.

Of other artists participating in the *Black USA* exhibition, such as Romare Bearden (1911–1988), Robert Colescott (1925–2009), and David Hammons (b. 1943), Wesseling's review states that "all their work has little expressiveness" and that there is only one artist who also works figuratively but whose work "transcends the anecdotal," Benny Andrews.[25] With this statement Wesseling authorizes Andrews's excellence and consequently his right to speak, judging from the position of her Western standards. This is a metaphor for Blackness: by excelling according to the Western idiom (cultural passing) and being authorized to be part of it, one transcends into the (*blank*) mainstream. Just like the gallery owner June Kelly, Benny Andrews as the Black voice confirming the validity of this position is quoted: "'visual arts, other than music, has not been part of Black culture,' a visual tradition is lacking here."[26]

Arguably, Overholland's *Black USA* exhibition was part of a larger worldwide conversation. Postmodernity, being receptive to Afro artists, opened up another layer of artistic engagement with Blackness in the Netherlands through the American lens. Taking the exhibition *Black USA* and its criticism as a point of departure, an image arises of Westernness as the vantage point of the objective gaze. Racial discrimination and skin color emerge as possible mitigating factors when it comes to the quality of the work, transcending the anecdotal. The idea of "negro art" is presented as distinctively different because apparently "the Black imagination speaks only to Blacks." To reiterate, this places Blackness and Afro-ness outside of Western (in the Dutch case, meaning *blank*/white) standards. Wesseling's review of *Black USA* expresses this generally held position and speaks of the push and pull between racial identity and quality of the work. With the work being placed outside of the West, it is apparent why, for Dutch Afro artists such as Wakaman, thinking through a new space became a vital question.

---

25 Ibid.
26 Ibid.

Just like the quality argument, the failure to account for Afro-ness as part of the Dutch visual language has a history. In the context of Dutch colonial relations, this way of coding the quality argument through a "native" Black voice was exemplified by the Surinamese artist Erwin de Vries (1929–2018), who was offered a solo exhibition (1998) at the Stedelijk Museum in Amsterdam. In an interview, he stated that before he went to the Netherlands he had never seen a real painting in Suriname.[27] By using the sentence "Eén echt schilderij had ik in Suriname nog nooit gezien" ("I had never seen one real painting in Suriname") as the title of the interview, the reporter continued to reproduce the particular framing of the quality argument that appeared in the early 1990 during the exhibition *Black USA*. The rhetorical technique of producing this narrative from the mouth of a "native" is deployed to bypass accountability for the point of view that art from Suriname does not have the same artistic validity as that in the West. Again, for the artist, expressing this difference sets him apart from the artists in his native Suriname and affirms his passing into Western cultural standards, albeit through the mechanism of ethnic cultural discrimination. Just like Rudi Fuchs's remarks on the exhibition *Twintig jaar beeldende kunst in Suriname* (*Twenty years of visual arts in Suriname*) (1996–1997) that Surinamese art is a "sluggish stuck-in-the-mud variety of Dutch painting,"[28] these examples point to ways in which the language around Dutch Afro art production is construed through the idea of cultural passing, the African American lens, and attitudes based on colonial superiority.

The agency in "cultural passing" can also be connected to a particular sense of performing the Dutch Afro condition within

---

27 Bart Kamphuis, "Eén echt schilderij had ik in Suriname nog nooit gezien," *Trouw*, December 14, 1996, http://www.trouw.nl/tr/nl/5009/Archief/article/detail/2661295/1996/12/14/Een-echt-schilderij-had-ik-in-Suriname-nog-nooit-gezien.dhtml.

28 Frénk van der Linden, "Museumdirecteur Fuchs: 'Het ergste van vreemdgaan is de ontrouw aan jezelf," *NRC Handelsblad*, November 2, 1996, http://www.nrc.nl/handelsblad/1996/11/02/museumdirecteur-rudi-fuchs-het-ergste-van-vreemdgaan-7330346.

the Western art idiom. The Curaçao-born Avery Preesman (b. 1968) moved with his parents to the Netherlands in 1970. In 1994 his abstract paintings won the second prize in painting during the prestigious Prix de Rome competition. Even though he expressed in 1995 that "[i]dentity bound to borders doesn't mean anything to him,"[29] in the essay "De bevrijder van de schilderkunst" (The liberator of the art of painting) he is said to have impressed with his

> ferocious paintings in which eggs, coconuts, coffee beans, and pebbles — references to his exotic native soil — [...]. Preesman paints in a very intuitive and free way, almost comparable to the way the American action-painter Jackson Pollock flung down paint on the canvas without a preconceived plan.[30]

In 1998, the then director of the Boijmans van Beuningen museum and chairman of the Theo Wolvecam prize for painting Chris Decron praised Preesman for liberating Dutch painting from "pure optical seduction and a nostalgic desire for the past."[31] Underscoring the art-for-art's-sake argument, the press depicted Preesman as a true artist. The fact that he was a young autodidact inspired by Joni Mitchell, Natural Born Killers, and Dutch youth icons,[32] with only two years' training at Ateliers (1996–1998) and a three-month residency at the Rijksacademie, appealed to the imagination.

But in 1999 Dutch Afro artists were officially reclassified as "allochthonous," and by 2001, when he had a solo exhibition at the Stedelijk Museum Amsterdam, the critique on his work had

---

29 Nicoline Baartman, "De dingen moeten verotten," *De Volkskrant,* March 3, 1995, http://www.volkskrant.nl/archief/de-dingen-moeten-verrotten~a413570/.

30 Sandra Smallenburg, "De bevrijder van de schilderkunst," *NRC Handelsblad,* October 31, 1998, http://www.nrc.nl/handelsblad/1998/10/31/de-bevrijder-van-de-schilderkunst-7420825.

31 Ibid.

32 Baartman, "De dingen moeten verotten."

changed accordingly, saying it had become too old-fashioned Dutch modern art, which

> in the tradition of Mondriaan prescribes sober art in which light, bare forms, and the line of the landscape play the principal part [...]. Preesman returned to the womb of the Dutch tradition [...] in short, entered into the painterly illusion.[33]

Art critic Hans den Hartog Jager concludes that Preesman

> doesn't have enough affinity [with] these Dutch limitations to arrive at original solutions [... and is] a searching artist who has become too conscious of the world. [... T]he spirit, the sparkle that made him into a great talent, has been crushed under this violence [of Modernism].[34]

Based on the press coverage from that period, the mixed-race Avery Preesman was heralded as a true intuitive abstract artist, with reference to his native soil but not his cultural heritage *per se*. Alluding to earlier generations that looked at African artistic expressions for liberation and catharsis, a closer reading of the criticism suggests that Preesman possessed a primal force that was able to transform the landscape. But when his work changed, it lost its appeal for the critics. Saying that he does not have enough "affinity" with the "Dutch limitations" in painting is of course code for his primal instinct (Afro-ness) getting in the way of his objectiveness (Europeanness). I propose the alternative reading that Preesman used his painting to work through his subjectivity as culturally passing for Dutch while being perceived as allochthonous in the new post-1999 paradigm. The reception of Preesman's work in the Netherlands offers just one

---

33 Hans den Hartog Jager, "Worstelen in plaats van sprankelen," *NRC Handelsblad*, December 19, 2001, http://vorige.nrc.nl//dossiers/stedelijk_ museum/tentoonstellingen/article1570693.ece.
34 Ibid.

example of artistic agency when subjected to the Dutch Afro condition in the twenty-first century.

Another example is Remy Jungerman (b. 1959) who, even though he was from the "second generation" of artists in the Netherlands, was not born locally. His studies in Suriname and education in Western and non-Western art history provided him with a sense of agency that his peers who were born and educated in the Netherlands may not have experienced in the same way. He acknowledges that (Surinamese) cultural upbringing played a large part in how he developed as an artist. Richard Price and Sally Price's *Afro-American Arts of the Suriname Rainforest*[35] was one of the few books available in the art academy's library in Suriname that inspired his way of thinking. During those days at the academy in Suriname, this book proved to him and his peers that the Modernists had "stolen" the visual language that was actually their heritage. The Modernists thus created their own language from the language that was available in Afro aesthetics. By using the image on the front of the Prices' book as the source for a large wall painting, in 1987 Jungerman reappropriated that visual language. He realized how the visual aesthetics that Africans took with them to Suriname could be used as a tool for communication in an international context. Essentially, he recognized this part of his cultural background as something that could be materialized in a global context as a way of exerting individual and collective agency. Having his cultural background acknowledged through the Prices' scholarship exemplifies how recognizing oneself in art and theory is useful for personal and artistic development. Years later it would allow him to create a (visual and theoretical) language that has agency of its own rather than by proxy.

During his studies in the Netherlands, Jungerman established contact with an older generation of Surinamese artists such as the celebrated Erwin de Vries (1929–2018), who by acting "with effect" had access to resources and an acknowledged personal

---

35 Richard Price and Sally Price, *Afro-American Arts of the Suriname Rainforest* (University of California Press, 1980).

agency in the art world. In addition, Jungerman had close contact with artists from the Srefidensie gallery such as Frank Creton (b. 1941) and Jan Telting (1931–2003), who, through collective effort, intentionally exerted their agency by carving out a space in the Dutch artistic landscape. The important thing for Jungerman in these contacts was being able to be in someone's studio and see that it was possible to be and become a "real" artist in the Dutch art environment. These interactions fostered how Jungerman came to see himself in relation to the art world and what might be possible in terms of his role. He concluded that every artist assumes a position and that this has consequences for how the visual work evolves and the type of agency the artist acquires, developing in tandem with the cultivation of a visual language, paired with the refusal or acceptance of a specific socio-political role. Jungerman's interactions with an older generation of artists made him very aware of the kind of example he set for younger artists, and he recognized how, with the power of resources and capabilities that he had, this could yield a purposeful collective form of agency with regard to the Dutch Afro artistic position.

Before 1999 Jungerman had risen to prominence because he was identified as Surinamese while creating installations that deviated from what was known from Surinamese artists. His position was different from Preesman's, who had risen to prominence before state policy directed attention to artists from "other" regions. The result of the 1999 developments in terms of the official designation of Dutch Afro artists as allochthonous was that, according to Jungerman, invitations to participate in exhibitions stopped coming in. The quality of Afro artists was suddenly determined by state welfare, which in turn affected the perceived quality of the work itself.

People forgot that you were already bought by the Stedelijk [Museum] and had quite some exhibitions to your name. [...]

However, in their experience, you were acquired because you were allochthonous.[36]

We were stunned because we were already in the picture. We were already taking part in Europe and had exhibitions in the Stedelijk and all of sudden you noticed you had nothing left.[37]

Although this cultural policy was geared toward advancing the position of "allochthonous" artists, it had an adverse effect on artists such as Jungerman and Preesman who had already been participating in the general art scene. They were now racialized, rendering their work subservient to their ethnicity. Even though their ethnicity had played a role before in relation to what was expected of them as artists, this policy change created additional challenges, leading to a scrutinizing of the visual language they had used until that moment. References to personal cultural background had now become suspect, as they were reinterpreted as devices to access public financial support owing to the artist's insufficient ability to participate in the general art discourse on their own.

Thus the policy change forced Jungerman and his colleagues into a position where they had to counteract the created (stereo)type evolving from affirmative action, questioning their visual language and approach. For Jungerman this question turned his gaze inward toward what constituted their original and personal contribution to the art world. He concluded that although they had a personal visual language, they were not connected to the wider world due to the visual language they used as artistic reference material or, at least, that that connection had been severed as a result of the new policy.[38] At the same time, due to their increased separation from the broader art world in the Netherlands, the latter could not longer process their additional frames of reference as personal input, viewing them instead as a dif-

---

36 Remy Jungerman, interview with the author, Amsterdam, March 15, 2016.
37 Ibid.
38 Ibid.

ferent (cultural) language that they did not understand and did not need to investigate or invest in. The stage provided after this political turn to ethnicity was simply too narrow. Jungerman concludes that all of these developments made him sharper, opening up new possibilities to produce work that fit into the narrative of the larger stage.[39]

Jungerman notes: "The images I was producing at that time were almost a reaction to be understood. It was like: I can also create an image that you can comprehend. An image that you literally understand. An image about current affairs."[40] This strategy worked well for exhibitions outside of the Netherlands but within the Netherlands he (just like Preesman) was no longer recognizable as a Surinamese ("other") artist, and his new approach did not noticeably change his position in the country. Though his work no longer fit the mold, he was still from elsewhere, the former colonies, while his newly found (international) culturally passing position confused curators who were grappling with the new environment that had arisen from the change in state policy.

It is here that the absurdity of assimilation into blankness, in the guise of Dutch cultural integration, is in full effect: culturally passing is sabotaged at the moment the racist construct of the quality argument can no longer be applied. So when Jungerman returned to using his Surinamese background in his work, he regained attention within the Dutch niche of "diverse" art.

Dealing with his changed positionality the cultural land-scape, Jungerman sought to create a framework in which his work could be understood from a curatorial perspective outside of the niche market. So by 2001, Remy Jungerman, Gillion Grantsaan (b. 1968), and Michael Tedja (b. 1971) seriously started to discuss their artistic position amongst themselves and with other (Afro) players in the field. Should they create their own stage? And, if so, how would such a stage function?

---

39 Ibid.
40 Ibid.

Finding Ways to Name the Self: The *Wakaman* Project

I have shown that the language about Afro art production in the Netherlands affirmed the validity of Dutch Afro art through African American art and colonial superiority. On the one hand, art is simply considered art with equal rules for everybody, which means that there should be no need to separate any specific group. On the other hand, there is the notion that artistic and qualitative relevance comes from the ability of the work to participate in the existing discourse and not from the ethnic background of the maker. The difference between these two seemingly similar ideas is based on who decides what is relevant. For the Dutch, African American artistic relevance was established outside of the Netherlands and therefore had authority. African American culture was perceived as distinctively different from both American and European culture, and hence culturally passing and blankness were not required in the Dutch context. Meanwhile, the Dutch were in control of deciding whether other (nonwhite) narratives and visual references were relevant to Dutch art discourse. In the transitoin from transculturality to diversity and with the cultural policy of assimilation in the guise of integration, appreciation of artistic expression that did not pass the cultural standard in the Netherlands thus seemed to be out of reach for Dutch Afro artists.

Tedja, Grantsaan, and Jungerman understood the political change of the late 1990s as a linguistic and visual problem pertaining to their subjectivity. As a result, the predicament of being an artist subject to the Dutch Afro condition, aiming to produce a discourse that considers the hybrid nature of one's subjectivity, required finding a (visual) language to speak about the self. This turned into a language derived from the desire to be integrated into the existing Dutch art world on its own terms, at a time when the alternative of establishing and maintaining a relation with the larger Afro diaspora art world was not yet common. The artists wanted to bring issues concerning visual arts with a Surinamese background into the public domain, and they combined forces under the name Wakaman.[41]

In my interview with Thomas Meijer zu Schlochtern, curator of exhibition space TENT in Rotterdam (1999–2006), I argued that the artists involved in the first Wakaman were demanding cultural citizenship through their art practice. Meijer zu Schlochtern agreed and supplemented this by saying that Tedja, who had been born in the Netherlands, stressed his Rotterdamness. Tedja thought it very important to emphasize this, while Jungerman, born and raised in Suriname, did the opposite. As Meijer zu Schlochtern noted, "When someone looks at them, they would not see that these two perspectives are very different because they just see two Black guys."[42]

Tedja, Grantsaan, and Jungerman chose the name Wakaman as it has many different connotations, such as stroller, wanderer, traveller, drifter, loafer, or tramp. In Surinamese vernacular, it is "a man who goes from one woman to the next or a hustler, street philosopher, someone cool."[43] In their early years they chose the interpretation of Wakaman as "someone who intentionally stays on the sidelines in order to be in a position to campaign behind the scenes [... because] a major discussion point was that a Wakaman is impartial!"[44] As curator of TENT, Meijer zu Schlochtern had received a mandate from the Arts Council Rotterdam, and later from the state, to promote local artists, and as such he supported the first Wakaman exhibition in TENT in 2005. In his contact with Jungerman and Tedja, Meijer zu Schlochtern thought their Wakaman concept would fit perfectly into what he had been programming and thinking about in recent years. When they contacted him, he recognized it as a new perspective coming from Black artists. For Meijer zu Schlochtern, Wakaman was part of the developments concerning the relation between the Netherlands and its former colonies and the larger

---

41 Remy Jungerman and Gillion Grantsaan, *Wakaman: Drawing Lines Connecting Dots* (Wakaman Project, 2009), 8.

42 Ibid.

43 Ibid.

44 Ibid.

framework of incorporating allochthonous people into Dutch society since the late 1980s.

During the first Wakaman exhibition, a "multi-evening" was organized on November 24, 2005. After the opening there was an interview under the heading "Ik ben zwart, rijk en… Nederlander" (I am black, rich and… Dutch[45]) conducted by Stephan Sanders speaking to the Wakaman artists, art historian Adi Martis, artist Felix de Rooy, and Meijer zu Schlochtern as curator. The announcement featured several quotes to start off the conversation.

> **Jungerman:** "I do not need to be immersed in Dutch culture, but I do want to be part of the financial system."

> **Grantsaan:** "I did not come here to continue Dutch traditions, but because of the survival of the fittest."

> **Tedja:** "All art is Black."[46]

The conversation raised a set of questions, such as: "Why polarize? Are we, perhaps, radicalizing? Is it about power? Money and power?"[47] After this discussion, the video *a/k/a Mrs. George Gilbert* (2004) by Coco Fusco was shown though initially, the documentary *Louis Doedel* (1999) by Nina Jurna had been scheduled.[48] The evening ended with one of the artists participating in the exhibition, Dwight Marica, playing live dub reggae.[49] The text accompanying the invitation read: "Black Art is not the exclusive domain of people of African origin. As a

---

45 "Programma multiavond 24 november," November 29, 2005, TENT Archive, Wakaman, Programma, 2005.

46 Ibid.

47 Jungerman and Grantsaan, *Wakaman*, 8.

48 "Wakaman achterkant flyer1," November 10, 2005, TENT Archive, Wakaman, Programma, 2005.

49 "Info voor 24 nov. Website," August 31, 2006, TENT Archive, Wakaman, Programma, 2005.

fact Black Art has nothing to do with the skin pigment of the artist."[50] It continued:

> WAKAMAN does not produce *hapsnap* [random stuff] that hardly needs effort. His art is not a game, no quickie, no blarney, not an appetizing story and no standard romance. The Wakaman produces his art with high concentration while he fantasizes what it would feel like to be a thousand prospective faces. He does not like *L'art pour l'art*.[51]

The shared skin pigment of the first Wakaman show opening on November 3, 2005 meant that they could not walk through the metropolitan globalized *Umwelt*, which they considered their reference point, as *bleekscheten* (whiteys),[52] but they did include an "expansion" of drawings, paintings, installations, and video projections[53] to the Wakaman show by inviting five female artists, Miek Hoekzema, Judith Heinsohn, Fabiola Veerman, Rose Manuel, and Juliette Tulkens.[54]

The accompanying text on the wall stated:

> This expansion of the Wakaman exhibition is more than the sum of its parts. By not taking skin pigment as its subject, but also consciously applying the gender debate to one another's work, an exhibition emerged in which artists and artworks attended to and criticized the communal reference point of the metropolitan, globalized *Umwelt*.[55]

---

50 "Alg zaaltekst," November 24, 2005, TENT Archive, Wakaman, Programma, 2005.

51 Ibid.

52 Ibid.

53 "Info voor website uitbreiding Wakaman," December 29, 2005, TENT Archive, Wakaman, Programma, 2005.

54 Ibid.

55 "Zaalbrief Wakaman uitbreiding probeersel," November 23, 2005, TENT Archive, Wakaman, Programma, 2005.

In an effort to contextualize the Dutch Afro condition and create a stage from which to operate, a side program that included debate and screenings of Spike Lee's film *Bamboozled* (2000) and Frank Zichem's *Anton de Kom, Wij Slaven van Suriname* (1999) accompanied the exhibition. While explicitly positioning themselves as Black artists, understanding that they needed to (re)present themselves to the world, the main question concerned their position in the visual arts landscape of the Netherlands. Wakaman responded to the language about their Dutch Afro condition as artists by presenting a diaspora framework in which they wanted to be understood. Even though the opening of the show was well attended, there was no reaction to their position (as explicitly Black) in the press or anywhere else. This may be one of the reasons why their presence and point of view was not well known in the larger Dutch art environment. Arguably, because it was "militantly Black" and did not adhere to the adage that art should be independent and free, there was no market in place to assign value to this position.

According to Roel Meelkop, who has been with TENT since 1999, the organization did not have a PR and communications team back then. Texts about exhibitions were written in the magazine *Tentplaza*. Exhibitions lasted four to five weeks, which the press considered too short. According to Meelkop, there was never any press coverage of the exhibitions. Only with director Mariette Dölle (2006–2016) a professional PR team was established, and exhibition periods were extended.[56]

This may be part of the explanation why there was no significant reaction to the Wakaman show, which "unpleasantly surprised" the organizers.[57] As a result, the artists looked into ways to develop their project further and investigate this "lukewarm reception."[58] They thought that one of the possibilities that made them less visible, understood, or accessible for the Dutch

---

56 Roel Meelkop, personal communication with the author, November 8, 2017.

57 Jungerman and Grantsaan, *Wakaman*, 8.

58 Ibid., 9.

public was that there were "almost no publications at the academies in Suriname and the Netherlands that examine the theories, methods, and spheres of influence for artists with a Surinamese background."[59] This spawned the idea of "THE BOOK," "which would have to be in every academic and institutional library, both national and international, [and] would put things into an international perspective and draw parallels with other cultures."[60]

Not long after the first Wakaman show, the artists were invited by the Netherlands Foundation for Visual Arts, Design and Architecture[61] to submit their ideas for the *Intendant Culturele Diversiteit* and were accepted into the two-year program.[62] The Wakaman proposal was concerned with "the problems of categorization, recognition, and interpretation that they encounter as non-Western artists living in the West."[63] The plan included an encyclopedic work with artists of Surinamese descent, with scholarly support provided by Adi Martis, associate professor of Art History at the University of Utrecht, which would address the (mis)reading of Afro Dutch works.

Exemplifying their predicament is the tension between the questions brought about by Wakaman and the circumstances that thrust them in the spotlight. The Wakaman artists, even those born in the Netherlands, were not seen as Dutch, but as Surinamese artists living in the Netherlands. Their background thus made them eligible to receive part of the €500,000 Mondriaan Fund budget that was reserved for diversity in 2005. Perrée and Jungerman point out that there were many cynical reactions and questions about why, all of a sudden, so much money had been made available for this idea. This had never happened

---

59　Ibid.

60　Ibid.

61　The counterpart of the Mondriaan Fund, focused on funding individual art practices.

62　Ibid.

63　"Wakaman Walks," *Intendant Culturele Diversiteit,* archived at https://web.archive.org/web/20160802083053/http://www.intendant.nl/intendant/english/projecten/o2/project.php.

before (or after) on this scale.[64] Such sums overwhelmed even the artists who benefited from this policy change, which, rather than empowering the Afro-Dutch condition of the artists, recognized their Surinameseness. In effect, the Dutch Afro artistic agency of the artists was nullified by geographically displacing them to a former colony. In exchange, they were granted a colonial form of economic agency, akin to development aid. Thus Wakaman could not claim ethnic variation in the national art content, which only recognized blankness as valid. However, once diversity was reframed in the context of art from other regions through the concept of world art, their concept and existence became workable in the Dutch context.

The Wakaman group subsequently converged in the exchange project *ArtRoPa* (2007–2011), which arguably implemented a form of artistic development aid. The Center for Visual Arts in Rotterdam and the Republic of Suriname initiated *ArtRoPa* as a four-year project aimed at strengthening the cultural infrastructure and enhancing the cultural dialogue. Meijer zu Schlochtern, who had previously provided space to Wakaman in 2005, led this project between Rotterdam and Paramaribo, the capital of Suriname.

In this environment, the 2007 presentation of the *Intendant Culturele Diversiteit* took place in the cultural center Podium Mozaïek in west Amsterdam. Perrée criticized the whole setup of the event, which supposedly underlined diversity while in reality only emphasizing the "otherness" of the presented plans. He observed that the same Mondriaan Fund, which several years earlier had been absolutely uninterested in diversity, was now encouraged through state policy, giving the impression of wanting to compensate for its prior negligence. Through these mechanisms, agency by proxy was provided to the artists and to the cultural center as a place of "importance," while the administering party held on to the racializing language of governmental cultural policy, which overshadowed the language of the cultural producers, neutralizing their collective purposeful

---

64 Rob Perrée, interview with the author, Skype, March 6, 2016.

agency through the power of resources that were controlled by the government's proxy, the art foundations. The eventual consequences of this approach can be seen in how the Wakaman group evolved.

Understanding this undermining of the Wakama group's agency as it became part of a wider conversation, its approach toward tackling concerns about categorization, recognition, and interpretation became a point of internal debate and eventually a source of friction between its founding members. Political exigency, not friendship, brought them together in conversation, action, and networking to overcome the position they were maneuvered into, being the source of their collaboration. Now, brought back into the fold of Dutch cultural politics, albeit via the (negative) mechanism of being explicitly racialized and the affirmative action that followed, their initial, collective plan fell apart and the group decided to part ways. Among other things, this split was based on a lack of clear agreement over responsibilities in the project,[65] which led to disagreement about how funds were to be allocated[66] and curatorial disagreement about inclusion of other foreign (non-Dutch or Surinamese) artists in the project.[67]

In August 2008 the three Wakaman presented a new plan based on the separation that had taken place. Michael Tedja created a curatorial plan of his own that did not include either Grantsaan or Jungerman.[68] The grant was equally divided, so that each artist could spend it on their part of the project. The Jungerman/Grantsaan project delved deeper into the "allochthonous" role in an effort to excel through the mechanism of being racialized. This approach basically acknowledged the quality argument while trying to undo it. Tedja fully rejected

---

65 Remy Jungerman, "Plan Remy extra," February 25, 2008, Wakaman Archive Remy Jungerman.

66 Remy Jungerman, "Brief Fbkvb," January 31, 2008, Wakaman Archive Remy Jungerman.

67 Michael Tedja, "Plan Michael," February 11, 2008, Wakaman Archive Remy Jungerman.

68 Jungerman, "Brief Fbkvb."

this social and linguistic framing through policy and proposed to "eat the frame." Effectively, both parties were engaged in producing a language about the way in which they had been framed, questioning their own otherness and its relation to Blackness and blankness. The fundamental difference in how to approach this new situation is apparent in the first few sentences of Tedja's book *Eat the Frame!*

> When the Dutch government supports a multicultural art project, it does not have the intention that the supported Dutch person with a background different from the so-called authentic Dutch returns to where he originally comes from. That he will find his roots if only he descends far enough into the jungle of his history, that he has to be in the same place, the ground on which his parents were born (or he himself) to truly know and understand who he is — this is a despicable idea. Those who claim that Black artists living and working in the West are derivatives of western thinking commit a grave error in thinking.[69]

After the split, *Wakaman gaat lopen* (Wakaman is going to walk) became the working title under which both projects proceeded with their own budget and autonomy.[70] The introduction to this new plan stated that while they were very different, "their Wakaman projects are concerned with the same element of art by non-Western people who live in the West, and the problems they face when it comes to categorization, recognition, and interpretation."[71] Among other things, the two Wakaman projects investigated these questions in a different way. Grantsaan and Jungerman focused on the artist relation between Suriname

---

69 Michael Tedja, *Eat the Frame! A Polymorphic Essay as the Catalogue of an International Art Exhibition in the Netherlands Anno 2009* (KIT Publishers, 2009), 11.

70 Remy Jungerman, "Programma details rj+mh-2," October 17, 2008, Wakaman Archive Remy Jungerman.

71 Remy Jungerman and Gillion Grantsaan, "Wakaman gaat lopen nieuw plan," August 5, 2008, Wakaman Archive Remy Jungerman.

and the Netherlands, while Tedja aimed to formulate questions around diaspora and displacement in an international context.[72]

Eat the Frame: Michael Tedja

In prepation for his *Eat the Frame!* exhibition, Tedja held an event called *Teach In* at the Boijmans van Beuningen museum in Rotterdam. He published a one-page newspaper-style leaflet called "The Daily Fucked Up Intendant" with the subheading "We are the garbage collectors of the mind. We air our dirty laundry."[73] In the article "It is like, It is like" he explains his thinking toward what was to become the notion of "eating the frame." Tedja spoke about a Wakaman as being a *hosselaar* (hustler), coining a new name for his part of the project, which took Suriname as its point of departure but was in search of the whole world. He argued against "trendy us/them thinking," which led to a provincial attitude toward the foreign and unpleasant, while he, being a cosmopolit, was in search of questions that were larger than himself. This was a time "in which art is degraded into a folkloristic disposable article […] and contemporary artists move like trapped allochtonenmuizen (allochthonous mice)." Tedja imagined a newspaper under the same name as the leaflet, *The Daily Fucked Up Intendant,* which could be read online, conceived as an imaginative framework around the exhibition that mixed fact and fiction and was produced by a mishmash of nationalities.

The exhibition took as a given that engagement in the arts is omnipresent. Rather than wither away, the artists looked for "existential ligatures" with others "beyond the Dutch and Surinamese borders through which the idea of a 'vision for the future' widens." For this he planned on inviting the art collective Otabenga Jones, aiming to create a polymorphic exhibition that denounced nationalist sentiments and would explicitly criticize

---

72 Ibid.
73 Michael Tedja, "The Daily Fucked Up Intendant," February 21, 2008, Wakaman Archive Remy Jungerman.

the "danger of the *Blut und Boden* rhetoric" of far-right political parties such as Trots op Nederland (Proud of the Netherlands), Vlaams Belang (Flemish Interest), or PVV (Freedom Party). Tedja argued that these parties were attractive for people who are "psychologically or morally neglected," who "then go search for an identity on the internet, [and] specifically this search for an identity based on occurrences from the past or a faraway country seems to become a characteristic of the information society." The exhibition wanted to show that such identities are fragile and cannot handle confrontation outside of cyberspace. Tedja insisted that these developments are a "negative exaltation," a "societal disaster which corrodes the arts from the inside out and willingly imposes a practical function so that it cannot carry out straightforward cultural criticism." He called this a "slave-mentality that is employed by some artists, civil servants, policy makers, directors, and traders." Quoting Jean-Paul Sartre, he mentioned that what is important is not what others do with us but what we do with what others do to us, and he wondered "where this massive need for historical identities — often victim identities, particularly with people who are not victims — comes from."

According to a review in the Surinamese newspaper *De Ware Tijd,* it was not easy for Tedja to find a location for his exhibition.[74] He proposed his exhibition plans to several institutions, which, despite an initially positive response, did not think that an exhibition on cultural diversity should include white artists and wanted to amend the line-up.[75] Tedja did not take this well: "It reduced the content of my plans to identity politics, while I wanted to make an internationally oriented exhibition that made connections between complex questions."[76] The end result was that Tedja staged the exhibition, with artists from the USA, Suriname, the Netherlands, and South Africa, at the commer-

---

74 Stuart Rahan, "Wakamanproject: Surinaamse kunstwereld is twee naslag-werken rijker," *De Ware Tijd,* Cultuur, July 11, 2009, B9.

75 Ibid.

76 Ibid.

cial gallery Nouvelles Images, including work by René Tosari, Carl Pope, Gean Moreno, Jean Bernard Koeman, Anton Vrede, Hamid el Kanbouhi, Dwight Marica, Miek Hoekzema, Mirjam Kort, Kaleb de Groot, and Moshekwa Langa.

The tangible result of Tedja's process is the bilingual Dutch/English *Eat the Frame! A Polymorphic Essay as the Catalogue of an International Art Exhibition in the Netherlands Anno 2009*[77] and the book *Hosselen: Een diachronische roman in achtenvijftig gitzwarte facetten over beeldende kunst in identiteitsdenkend Nederland anno 2009*[78] (*Hustling: A Diachronic Novel in Eighty-five Jet-black Facets about Visual Arts Identity-thinking Netherlands in 2009*). The connection between the two publications is explained in the first pages of *Eat the Frame!*:

> As the exhibition was developing, Michael Tedja wrote the fictional story "Hosselen" [...]. The main character is a young curator busy preparing an international exhibition. His path through life is marked by various twists and turns. The novel is written in facets. And just like a diamond, a brilliant, which has 58 facets, the book is composed of 58 chapters, each telling a story about art and the art world in the Netherlands. By the end of the book, the young curator steps out of the framework of the story and so exits the fiction. [... T]he catalog of the exhibition is the final chapter of "Hosselen." *Eat the Frame!* is now a reality.[79]

Hosselen is a collection of "texts and images somewhere between fiction, non-fiction, poetry, pamphlets, reproductions of artworks, picture stories, collages, diagrams, and drawings."[80] Critic Albert Hagenaars states:

---

77 Tedja, *Eat the Frame!*, 11.
78 Michael Tedja, *Hosselen: Een diachronische roman in achtenevijftig gifzwarte facetten over beeldende kunst in identiteitsdenkend Nederland anno 2009* (KIT Publishers, 2009).
79 Ibid., 5.
80 Rob Perrée, "Michael Tedja, Hosselen," *Kunstbeeld,* 2009, http://robperree. com/articles/702/michael-tedja-hosselen.

Cast in many different shapes, it specifically deals with identity, art, and the numerous connections and discrepancies between the two. Subjects such as ethnicity, shattering existing structures, and the relation between form and content are reviewed. Tedja's provocative style is as diverse as his themes; concepts such as "diachrony" and "Kantian accuracy" are mixed with street language and group jargon. The perspective constantly changes on the basis of "facets," without losing the main thread and the reader is left with a lot to interpret.[81]

Perrée adds that Tedja's "perspective on art, the art world, and sociall incidents" can be distilled from the essays and these "will be experienced by many as exaggerated, but this is because before him, others did not have the courage to express them."[82] He adds that, when Tedja speaks about *Eat the Frame!* he is referring to Dutch art funds that have to invest in politically correct projects or lose their state funding, and consequently are forced to make a distinction between white and Black artists, thereby stigmatizing the Black artists who comply by performing Blackness within the established framework.[83]

The catalogue was co-published by KIT Publishers, which at that time was part of a large Dutch colonial institution, het Tropenmuseum, and the new publishing house The DFI (Daily Fucked Up Intendant) Publishers, established by Michael Tedja during the process of writing *Hosselen*.[84] Here again it is stressed that

The DFI is an imaginative framework. It places art in an international perspective. Parallels are drawn. It represents a way of thinking which, like a writhing snake, develops organi-

---

81 Albert Hagenaars, "Michael Tedja — Hosselen," *Werkgroep Caraïbische Letteren*, April 27, 2010, http://werkgroepcaraibischeletteren.nl/michael-tedja-hosselen/.

82 Perrée, "Michael Tedja, Hosselen."

83 Ibid.

84 Ibid.

cally and naturally. A poetical view born of a multicultural spirit.[85]

Through writing and theorizing, Tedja established the context in which the exhibition had to be placed. With *Eat the Frame!* he pushed back against the Dutch Afro artistic position that was invalidated through policy and placed him outside of the Dutch artistic context. As a curatorial practice, he actively resisted the existing narrative by suggesting to "eat the frame." Sticking to his principles, this also meant that a commercial gallery rather than a museological environment was the space in which his perspective found resonance.

Drawing Lines, Connecting Dots: Remy Jungerman & Gillion Grantsaan

Jungerman and Grantsaan aimed to question the Surinamese/Dutch diaspora and elucidate underexposed perspectives.[86] With the title *Wakaman: Drawing Lines Connecting Dots* they aspired to produce an essential contribution to the "gnashing cultural and social discussions": "As artists we can and want to exert influence on some relevant and recurring elements: categorization, recognition, acknowledgment, frame of reference, and interpretation in art and the discussion of art."[87] As curators they did not set out to make a difference between the local and the global context, because they embodied both.[88] They imagined a participatory and public character for the project and, to make this happen, they set themselves the task of actively looking for critique off the beaten track, making intensive use of

---

85 Ibid.

86 Remy Jungerman and Gillion Grantsaan, "Plan van aanpak Remy Junger-man en Gillion Grantsaan," August 5, 2008, Wakaman Archive Remy Jungerman.

87 Ibid.

88 Ibid.

the internet.[89] One of the ways they imagined doing this was by establishing a website and by publishing a book.

While developing their thoughts, Jungerman and Grantsaan decided to hold the Wakaman exhibition in Suriname. The idea for the exhibition involved the creation of couples consisting of an artist of Surinamese descent living in Suriname and an artist of the Suriname diaspora living elsewhere. Jungerman and Grantsaan established the artist couples Marcel Pinas and Charl Landvreugd,[90] Kurt Nahar and Iris Kensmil, and Ory Plet and patricia kaersenhout. The instruction was that each artist would make an autonomous work as well as a contribution toward a collaborative piece. As the budget did not allow room for transport of artworks to Suriname, the organisers advised the artists to communicate in advance their needs for the production of their work and bring as much material as possible from abroad.[91] The exhibition was meant to show the process toward the collaborative piece. With the geographical distance between the artists, the process consisted of email and regular mail exchanges that were to be curated into the exhibition. In the process journalist Nina Jurna and producer Ada Korbee supported the artists in Suriname, while project leader Manu Hartsuyker supported those in the Netherlands. Art historians Adi Martis and Rob Perrée, author and curator Chandra van Binnendijk, and writer Marieke Visser worked on the accompanying publication.

In the process many thoughts about being Black in the visual arts were communicated back and forth. During the meetings the question was raised whether "Black art" existed or not.[92]

---

89 Ibid.

90 At that time, I was doing my BA at University of London, Goldsmiths. While looking for other artists of Surinamese descent, I found Remy Jungerman and Marcel Pinas on the internet and sent them an email. They both replied very enthusiastically. In 2008, the year that I moved to New York to pursue an MA, I was invited to come to join the *Wakaman* project.

91 Remy Jungerman, "Brief aan Wakaman Koppels," January 4, 2009, Wakaman Archive Remy Jungerman.

92 patricia kaersenhout, "Brief Patricia," October 31, 2008, Wakaman Archive Remy Jungerman. Subsequent quotes are from the same letter.

These thoughts developed in the vacuum of the Dutch art environment around the same time as the *Be(com)ing Dutch* project by the Van Abbemuseum. For the artists, theories on the subject and, for example, information about the Black Arts movements in the United States and Great Britain were not readily available. With this in mind, it is clear why Jungerman observed that it would be great if a "Black art" movement had emerged "in the vein of impressionism or surrealism or any other ism. It would mean that a group of Black artists had produced an idea that would give Black art a place in an art-historical context." This thought occurred to him because he googled the term "Black art" without finding any significant result except some "bad art." Jungerman asked how this was possible and "why Black artists are more concerned with their identity and surviving in a white art scene before coming to the development of an art movement." Then there was also the "phenomenon of Black artists who do not want to be identified with Black art whatever that may be." They were working in an environment of a cultural policy that was invested in such pervasive blankness that it prevented the emergence of a new language. In this moment Jungerman expressed the ambition to arrive at a "universal form-language that carries with it all the elements of his Blackness. After all, art is also economy."

The election of Barack Obama as the first Black US president in 2008 also had an impact on the sense of self in artists such as kaersenhout (b. 1966). She felt relief accepting herself as a Black woman living in white society. In her words:

The constant tight-rope walking and trying to keep the balance between different worlds in which I seemingly move effortlessly. It feels like for a moment I don't have to but can finally just be.[93]

---

93 patricia kaersenhout, "The Poetry of Being," November 7, 2008, Wakaman Archive Remy Jungerman.

To "just be" opens up critical space to question her practice. She wonders whether her work has evolved to what Chris Ofili called "ghetto art" when criticizing the British Black Art movement.[94] She asks,

> Can we as Blacks still hang on to the blues? Is Black art progressive enough? Or do we, as Black artists, get inspired to see ourselves through different eyes (now that Obama is president)? Is there going to be an enormous shift of roles on the world stage? Are we going to be looked at differently and in which way will this influence our work?[95]

kaersenhout has no real answer to these questions at this time but reminds us that, if the roles were to change, "the oppressed become the worst perpetrators"—a chilling thought.[96] Conclusively, the thoughts that developed during the *Wakaman: Drawing Lines Connecting Dots* project occurred with an awareness of what was happening in the global art world in relation to identity thinking, while at the same time being unaware of the large Black diaspora art movements of the past. The artists understood their Afro-ness in the limited space of the Dutch art environment, including the former colonies.

The invitation for the opening of the exhibition *Wakaman: Drawing Lines Connecting Dots* in Fort Zeelandia, Paramaribo, made a point of centering Suriname as a point of departure and establishing the exhibition's international character by naming New York, Copenhagen, Paramaribo, and Amsterdam as the places where the artists work. It was promoted as a surprising dialogue between the artists, departing from the question "What is contemporary Surinamese art?"[97] By framing this question internationally and in accordance with the Dutch

---

94 Ibid.
95 Ibid.
96 Ibid.
97 Wakaman, "Uitn. Wakaman tekst," February 6, 2009, Wakaman Archive Remy Jungerman.

logic regarding Dutch Afro artistic production, the Dutch artists were firmly located outside of the Netherlands. This implied that validation of their artistic practices originated in a different environment.

During his opening speech, Jungerman articulated some of the questions that inspired the artists as a way of giving context to this Surinamese framing: To what extent were the artists' works influenced by their past, present, and place? What was the function and position of their art in Suriname, the Netherlands, the Caribbean, and the international art world? How could they position Suriname in the international art world through their actions? And, lastly, to what extent could Paramaribo serve as a center for visual arts?[98] The side program included several talks with local artists on artist initiatives in Suriname, a lecture by Adi Martis on Caribbean art, and a viewing of Tessa Boerman's documentary *Zwart Belicht* (*Black Illuminated*) (2008), which looks at the hidden story of Black figures in the paintings of Peter Paul Rubens and his environment.[99] Even though Grantsaan had left the project by then, he is listed as one of the organizers.

In contrast to Tedja's idea of eating the frame, Jungerman and Grantsaan took a "back to the roots" approach, meaning that they took Suriname as their starting point to "find out where inspiration comes from and to gain insight into ourselves."[100] In the form of a dialogue they wanted to "tell the story of contemporary Surinamese art and thereby clarify any possible enigmas in our work for all Surinamese, the Dutch, and the rest of the world."[101] They were trying to decode a Black source from which to theorize contemporary Dutch Afro aesthetics. In this process, Jungerman and Grantsaan aimed to center the artists living in

---

98 Remy Jungerman, "Opening FZ," February 20, 2009, Wakaman Archive Remy Jungerman.
99 Wakaman, "Uitn. Wakaman tekst,"
100 Jungerman and Grantsaan, *Wakaman*, 9.
101 Ibid.

Suriname and in preparation set up meetings in Suriname with relevant parties.[102]

This strategy was in line with the Dutch transcultural approach of mutual influence that recognized both groups of artists as culturally different from each other. Simultaneously, by centering Suriname, the approach took on a world-art view toward the artists involved, including the Dutch Afro artists, which underscored their difference from cultural Dutchness. For the Dutch Afro artists, this was arguably a move into a diaspora space of engagement that could position them on the world stage, away from the Dutch cultural environment. Because of the international working field of the Dutch Afro artists, the Surinamese artists could then benefit by proxy. It was a bold move with which Jungerman and Grantsaan effectively aimed at moving the center of gravity to South America, relocating the source of agency for the Dutch Afro (Surinamese) artists there, which was the opposite of the tendency that Jungerman had noticed in 2007. He explained that at that time many Dutch institutions had done collaborations with Suriname and that these had often been one-sided, meaning that groups of Dutch artists got the opportunity to work in Suriname, but the favor was only returned to a handful of Surinamese artists.[103]

Adi Martis argued:

Improved communication, increased mobility and changes in the art discourse mean that they are part of an informal, international network that also includes their fellow artists in the Diaspora. The contacts between Gillion Grantsaan, Remy Jungerman, the Wakaman pairings and others involved in the projects reflect this cooperation in miniature; the lines of communication run from Accra, Boxtel, Amsterdam, Cairo,

---

102 Ibid., 10.
103 Remy Jungerman, "Culturele uitwisseling/plan Suriname," October 5, 2007, Wakaman Archive Remy Jungerman.

Cape Town, Copenhagen, London, New York, Paramaribo, Rotterdam, Utrecht and Vermont.[104]

To underscore this move toward relocating the source of agency, the initial publication concept for the whole Wakaman group was to create a book in the form of a "standard" work about the development of Dutch/Surinamese art in a global context: *From 1700 to Wakaman.*[105] This publication would be able to place contemporary Dutch Afro art production in a historical context by rewriting Surinamese art history and mentioning people like Leo Glans, who was admitted to the Rijksacademie in 1930 and was the first person of Surinamese descent to graduate from this institution.[106] The final book *Wakaman: Drawing Lines Connecting Dots* (2009) became less encyclopaedic. Martis writes:

> This book is not an account of a nostalgic return to the past and to the source. It is the account of a process of collaboration between different artists of Surinamese origin who have made a breakthrough during the last two decades and comprises field notes, the lines of art they are setting out for the future.[107]

The book starts with the phrase "Yesterday I met Wakaman." on a single page before it opens with Grantsaan's story "Redi musu."[108] This fairytale features a protagonist who is guided to the center of the (art) market by Little Red Riding Hood. The title of the story "Redi Musu" translates as "Red Hat" or "Scarlet Cap" and is understood as the Sranan Tongo translation of "Lit-

---

104 Adi Martis, "Wakaman Goes Caribbean," in *Wakaman: Drawing Lines Connecting Dots,* by Remy Jungerman and Gillion Grantsaan (Wakaman Project, 2009), 22.
105 Remy Jungerman, "Van 1700 tot Wakaman," February 11, 2008, Wakaman Archive Remy Jungerman.
106 Remy Jungerman, "Vergadering 17 december Café de Jaren," December 18, 2007, Wakaman Archive Remy Jungerman.
107 Martis, "Wakaman Goes Caribbean," 25.
108 Gillion Grantsaan, "Redi musu," in Jungerman and Grantsaan, *Wakaman.*

tle Red Riding Hood." At the same time, Redi Musu was also the name given to the cruel and ruthless eighteenth-century enslaved Africans in Suriname who were deployed to hunt the runaway enslaved people in the forest of Suriname and was synonymous with the word traitor. Redi Musu leads the protagonist into the market (public domain) and shows him all the stalls (art institutions). Worrying about the big bad wolf, the protagonist wonders when the story will end. Redi Musu answers him by saying that everybody has already asked, in German, "Wo ist mein Zuhause? Oder; was ist das Zuhause? Heimat?" ("Where is my home? Or; what is home? Homeland?").[109] The protagonist continues:

> "Yesterday I met Wakaman and asked why they had come, what they wanted to see. From their clothes and the way they talked I deduced that some were not from around here and yet were not strangers. Or maybe they were, since they were not here to look at anything, they were here to be looked at, not to buy but to sell. [...] even the jester has his place in a story."[110]

But Redi Musu is telling the protagonist that "More Money More Money Dumas is not from these parts, but belongs now, just like you. And she's doing just fine!"[111] Which is exactly what Wakaman wants too. Grantsaan continues:

> Because of the way they perceive this fairy-tale, Wakaman's trade has almost no quantifiable effect on the public domain or the market as they wander round. Their thoughts drift like stray vendors who only occupy space and set up their stalls after closing time and hastily dismantle them when the mainstream customers flood back again in the morning. Wakaman is not a countermovement but a movement;

---

109 Ibid., 3.
110 Ibid.
111 Ibid. This is a reference to South African–Dutch painter Marlene Dumas.

a visual sinuosity between the lines of the market and the interpretation of the storyline of our fairy-tale. [...] Therefore, Wakaman explains nothing. In this market Wakaman tells stories in its own language about the stratification of people as a collage of worlds. Wakaman is like the fairy tale of the invention of the can before there was a can opener, or of the compass before anyone knew the magnetic pole was by Greenland or the use of nuclear power before we know what to do with the waste.[112]

The protagonist ends by asking Redi Musu whether she is asleep. Even though arguably the project mimicked earlier transcultural projects in the Dutch arts, the book thus starts with an accusation against the "well-meaning" people and a critical approach toward the Dutch art system in which the Wakaman artists operate.

In the book *Wakaman: Drawing Lines Connecting Dots*, Grantsaan makes an effort to theorise a notion of what could become a Dutch Black Art Movement, asking:

> isn't there anyone out there genuinely hot for that real black thing? And am I, a black visual artist, capable of generating that drive that gave birth to Calypso, Funk, Hip Hop, Blues, Mambo and of translating this drive into visual art?[113]

> Black Art.
> Black art is a product of black consciousness.
> Black art is elitism and there to be judged on its quality.
> Black in Black art means to be political.
> Black art is an innovative synthesis of two or more Weltanschauungen [world views].
> Black art is not the exclusive domain of people of African origin. As a fact Black art has nothing to do with the skin Pigment of the artist.

---

112 Ibid.
113 Jungerman and Grantsaan, *Wakaman*, 25.

> But with the dreams that keep following me: Dream A, B
> and C.
> Dream A is for producing images for my political ideals and
> black socio-cultural information.
> Dream B stands for shocking the world with innovative
> images.
> Dream C wants to inscribe my fellow immigrants in the
> course of European history.[114]

As one of the invited artists in this project, I articulated the idea
of the imagined normal space as *alakondre* (Surinamese for "all
lands"), contextualized as being

> centred and decentred at the same time, located in the space
> outlined by rhizomatic lines of flight [...]. A fragmented
> whole like a broken mirror with many pieces reflecting Ala-
> kondre back into space. The reflection is in all different direc-
> tions except for where one would expect it to take root. For
> taking root in one place is ending the route. [...] I challenge
> the impossibility of taking roots in the fragments, taking
> roots in the lines of flight, taking root in the route and pro-
> claim myself Wakaman.[115]

Effectively, the entire book was concerned with imagining different spaces and strategies from which to operate. Surinamese
artist Luciel E. Becker speaks about *WildcoastArt* and defines
himself as a Wild Coast Man who "is a product of the creative force inherent to our [Surinamese] cultural diversity."[116]
Rob Perrée makes a connection between Suriname and the
USA, questioning the idea of Black artists in various stages of

---

114 Ibid.
115 Charl Landvreugd, "Waka Waka Waka #1," in Jungerman and Grantsaan,
Wakaman, 50.
116 Luciel E. Becker, "WildcoastArt: A New Concept, a New Result," in Jungerman and Grantsaan, *Wakaman*, 28.

"Obamazation."[117] stanley brouwn is recognized and included with a blank page stating his name in the bottom-right corner.[118] Chandra van Binnendijk writes about the 1980s' Surinamese artists' collective *Waka Tjopu*. The rest of the book provides an overview of the participating artists' communication, background, and the result of the exhibition. After the release of the book, the project group made an effort to get it into the hands of art historians and librarians in the Netherlands, Suriname, the USA, Jamaica, Cuba, Trinidad and Tobago, Curaçao, Aruba and Bonaire, France, and the UK.[119] For the presentation of the book in the Netherlands, they invited the Dutch press: *De Volkskrant, Trouw, Kunstbeeld, Parool, NRC Handelsblad, AD, Financieel Dagblad, Metropolis M, Museum Tijdschrift,* and *Vrij Nederland.*[120] None of them replied to the invitation. In the end the book was only reviewed in *Museum Tijdschrift*:

> The strength of this book is that the artists speak for themselves and are not afraid of self-criticism. They have cast off the role of the victim and show that there is not a simple univocal solution.[121]

Besides this article, the *Wakaman* project and Grantsaan and Jungerman's book received some attention, particularly online and on the radio, but not from any of the established cultural media outlets.

---

117 Rob Perrée, "Suriname and the USA: Black Artists in Various Stages of Obamazation?," in Jungerman and Grantsaan, *Wakaman*.

118 Jungerman and Grantsaan, *Wakaman*, 35.

119 Wakaman, "Distibutie boek Wakaman 2 feb 2009," July 5, 2009, Wakaman Archive Remy Jungerman.

120 Wakaman, "Uitnodigingen en aanmeldingen," July 4, 2009, Wakaman Archive Remy Jungerman.

121 D. Pieters, "Passant," Museumtijdschrift, October 21, 2009, Wakaman Archive Remy Jungerman.

Undoing the Name, Finding Ways to Name the Self

Passing the cultural standard or, even better, creating a new one, begins by undoing the name that was given to immigrant background subjectivities in the assimilation process and finding ways to name the self. The Wakaman artists came into existence by being specifically categorized as "allochthonous." Through curatorial practices, they tried to produce a language that addressed their subject positions as Dutch Afro artists, but it was precisely through the difference in how this position was experienced and negotiated that the group fell apart.

For Jungerman, there has always been a conflict within naming oneself. When he is presented, one museum speaks of the Dutch–Surinamese artist while the other speaks of the Surinamese–Dutch artist. He believes, being born and raised in Suriname, that while this is always a part of him, the naming strategies he is confronted with do not cover the precise feeling he has about his position as a human subject and artist within the system. He notes that, even if one wanted to fully embrace Dutchness, the cultural climate in the country does not allow it. Being linguistically (re)produced as Other is a large part of this. In our interview, it becomes obvious that this question about naming and, through naming, declaring a cultural and political position is an extremely difficult exercise problematized by the push and pull between head and heart, private and public. To the question whether he would prefer a situation of naming beyond ethnicity, he fully agreed. Self-naming is a set of strategies depending on cultural, political, personal, and economic involvement and desires. For artists born or raised in the Netherlands it is not a matter of cultural passing, because they know that Dutch culture is their culture and feel that they have a say in what it looks like. The feelings of entitlement connected to their cultural Dutchness and, if you will, perceived blankness or Dutch neutrality, complicate the political, personal, and economic aspects. Even though there is a generational difference in cultural ownership of what it means to be Dutch and different feelings of entitlement, all generations are approached as the same and are forced to take a position based on the same mechanisms of possible exclusion. These choices seem easier for other Afro artists who live and work outside of the Netherlands but operate in the Dutch and European market. To think the self through language then becomes an exercise in balancing out all these different interests.

The Jungerman/Grantsaan duo embraced the otherness and tried to unpack the Dutch Afro condition from a geographical position, effectively discussing the in-between space, decolonizing it in an effort to balance out the status quo. Tedja, alternatively, immersed himself in the in-between and, in an effort to transcend it, proposed to *Eat the Frame!* His effort was to destroy the frame that makes the status quo possible. Both sides tried to artistically negotiate their subject position in the Dutch Afro condition through curatorial practices. Their different approaches were both actively geared toward changing their positions in the landscape and had different effects on the Dutch artistic environment and the artists involved.

With the three publications — Jungerman and Grantsaan's *Wakaman* and Tedja's *Hosselen* and the *Eat the Frame!* catalog — Wakaman succeeded in centering Afro artists' subjectivity and work. They established a trilogy that needs to be read and analyzed as contemporary Dutch Afro art theory.

As a consequence of these developments, and from a Dutch Afro position aiming at establishing a different normal space, the Dutch Afro condition has now been furnished with two distinctive Afro examples of curating contemporary art in the frame of the Dutch context. Both have to deal with the narrative that is based on the developments in the Netherlands through thinking about African American art and the development of state policy and its consequences. One way of curating is to inhabit the institutional discourse that has developed over the years concerning the position of the Dutch Afro artist in the landscape and trying to change the position of the artists from the inside out. The other comprises the self-initiated exhibitions that aim to establish Dutch Afro artists' production beyond ideas of the quality argument and away from the existing framework — in other words, to eat the frame. From an Afro perspective, both aim to further the Dutch Afro artistic position in the Dutch art landscape by means of a curatorial practice, which I call *action curating*.

5

Cultural Multiplicity as Default: Action Curating Dutch Afro Subjectivity

The Lived Experience of Dutch Afro and Migrant Artists Native to the Netherlands

So far, the central question has been whether it is possible to read Dutch Afro artistic production as native to the Netherlands. Focusing on the Dutch particularities, my intention has been to move toward a language that takes into account the subjective experiences of Dutch native artists, curators, and critics as a tool to balance out the current institutional language on inclusive museum practices. My proposed method has been to depart from "the prevailing British and Americo-centric discourse"[1] and to concentrate on the production of language that considers the specifics of local Dutch sensibilities. I now want to conclude by providing insight into the way artists, curators, and directors positioned themselves in relation to this question and method on May 27, 2017 by means of a *krutu*.

---

1   Paul Gilroy, "Foreword: Migrancy, Culture, and a New Map of Europe," in *Blackening Europe: The African American Presence,* ed. Heike Raphael-Hernandez (Routledge, 2004), xi–xxii.

A *krutu* is a gathering where issues of governance and law are brought before the members of society. It sets out from the assertion that we belong to a single community and therefore, in this context, it should not be interpreted as an intercultural meeting, but as a meeting that embraces the inherent cultural multiplicity as its default position. The head of the *krutu* is normally the leader of the specific community who listens to all parties and then retreats with the advisors or elders to consider all the facts and opinions brought before the *krutu*. In our specific case, I considered the leader to be the current Dutch art world with its need to diversify and the advisors the communities of cultural producers present. Essentially, I considered the Dutch art world to be a subjectivity whose decisions are advised by, informed through, and executed by the cultural producers. I conceived of this method as a possibility for departing from the usual abstract conversation in the Dutch visual arts landscape revolving around the effect of the perception of race and ethnicity when discussing diversity and quality in the arts. Taking my cue from action research,[2] understanding the *krutu* as a contemporary discursive curatorial project emerging from a migrant experience, with the specific aim of changing the status quo, is action research transformed into *action curating*.

In the open session of the *krutu,* twenty-six invited artists, curators, directors, and critics individually presented a three- to five-minute response to the question: "What would your considerations be toward developing a language that considers work made by Dutch artists with a migrant background as culturally Dutch?" The question aimed to uncover thoughts that could lead to useable language to reimagine the Dutch art landscape. As expected, the answers in this open session were not radical and stayed within the lines of respectable diversity rhetoric.

In the second, closed part, the same question was addressed in a private and focused session through multiple subquestions. Like the open session, it was set up as a multilogue, meaning

---

2   Jean McNiff and Jack Whitehead, *Action Research: Principles and Practice,* 2nd ed. (RoutledgeFalmer, 2002).

that participants were encouraged to listen to what was being said, without trying to internally or verbally produce a response. The way to make this happen was that one was only allowed to respond to the question and not to the previous speaker. The underlying idea was that, when contemplating the question, actively listening and postponing any thoughts about what someone else said, a (minor) shift could occur in how the Dutch (visual) arts landscape is perceived through a multitude of voices. The questions that were asked concerned tracing historical conditions, how these developments were experienced, and how the participants inhabited the current situation and might imagine the future.[3]

The results confirmed my own conclusions: namely, that language is one of these discursive spaces where what is considered Dutch culture has become racialized. It was in this verification process of culture as racialized that the closed session of the *krutu* in particular was different from other public programming around diversity. It gathered all research within one consolidated forum by rearticulating long-standing issues around race and culture in 2017. In so doing, it became apparent how invested all participating subjects were in the Dutch self-image and consequently demonstrated the cultural nativeness of all participating subjects, including the Dutch Afro ones. Testing the key questions, understanding how they were reformulated by the community underscored the need and demand for a different type of discourse and curatorial practice.

Krutu: Action Curating in Practice

As the initial invitation from the Van Abbemuseum to the participants stated, the *krutu* was set up to focus on artistic "linguistic and curatorial strategies surrounding art made by Afro subjects in the Dutch context," and "used to unpack the con-

---

3   For reasons of confidentiality, the remarks of the closed session will be referenced through respondent numbers either in-text or in the footnotes. Respondents in the open session are identified in-text.

cepts, sensitivities and artistic expressions that are typical of the [Dutch] region." As respondent no. 16 said:

> The Krut'krutu (Krutu) provides a way of thinking through this difficulty because one can listen without having to formulate an answer. This gives the space to listen to what is being said without having to place it within one's own frame of reference.

Speaking about local Afro-ness in Dutch was a deliberate method as it underscored the inability of the Dutch discourse to speak about race in the arts. This approach was in contrast to most Dutch gatherings, which, when considering diversity and inclusivity in the visual arts, were held in English because of the invited guests or (presumably) non-Dutch audience present. This encouraged the participants, who were mostly not trained in Dutch theoretical language either, the audience, and myself to think and express our sensitivities by speaking our native tongue. The change that occurred in me and the participants coming out of this discursive curatorial project, driven by a migrant background experience, underscored the significance of action curating while demonstrating the need for Dutch-specific language. Both are needed in the Dutch art world to create a different environment that is capable of analyzing the visual production of Dutch Afro artists as native to the Dutch artistic landscape. The terminologies that have emerged as useful in this book arise from that same space as the imagined normal space: the space between languages, an inherently hybrid space that emerges from the fold where a different meaning arises in the derailment between languages.

What I suggest is that when in its original form the meaning of a particular word cannot be directly transferred from one language to another, the agency it has in one language cannot be transferred either. As a consequence, agency and meaning are left in the fold/in-between space to be appropriated, and thus describe the inherently hybrid space. As a referent to the meaning the word has in the language from which it originated, it then expands on it to create the conditions in which the imagined normal space can be conceptualized.

Terms such as "cultural nativeness" and "blankness" therefore should not be read as newly minted terms, but rather as linguistic flashes, born out of inherent hybridity, suggesting the existence of an imagined normal space.

The current landscape of Dutch art critique does not provide space for establishing Afro nativeness. In this experience the contemporary Dutch Afro subjects are arguably comparable to the post-WWII Black British and the African Americans of the first great migration (1916–1930). Colonially inspired beliefs and the subsequent differing treatment of Afro subjects are so virulent that imagining any sort of (Dutch) Afro subjectivity has to somehow take this into account. The presence of this structure permeates all communication about a Dutch Afro subjectivity as culturally native to the Netherlands.

To open up this communication, close assessment of the Dutch language is a method to unearth obscured problems and bring to light underlying cultural sentiments. The impact of this method is so strong that during the *krutu* it was suggested that one of the problems of being "forced to speak and hear everything in Dutch [is that it] reeks of nationalism."[4]

The assumption of nationalism, which is strongly tied to the notion of fascism, was that it would neglect looking beyond the Netherlands and learning from it. Yet it is precisely this looking beyond the Netherlands that has stifled the development of local concepts and language about Dutch pain connected to its histories. The looking beyond, specifically to the United States, involuntarily has negated the crucial differences in views on race. Art critic and curator Ferdinand van Dieten observed that the American situation is a "colonial society in which the colonizers are still in charge. A society where the white underclass is an associate-colonizer. Dutch racism does not go to this extent of mortal fear but is one of exclusion and disadvantage." He stated that the challenge is to keep wondering whether our

---

4   Respondent no. 23, *Krut'krutu*, closed session, May 27, 2017.

language is capable of speaking that difference when the Dutch underclass does not have a group beneath them but one that is imagined against them. Van Dieten remarked that those who experience this difference and can indicate how it is experienced on an emotional level must first do this work in the development of language. He concluded that "the underclass racism is not that important for the Dutch art world. It is mainly colonial superiority, which can be found at the top layers of society, which includes the arts. It is constitutive of the elite culture which does not account for its role in world history but looks at a formal analysis of its own living environment." In the words of anthropologist Marcus Balkenhol, "[w]hat counts as Dutch is considered to be what white people do."

Curator and director of TENT in Rotterdam, Anke Bangma, questioned whether conventional language could be a tool to actualize who belongs to Dutch culture. In the participant group, it became clear that language and the visual should move to a modus of relations, away from this societal racialized view that favors whiteness. One of the resulting ideas was that the Dutch cultural community that is Afro belongs to the present and the future of Europe and the Netherlands. To get there, Van Dieten wondered whether there is a language in Dutch, with a consciousness of the future, such as Du Bois's double consciousness. Curator and critic Vincent van Velsen imagined it as a consciousness that disavows the polar system of Western/non-Western — one that moves away from hyphenated identities that mathematically imply that the second part is subtracted from the first. In his words, "a language that foregrounds the togetherness of these words that is closer to the truth, meaning Surinamese *plus* Dutch."

This sort of plus-language, not yet existing in the Dutch context, creates a new symbolic meaning with a future. This is the sort of language that is needed to give shape to the imagined normal space. For this language to come into being, curator and scholar Chandra Frank put forward the following questions:

> How to create a language that puts language at the center and is not confined to white Dutch-ness? How do we describe, analyze, and what aesthetics do we see and acknowledge? How do we organize [exhibitions]? What does it mean to be here, which includes a "there" that is brought here?

This highlights the importance of action curating as a strategy rooted in a migrant-background experience. The question of the open session was: "What would your considerations be toward developing a language that considers work made by Dutch artists with a migrant background as culturally Dutch, as native?" Translating this into Dutch was problematic. The translation of the word "native" to Dutch is literally the word *inboorling/ inheems*. These words allude strongly to colonial history, which is still a painful and ignored issue, and have heavily negative connotations. During the process, I translated culturally native in a way that I thought would position it in the contemporary Dutch discussions about belonging by using the term *cultureel autochtoon* (culturally autochthonous). Whereas autochthony is already claimed by whiteness and connected to geography, "cultural autochthony" as an innovative construction in contemporary art could be located in the art and cultural world of the Netherlands. However, as Nira Yuval-Davis states, autochthonous politics are about claiming "We were here before you, and therefore we belong and you do not!"[5] Consequently, "cultural autochthony" became a new, albeit problematic, term, which we could fill up with meaning and give shape to what it means to be Black in the Netherlands.

Now, in hindsight, the Dutch notion of *cultureel eigen* or *cultuureigen* (culturally proper) appears more appropriate as it signifies being inherent to a culture and is separated from the (racial) project of a "politics of belonging"[6] that is signified by

---

5   TBA21 Thyssen-Bornemisza Art Contemporary, "EPHEMEROPTERÆ
     V - Nira Yuval-Davis," *YouTube*, November 18, 2016, https://www.youtube.
     com/watch?v=fL8rvvCipFM.

6   Ibid.

the word "autochthony." In Dutch, Dutch Afro art as cultuureigen makes sense and can be explored, while the idea of "culturally proper" does not exist in English. With this proposition, Frank's question about how to create a language that puts language at the center and is not confined to white Dutch-ness is exemplified through action curating as a discursive exercise. It is an exercise in language that goes against the grain of the Dutch tendency to simplify art speak in order to appeal to large audiences. As Van Dieten noted, "[m]aybe dulling language is a tool of the Dutch elite to mask differentiation in consciousness."

Following this premise, it can be argued that looking for Dutch language and concepts to discuss the issues raised, due to the assembly of art professionals, essentially maintains this differentiation. Alternatively, the *krutu* undid this differentiation by working toward an inclusive linguistic model based rooted in the diversity of the group rather than in the extant art-historical narrative. Exchanging an international word such as "autochthonous" for *cultuureigen* in the artistic discourse evidences the Dutch language as a method to conceptualize local sensibilities. In an effort to eventually locate Dutch Afro artistic output as native, addressing historical linguistic and curatorial Dutch tropes through this form of conceptualization proved useful.

Narratives + Space – Race

How museums experienced the changes in the cultural field and historically interpreted diversity in such a way that it excluded Dutch Afro-ness as a native subjectivity has been discussed in Chapter Three. Demonstrating that this continues to be a problem, curator Martijn van Nieuwenhuyzen mentioned that in 2017 there was little discussion about what cultural difference means in Dutch museums. He argued that since the 1960s the Dutch art canon has not been revisited and that hiring curators with a migration background to finally rewrite it could make a difference in perspective. Curator and director of Framer Framed, Josien Pieterse, noted that this could be done by "developing a way of working that is based on a diversity of narratives with different curators." She also stated that getting the work into the institutions is made difficult by the current theories that are the basis for institutions and education:

> After analyzing these, the question is how do new practices develop by providing autonomy in the exhibition space? Bureaucratic frames of new public management in an organization, value frames in exhibitions and communication frames. How do you arrive at a language that deconstructs the top-down development of language?

These remarks respond to my questions about the museums, the canon, cultural perspective, current theoretical frameworks, language, heritage, neutrality, objectivity, and redistribution of space that have been discussed in the previous chapters. They are rephrased through the voice of the community and, by highlighting narratives and space rather than race, arguably support the argument of embracing Dutch culture thinking as a tool toward the imagined normal space. Getting there means constructing a different language based on close examination of local sensibilities, such as our investment in the idea of a non-racial, equivalent, and meritocratic society.

The role of the Van Abbemuseum in this process was that, as a sequel to the *Be(com)ing Dutch* program (2006–2008), they organized the ten-day *Be(com)ing More* caucus in 2017. For *Be(com)ing More,* they invited artists, organizers, and thinkers working in the Netherlands to author distinct days and moments. The museum believed that at this critical juncture in 2017 of the growing Black Lives Matter movement (which went in tandem with an ever-growing Dutch Afro awareness), it was vital to listen, consolidate, and share. The eventual *Be(com)ing More* program represented the museum asking how art could provide a productive, critical space where solidarities are formed and political visions rehearsed. In other words, it asked: "How can we become more?"[7]

---

7   Van Abbemuseum, invitation email Krut'krutu, April 29, 2017.

With *Be(com)ing More,* rather than expressing their opinion as they had done during *Be(com)ing Dutch* ten years earlier, the museum decided to see first which cultural producers in the visual arts with a Black or migrant background could be involved in the process. According to curator Annie Fletcher, the decision was made not to speak as the museum but rather to share the institution with people who are important for them and have something urgent to say and discuss through intervention. In the final program the museum acknowledged the changed environment where migrant-background critics were demanding their cultural citizenship. The program included Gloria Wekker, Iris Kensmil, Bijmerpark Theater, Hip-Hop Huis, University of Colour, and myself, among others. In the process the museum provided space and extended museological legitimacy to different forms of knowledge and experiences and addressed the criticism that had been articulated with regard to the *Be(com)ing Dutch* caucus ten years previously. The idea of the *krutu* as action curating was to collaborate with the Van Abbemuseum in an exploration of how an institute could contribute more holistically to the production and empowerment of plural subjectivities. What it did was "redistribute the space of which we know it exists," as cultural critic Simone Zeefuik proposed during the *krutu,* and made an effort to "arrive at a language that deconstructs the top-down development of language," as Pieterse suggested.

For Bangma, making a step in the direction of the previously proposed plus-language becoming self-evident within art institutions also meant looking at where that institution was located and wondering what it should be or could become. Pointing out the problem of language and explaining it when making an exhibition is key in an institutional context where the audience is mainly white. Therefore, according to Els van der Plas, director of the National Opera and Ballet, explicit use of current language was a way of creating a new language. Amsterdam Museum curator Imara Limon added that "this language should not be construed as a reaction or addition to the white Western idiom but rather as a language that stands on its own and show the inadequacies in the current institutional language." From Bangma's position as a director based in the most diverse city of the Netherlands, Rotterdam, an institutional and curatorial position should therefore not be fundamental but situated and practical: "It is not about discussing stuff but concrete actions toward settling the semantic difference between Dutch [white], foreign, and artists with a multiple background [Dutch with a migrant background]."

The development of this terminology or language makes explicit the imbalance in collections and curatorial decisions. Respondent 20 added that speaking it is a way of starting to change the *normaalwaarden* (normal values) that are in place, though from an institutional perspective such a language is often considered too niche and problematic to inform and attract (the mainly white) visitors. With this remark, the respondent alluded to the "innate incomprehensibility" of work dealing with Dutch Afro "life-feeling" (i.e., Black experience) that remains an impregnable fortress for Dutch art critique and the curatorial practice.

In popular culture, however, this making explicit (of whiteness) already happens. The language used by musicians is inspiring yet has found no translation in the visual arts environment. Tent curator Mariette Dölle stated that this inclusive language originating in the music industry is energetic and should be incorporated in speaking about art, while Pieterse noted that this popular culture language is looking for "renewed commonality." It creates what Van Nieuwenhuyzen called "elephant tracks" that disrupt the rigid system and construct free zones that do not acknowledge extant institutional formats, becoming a meeting ground for artists with different backgrounds. Here, new formulas for artistic criteria can be encountered without being immediately categorized. These "elephant tracks" are the in-between space where this subjectivity is shaping the new normal space, which at this time remains imaginary.

It is in this space where white cultural workers (researchers, etc.) can recognize that whiteness is also a color and a position from which to do research and create art, resulting in recognition of the self as a racialized and nonneutral position, as respondent 5 suggested. From the current institutional point of view, when racial background poses as culture, whiteness is passing for Western culture. Culturally passing implies that one element (ethnicity or race) can be disregarded because there is a space surrounding it in which an articulation can be formed. Respondent 14 argued that, in that sense, the contemporary populist Dutch self-image is culturally passing for Western universalism and blankness with a disregard for its colonial past. Once this is recognized, the museum can become a space of histories, rather than a space for a single universalist view. This space of "histories" that the museum became with the *krutu* was rightly criticized by respondent 9. They stated that this context of the museum was forced upon the participants and was not necessarily a context that is essential to achieve appreciation for the discourse on Afro-ness in the Dutch arts. However, as redistributed agency by museum proxy, it did answer to the cultural, social, and spatial entitlement that is experienced by Dutch Afro artists and consequently inscribes itself in the Dutch national self-image of nonracial equivalence.

The tension between this entitlement and inhabiting the national self-image raises the question whether Dutch Afro art can be located as native to the Dutch artistic landscape, following the question whether migrant-background Dutch subjects can be located as native to the local environment. This opportunity of the *krutu* allowed for returning the existing research and the questions back to the institutional context, which worked through similar questions in the past, in which Dutch art criticism moved from exotic and mystical in the early 1980s to a postcolonial context that included world art at the beginning of the twenty-first century. In this process there was an (internationally oriented) focus on the contrast between so-called traditional art practices and Western art practices, a cultural difference between Black and white. The critique focused on "identity" and the perceived inability of non-Western (particularly Afro) modern artists to attain the same quality standard as their Western (white) counterparts. This trajectory produced the key argument in the appreciation of works, which is the false binary between ethnicity and quality that is defined as the quality argument. As a curatorial question, Okwui Enwezor tackled this issue in *Documenta XI* (2002) with its theme of "cultural identity"[8] in the postcolonial era, when he insisted that issues faced by African artists are similar to those faced by artists in the West.[9] And that "it is totally imaginable that Documenta is not the right platform for many artists."[10] I argue that with this line of thinking Enwezor destabilized the quality argument by proposing that Western art institutions are insufficiently equipped to grasp the full complexity of current cultural identities.

Becoming and Refusing to Be (Artistically) Black: From Racialization to Culturalization

Factual evidence gathered during the *krutu,* however, does not compensate for the lack of concepts and language to speak about the Dutch Afro experience and the paradox of simultaneously becoming and refusing to be (artistically) Black. Previously I proposed a privilege of existing in a normal space where Blackness exists without reference to whiteness.[11] Back then I understood this as stemming from a subjectivity that conceives itself as self-evidently privileged, regardless of the construction of the dominant society that judges on the basis of race. It is this kind of imagining that became a problem for later generations for whom, according to Yuval-Davis, "belonging is about feeling safe, feeling entitled to particular rights and roles, [and] is composed of emotional, cognitive, and normative dimensions."[12]

---

8   Rob Perrée, "Directeur Okwui Enwezor geeft visie op zijn Documenta: 'Ik dans niet voor geld,'" *Kunstbeeld* 26, no. 5 (2002): 7.
9   Ibid.
10 Ibid., 9.
11 Wayne Modest, "On the Self-Evidence of Blackness: An Interview with Charl Landvreugd," *Small Axe: A Caribbean Journal of Criticism* 18, no. 3 (2014): 133–34.
12 TBA21 Thyssen-Bornemisza Art Contemporary, "EPHEMEROPTERÆ V - Nira Yuval-Davis."

Over the years I came to understand this as the previously mentioned entitlement that is rooted in Dutch (colonial) cultural nativeness. It took me so long because the Dutch language does not have a word for this feeling in common parlance. In Dutch, *entitlement* translates as the "right to" and, when we start speaking about cultural rights, the debate quickly takes on an ethnic (or religious) motif, moving in the direction of the dreaded nationalist rhetoric.

Looking at this being confirmed and discussed during the *krutu* suggested that the level of cultural entitlement depends on the extent to which a sense of belonging to and being part of Dutch culture is experienced. Balkenhol noted that, since the 1980s when minorities came under pressure to integrate into Dutch culture, culturalization has had a large role in speaking about the multicultural society, while critic, curator, and crown member of the National Culture Council Board, Ozkan Gölpinar, added that culturalization meant that there has been a main theme to art projects in the past twenty years: "Keep your hands off our traditions!" Gölpinar continued by saying that, as a consequence, for people with a migrant background, "a place in tradition is not obtained easily as one is never invited in wholeheartedly," and that, as a way of circumventing this predicament, one could "wholeheartedly embrace Dutch culture, the culture of one's lifelong surroundings, and totally inhabit it, in a way that it is in your pores and cannot be washed off."

Becoming, or self-evidently being, encultured brings with it entitlement in social interactions (social entitlement) that is not automatically acknowledged. Lived experience shows that being encultured and the resulting social entitlement do not equate to a position to decide what tradition is or what the Dutch visual art landscape may become. What is needed to make that happen is what Gaye Theresa Johnson conceptualized in 2013 as *spatial entitlement*. Speaking about postwar Los Angeles, she describes this as

> the spatial strategies and vernaculars utilized by working-class youth to resist the increasing demarcations of race and

class [...] spatial entitlement entails occupying, inhabiting, and transforming physical spaces, but also imagining, envisioning, and enacting discursive spaces that "make room" for new affiliations and identifications.[13]

When read through this argument, the action research done of the *krutu* was curatorially executing spatial entitlement — in other words, action curating. From this perspective and specific problem space, then, using the cultural to locate Dutch Afro subjectivity as culturally native to the Netherlands can be done through different forms of spatial entitlement. During the *krutu,* artist and activist Quinsy Gario simply created a visual and performative image of eating a mango with the skin still on, as is done in certain parts of the Caribbean. By doing so, he challenged the discursive practice of presenting a statement about Dutchness in the institutional setting of a "symposium." The power that lies in nonverbal communication forced the viewer into a different frame of reference, moving into what, according to artist Antonio Guzman, "Yoruba tradition teaches us, namely that language is a matter of symbolism." This can also be internalized through inhabiting the performance. Remy Jungerman proposed closing off everyone's ears with the palm of their hands. Having done this, one tapped on the back of one's head several times. After taking the hands off one's ears, Jungerman mentioned several Surinamese Maroon place names and asked the audience to imagine what these places looked like. What happened was that, because the language was not understood by the majority, the names of the places became sounds to them. Ending with the name Libatongo. which means "the language of the river," one wondered what the sounds did to the imagination and what sort of language this river produced.

In the context of the *krutu,* these two challenges were examples of how Dutch Afro artists could exert influence on

---

13 Gaye Theresa Johnson, *Spaces of Conflict, Sounds of Solidarity: Music, Race, and Spatial Entitlement in Los Angeles* (University of California Press, 2013), 1.

the Dutch art scene through linguistic, visual, and sonic confusion that sharpens the mind while conjuring questions of doubt and inconvenience or nuisance. With this doubt, the artist moved into what artist and womanist patricia kaersenhout called "worlds of the swinging paradox where one is considered Blacker and sometimes less Black depending on circumstance." It is this doubt that arrives through executing and inhabiting spatial entitlement. It comes from entering unknown and uncomfortable terrain by means of the imagination, which is necessary for the construction of the imagined normal space that is desired by cultural entitlement.

Depending on the social history and historical connection to the Netherlands, the way in which cultural and spatial entitlement is experienced is different for the various Dutch migrant groups. Respondent 22 made a point out of noticing that the majority group question of diversity runs parallel to the question of self-reflective inclusivity for people of Afro descent (or migrant backgrounds) when thinking about becoming self-evident in the Dutch art world. Culturally passing as Black Dutch, which entails being considered encultured enough for cultural stereotypes to be relatively mitigated, often means being equated with Surinamese Dutch. According to respondent 15, this means acknowledging that Surinamese ethnic privilege, granted by white Dutch society at large based on the level of assimilation, puts forward the question of how Blackness is populated in the Dutch community, Respondent 4 asked: "Is it even possible to be considered part of this (Afro) artistic community when one is not part of the Afro community coming out of the Dutch colonial past?"

With a nonexisting coherent social or political community among people of African descent, the question was asked how trust can be built and who is being exploited when, as respondent 15 wondered, Afro Caribbean subjects use the African body to establish a back-to-the-roots feel in the arts while not having compassion for the refugees of African descent and voting for the PVV (Freedom Party)?[14] Considering my own Surinamese background and enjoying this Surinamese privilege, suspicion was rightly cast on my motives. In other words, what efforts did Dutch Afro artists and curators of specifically Surinamese descent make to produce an Afro-inclusive image of Dutch Blackness in the arts? What this interaction demonstrated is that, partly due to different privileges granted to different Afro ethnicities, a general Dutch Afro cultural citizenship cannot be achieved solely based on feelings of entitlement or racial identification. Afro ethnicity linked to cultural background is the defining factor in the acknowledgment of entitlement and consequently creates a hierarchy of belonging within the larger Dutch Afro community. In order to be able to interethnically speak within the Dutch Afro community about this hierarchy, we will have to develop local concepts and language.

The New Native: Self-Evident Hybridity

The curatorial propositions made by Afro artist–curators in the Netherlands followed a trajectory of self-determination that relates to Stuart Hall's historical account of Black artistic moments as a spiral retelling. Starting with the Srefidensi group (1970s) establishing a gallery space for Caribbean artists and Cosmic Illusion (1980s) organizing exhibitions that aligned the artists with the then prevailing Modernism of the New York–Cologne axis, we arrive at Felix de Rooy with the exhibition *Wit over Zwart* (1989), which showed the colonial legacy of racism through objects. This exhibition formed a curatorial turning point by centering the troublesome race–culture axis in the Dutch artistic landscape. Wakaman (2000s) questioned how this legacy informed the perception of their subjectivity and the work they produced, looking for new curatorial routes that centred their own experience. With the *krutu* (2017) the Wakaman curatorial arguments were transformed into action curating as

---

14 This remark refers to the city of Venray, which has a large community from Curaçao and is the largest Freedom Party stronghold in the Netherlands.

a method that affirms Afroness as native to the Dutch artistic landscape.

This forty-year trajectory effectively comes full circle in negotiating the usefulness, effectiveness and form of an artistic environment of affirmation, postulating a new, 21st-century beginning of curatorial strategies that is historically grounded and through the accelerated return of Afro and migrant experiences into the knowledge base shapes a different environment. With this in mind, artist Silvia Martes stated in an interview:

> As an Afro person, how much is one influenced by being born in the Netherlands and almost only seeing *blank* [white] people around, and in the media? Is it even possible to think from a space of Blackness when you live and come from this situation? [...] I think it would be wonderful to create films about normal people, about the everyday with people of color. That isn't asking too much, is it?[15]

With this statement Martes made clear that, when the racial assumptions are stripped from the work, it falls into the broader category of a migrant experience of being surrounded by a majority group. The tool to locate Dutch Afro art production as native to the Dutch artistic landscape can then be recognized as an aesthetic of belonging brought about through the digital, emerging from a Dutch immigrant background.[16] For Dutch Afro artists this immigrant background means that, due to "cultural difference," work dealing with Dutch Afro "life-feeling" (identity) is considered incomprehensible and consequently proves to be an impregnable fortress for Dutch art critique. Stressing this argument, Van Velsen comments that the ethnic fetishism emerging from this form of analysis denies Dutch *cultuureigen* (culturally proper, autochthonous) agency

---

15 Silvia Martes, interview with the author, Skype, March 31, 2016.

16 Regarding "migrant esthetics," see Graham Huggan, *Interdisciplinary Measures: Literature and the Future of Postcolonial Studies* (Liverpool University Press, 2008).

to artists with a migrant background, informing how they are approached and consequently speak about themselves. Their biographical migrant narrative "is brought in as new and as a way to increase [autochthonous] knowledge and economics." This idea is solid and hinges on what Van Rosmalen called the *daardroom* (there-dream), which entails seeing the artists as being from "there" even though they may only have "second-hand experiences located in the country of origin."

This manner and language of framing is, in Bangma's words, reiterated through "patterns in press releases and writings on the artists" that construct local artists with a migrant background as having a "background" while the others (white artists) are floating around in an autonomous space. The local migrant-background artists do not get the same type of appreciation as "an enrichment of the Dutch artistic landscape and her international stature" as does an American or Lebanese artist who comes to study in the Netherlands and is consequently considered an international artist: "An artist born in the Netherlands and drawing from their transnational background is not viewed as contributing to the international character of the Dutch art scene."

Bangma further points out that those "artists with a multiple background are always discussed in terms of symbolism and tradition [i.e., paganism] and the work of artists with a so-called single background discussed in terms of agency and artistic experiment." It is a culturally specific language of autonomy that seems unable to speak about art and culture without thinking personal ethnic and cultural background. This treatment of "autonomous" artists linguistically reduces culturally multiple-background native individuals to a single, lesser narrative.

In the 2010s, Dutch Afro awareness produces a movement with many different organizations working toward including Afro-ness in the understanding of what this Dutchness is. Even though it cannot be compared to the civil rights movement, this awareness develops using similar methods of art and activism. Supported by digital media, this evolution occurs in tandem with worldwide Afro awareness, as exemplified in moments such as #BlackLivesMatter (2013), #RhodesMustFall (2015), and Black Twitter. In effect, Ron Karenga's 1968 questions are reiterated: "Whose vision of the world is finally more meaningful, ours or the white oppressors? What is truth? Or more precisely, whose truth shall we express, that of the oppressed or the oppressors?"[17] No matter whether it is done through the racial component or through the cultural elements, the imaginative language that artists and activists produce with their works renders the edges of the imagined normal space and new contemporary artistic environment visible.

In response, the action-curating approach operates in a broader Dutch field where the majority group is struggling with the idea of cultural diversity, which is a strong concern for the majority group that is unwilling to understand itself as a part of the multiplicity over which it is losing control. In Dutch (cultural) institutions the often unconscious desire for ethnic dominance results in cosmetic solutions that require a "Black person in the annual report," as respondent 19 phrased it. This way of dealing with diversity has become a way to demonstrate awareness without actually making a change toward a multiplicity of voices on an executive level. As it centers whiteness, this diversity discussion is at odds with the growing minority and Afro awareness of this time. Consequently, in thinking cultural diversity, it is of more concern to the museum to include Afro-ness in its program and exhibitions than it is for Afro-ness to be concerned with the museum.

When Afro artists come with explicitly Black concepts, they create a paradox in the Dutch artistic landscape that is focused on institutional recognition, the local, and the global. With these concepts they culturally pass as (international) Black, which is recognized by funding bodies that invest in their practice. But by not complying with the rules of blankness and presenting themselves in this way, the artists are not recognized by the local institutions as specifically relevant to the Dutch artistic

---

17   Larry Neal, "The Black Arts Movement," *The Drama Review: TDR* 12, no. 4 (1968): 30.

discourse and their artistic and curatorial expertise is neglected by those institutions when it comes to issues of "diversity" in the Netherlands, as respondent 4 indicated.

Consequently, these artists develop careers that are more acknowledged as Dutch outside of the Netherlands than they are locally. Combined with the Dutch reaction to the production of explicitly Black concepts, a hierarchy of belonging is then produced that advances artistic loyalty to global Black culture, which in turn influences the local understanding of aesthetics and identities that are not part of the mainstream Dutch art market. There is a strong relation between recognition, representation, and the production of Dutch Afro subjectivity through the works of such artists, effectively perpetuating the dominance of English-language discourse in the development of local concepts and language.

The work that comes out of this commonality creates "elephant tracks" that disrupt the system. With Dutch Afro artists being recognized in a discussion about global Blackness and having the power to represent themselves through social media, the function of structured cultural authorities becomes of less importance in shaping Dutch Afro-ness. Stimulated by the developments in popular culture, the result is an art that is deeply immersed in the Dutch Afro condition as an experience. The variety of works emerging from this produce the shape on which the Dutch Afro condition is molded in an effort to change how it is experienced. It is spatial entitlement at work through pieces of art that become a metonym for social and political activism ("artivism") that is driven by cultural entitlement. The relation of this artivism to fine art or cultural practices of blankness is often limited to a promotional link, but its intertwined relation with digital spaces is the social link between high-impact popular culture and low-impact "high art."

During the *krutu,* cultural entrepreneur Ricardo Burgzorg remarked that any new outlook should reassess the quality argument that is used as an easy tool of exclusion. Unwillingness to do so and therefore a lack of understanding have placed Dutch Afro artists in the artistic space of the less qualified rather than a minority that is Dutch. Willingness to scrutinize this circumstance becomes an exercise in recognizing the locals as fundamental agents in rethinking the current art environment. As part of this willingness, the use of a quality argument by directors, curators, and other art professionals should be carefully grounded in the understanding of a "visual language that one is not used to and may be hard to understand with the specific Western visual language as a frame." For Jelle Bouwhuis it is matter of "decolonizing liberalism and the enlightenment as a way of looking at the museological world. [...] a new language may be found in critique or affirmative sabotage." Imara Limon concludes that the current limited vision on language and the visual signifies the whiteness of the institution, which needs to be made explicit by plastering on the wall: "White Institute."

Demonstrating that it is a white-centric, non-racial equivalence meritocracy, according to respondent 20, such a gesture would create movement so that in the future such explcitness will no longer be necessary. Respondent 16 asked: "A big issue in this process is to always make apparent again why and for whom?" Explicitness in this current moment is important because curators have to be aware "of how to speak about working (with) black artists, the practicalities of press release, representation and what is being achieved," respondent 16 added. In this process of establishing a new environment where race and ethnicity do not drive the arguments around the quality of the work or its belonging to the Dutch art environment, it is crucial to consider the implications of mentioning someone's ethnic background. The curatorial criteria for selecting an artist should be based on looking at, speaking and comparing with other artists, respondent 13 suggested. The question, therefore, is not whether the transformation needs to take place, but rather how? There is no single answer to this and it needs to be re-asked continuously to produce a different playing field.

Respondent 18: "It would then be advisable to look for what that is here and now, in that space, in the broader cultural field. The different forms of knowledge form this broader field."

Respondent 16: "It is really about everything from what you think you are as an institution, which is not yet understood."

Respondent 17: "Doing this, Dutch cultural institutions may learn to 'speak a language that speaks to many identities.'"

This was emphasized by the publicity for *Be(com)ing More,* which also stated "Be(com)ing More Black" Respondent 15 asked:

How does one become more Black? Is it something the institution really wants to do? What do we become when we become more Black, how do we become more Black, how can we have become more Black?

These questions point toward the agency exercised by institutions, curators, and critics in allowing Dutch Afro-ness, expressed as Blackness, to culturally pass into their understanding of the art world. This was an art world where the studio space in which the closed session of the *krutu* was held and which was carefully rearranged to accommodate the gathering failed to prevent the lighting from blinding some of the participants. This brought forth the question for whom the space was designed and what it was supposed to do in the first place. Rightly, my Afro-ness did not exclude me from being scrutinized for trying to pass the space as Afro-sensitive within a white institution. My Surinamese and educational background allowed me to culturally pass, but the agency that was provided to me by proxy did not allow for a full cultural translation and molding of the space into one that was right for a *krutu*. Even if it was conceived as action curating with the intention of bringing about minor changes in the status quo, it was still catering to a majority group idea about diversity. With all the best intentions on the part of all parties involved, with an invited Dutch

Afro curator, the diversity in a museum and "White Institute" is limited to *passing for* rather than *being* inclusive. It is symptomatic for the Dutch environment where even an institution like the Van Abbemuseum, which ten years after Gitta Luiten called for a close look at its structure, still did not have a curator of color. In such a construction the museum is not a home base but rather a place where others make place and the discussion goes back to considering the Dutch Afro condition in relation to the art world.

Alternatively, reaffirmed through the *krutu,* a "Black" space would provide an environment in which conceptualizing identity could be done without being damned if you don't and problematized when you do, in the words of respondent 21. While looking for a cultural space that could be outlined through language, the participants in the *krutu* formulated that creating one's own physical spaces was a necessity. They added that this space was desired and there was the conviction that there was an audience for something that was not a white cube. In terms of content, it could be, in the words of respondent 3, "a place where the visual language, body language, scent, color and hair are understood."

This proper space was imagined as a space where Afro-normative thinking was central, where Dutch Afro people could find out for themselves what Afro-ness was and how it could be inclusive. A space, respondent 22 continued, where it was possible to invent ways to distance oneself from the burdened colonial background and understand what migrating through different spaces resulted in. Looking into what such a space entailed was part of the work that could be done, informing other art institutions in their quest for a truly inclusive curatorial program.

I am explicitly making an argument toward a curatorial practice that is rooted in a migrant experience rather than one based in the institution as it is now. I am convinced that this is what we have to move toward to make the idea of the institution viable for coming generations. The point of departure of hybridity as degree zero is confirmed in the racial and ethnic mix that culturally identifies in a location, which in the past did not include those physical markers. This has to be the basis for everything one thinks about when it comes to the future. The idea of the singular identity does not hold up. Examining this needs theory and practice to go hand in hand in this contemporary period when we are training for the not-yet. It is a matter of writing and doing until we find a way that actually works as an idea of an institution or a curatorial practice.

While there is a need for autonomous cultural institutions where the normal space is not imagined, there is great hesitance toward a culturally ideological split from Dutch society with deliberately separated artistic environments — in other words, a racially driven separated cultural nation. This idea is considered sinister (respondent 1), summoning ideas of a dystopian sci-fi movie (respondent 19), which is scary and sounds like the United States (respondent 3). These reactions are a direct consequence of the sensibilities in Dutch Afro culture where many people have partners, family, and a social life comprised of different ethnicities. It is also a major underlying force in the paradox of simultaneously becoming and refusing to be Black, claiming Afro-ness as a native cultural position while refusing to become Black as an oppositional position. The understanding of the multi-ethnic and multicultural subjectivity that understands itself as Creole results in understanding emotive moves through culture, time, and space in terms comparable with other nations rather than understanding them as spatial movement of migration. A separate nation would create safety but not progress. A podium would allow for multiple paradigms while also allowing white people to learn how to shift gears when entering a space, respondent 3 added.

The question of whether Dutch Afro artists can be located as native to the Dutch artistic landscape is therefore answered with the question of whether the Netherlands is able to recognize and honor the social, spatial, and cultural entitlement that is experienced by these artists. All participants agree that there is no time to wait until this happens or we are invited again by a museum. We have to invite ourselves.

Bibliography

Archives

"Alg zaaltekst." November 24, 2005, TENT Archive. Wakaman, Programma, 2005.

"De Wakaman maakt geen hapsnap." October 19, 2005. TENT Archive, Wakaman, Programma, 2005.

"Info voor 24 nov. Website." August 31, 2006. TENT Archive, Wakaman, Programma, 2005.

"Info voor website uitbreiding Wakaman." December 29, 2005. TENT Archive, Wakaman, Programma, 2005.

Jungerman, Remy. "Brief aan Wakaman Koppels." January 4, 2009. Wakaman Archive Remy Jungerman.

———. "Brief Fbkvb." January 31, 2008. Wakaman Archive Remy Jungerman.

———. "Culturele uitwisseling / plan Suriname." October 5, 2007. Wakaman Archive Remy Jungerman.

———. "Opening FZ." February 20, 2009. Wakaman Archive Remy Jungerman.

———. "Plan Remy extra." February 25, 2008. Wakaman Archive Remy Jungerman.

———. "Programma details rj+mh-2." October 17, 2008. Wakaman Archive Remy Jungerman.

———. "Van 1700 tot Wakaman." February 11, 2008. Wakaman Archive Remy Jungerman.

———. "Vergadering 17 december Café de Jaren," December 18, 2007, Wakaman Archive Remy Jungerman.

Jungerman, Remy, and Gillion Grantsaan. "Plan van aanpak Remy Jungerman en Gillion Grantsaan." August 5, 2008. Wakaman Archive Remy Jungerman.

———. "Wakaman gaat lopen nieuw plan." August 5, 2008. Wakaman Archive Remy Jungerman.

kaersenhout, patricia. "Brief Patricia." October 31, 2008. Wakaman Archive Remy Jungerman.

———. "The Poetry of Being." November 7, 2008, Wakaman Archive Remy Jungerman.

Luiten, Gitta. "Gathering." January 26, 2007. Van Abbemuseum Archive, Symposia; Be(com)ing Dutch: The Gatherings, Algemeen, 2007.

Pieters, D. "Passant." Museumtijdschrift, October 21, 2009. Wakaman Archive Remy Jungerman.

"Programma multiavond 24 november." November 29, 2005. TENT Archive, Wakaman, Programma, 2005.

"Suriname deelnemers." September 21, 2005. TENT Archive, Wakaman, Programma, 2005.

Tedja, Michael. "Plan Michael." February 11, 2008, Wakaman Archive Remy Jungerman.

———. "Wakaman geredigeerd." October 19, 2005. TENT Archive, Wakaman, Programma, 2005.

———. "The Daily Fucked Up Intendant." February 21, 2008. Wakaman Archive Remy Jungerman.

Van Abbe Museum. "Annex 2, Persbericht Stimuleringsprijs voor Culturele Diversiteit Van Abbemuseum Eindhoven & Stichting InterArt Arnhem." Van Abbemuseum Archive, Symposia; Be(com)ing Dutch: The Caucus, Persberichten, 2007.

———. "Appendix 3: Re-Imagining the Collection, The Van Abbemuseum Proposal for 'Stimuleringsprijs Culturele Diversiteit.'" April 19, 2006. Van Abbemuseum Archive,

Symposia; Be(com)ing Dutch, Voorbereidingen, Algemeen, 2007.

———. "Persbericht Stimuleringsprijs voor Culturele Diversiteit Van Abbemuseum Eindhoven & Stichting InterArt Arnhem." Van Abbemuseum Archive, Symposia; Be(com)ing Dutch: The Caucus, Persberichten, 2007.

———. "Press Release November 2007." Van Abbemuseum Archive, Symposia; Be(com)ing Dutch: The Caucus, Persberichten, 2007.

———. "The Van Abbemuseum Proposal for 'Stimuleringsprijs Culturele Diversiteit.'" April 19, 2006. Van Abbemuseum Archive, Symposia; Be(com)ing Dutch, Voorbereidingen, Algemeen, 2007.

Vossen, M. "Bijlage 2, Aanvraag Stichting Doen – Ref. 07uit16754." July 12, 2007. Van Abbemuseum Archive, Symposia; Be(com)ing Dutch, Voorbereidingen, Algemeen, 2007.

———. "Toelichting Caucus Stichting Doen." August 22, 2007. Van Abbemuseum Archive, Symposia; Be(com)ing Dutch, Voorbereidingen, Algemeen, 2007.

Wakaman. "Distibutie boek Wakaman 2 feb 2009." July 5, 2009. Wakaman Archive Remy Jungerman.

———. "Uitn. Wakaman tekst." February 6, 2009. Wakaman Archive Remy Jungerman.

———. "Uitnodigingen en aanmeldingen." July 4, 2009. Wakaman Archive Remy Jungerman.

"Wakaman achterkant flyer1." November 10, 2005. TENT Archive, Wakaman, Programma, 2005.

"Zaalbrief Wakaman uitbreiding probeersel." November 23, 2005. TENT Archive, Wakaman, Programma, 2005.

Publications

"Aantal bezoekers Nederlandse musea gestegen." *NRC Handelsblad,* January 17, 1990. https://www.nrc.nl/ nieuws/1990/01/17/aantal-bezoekers-van-nederlandse-musea-gestege-6921606-a126352.

Adès, Dawn. "Kunst uit Latijns-Amerika." *Kunstbeeld* 13, nos. 7–8 (1989): 32–35.

Adusei-Poku, Nana. "The Multiplicity of Multiplicities: Post-Black Art and Its Intricacies." *Darkmatter,* November 29, 2012. http://www.darkmatter101.org/site/2012/11/29/the-multiplicity-of-multiplicities-%E2%80%93-post-black-art-and-its-intricacies/.

Andriessen, Theo, and Sirano Zalman. "Voorwoord." In *Double Dutch Educatief Project: Inleiding bij het didactisch werkboek.* Stichting Kunst Mondiaal, 1991.

Baartman, Nicoline. "De dingen moeten verotten." *De Volkskrant,* March 3, 1995. http://www.volkskrant.nl/archief/de-dingen-moeten-verrotten~a413570/.

Baartmans-van den Boogaart, Joep (Johanna). *Zover het oog reikt: Trans-culturele invloeden in het werk van zes Brabantse en zes van oorsprong niet-westerse kunstenaars.* Provincie Noord-Brabant, 1988.

Balibar, Étienne. *We, The People of Europe? Reflections on Transnational Citizenship.* Translated by James Swenson. Princeton University Press, 2004.

Bearden, Romare, Sam Gilliam, Jr., Richard Hunt, Jacob Lawrence, Tom Lloyd, William Williams, and Hale Woodruff. "The Black Artist in America: A Symposium." *Metropolitan Museum of Art Bulletin* 27, no. 5 (1969): 245–61.

Becker, Luciel E. "WildcoastArt: A New Concept, a New Result." In *Wakaman: Drawing Lines Connecting Dots,* by Remy Jungerman and Gillion Grantsaan. Wakaman Project, 2009.

Beek, Marijke. *Black USA: Overholland.* Lecturis, 1990.

van Beek, Willem. "De gelukkige familie van Houcine Bouchiba: Onder de Afrikaanse zon." *Kunstbeeld* 25, no. 3 (2001): 20–23.

———. "U-ABC: Beeldende kunst uit Latijns-Amerika." *Kunstbeeld* 13, no. 10 (1989): 14–17.

van den Berg, Nanda. "De kunst van het weglaten: De positie van allochtone beeldend kunstenaars." *De Gids* 157 (1994): 69–77.

Berk, Anne. "De Apartheid voorbij: Vrije vlucht van kunst in Zuid-Afrika." *Kunstbeeld* 21, no. 2 (1997): 18–19.

———. "Indonesiërs en Hollanders in Lakenhal: Oriëntatie op het eigen-aardige." *Kunstbeeld* 20, no. 5 (1996): 42–43.

Bhabha, Homi K. *The Location of Culture.* Routledge, 1994.

van Binnendijk, Chandra. "Waka Tjopu Visual Artists' Collective." In *Wakaman: Drawing Lines Connecting Dots,* by Remy Jungerman and Gillion Grantsaan. Wakaman Project, 2009.

Birch, Eva Lenox. "Harlem and the First Black Renaissance." In *The Harlem Renaissance,* edited by Harold Bloom. Infobase Publishing, 2004.

Blakely, Allison. "Coda: Black Identity in France in a European Perspective." In *Black France/France Noire: The History and Politics of Blackness,* edited by Trica Danielle Keaton, T. Denean Sharpley-Whiting, and Tyler Stovall. Duke University Press, 2012. DOI: 10.1515/9780822395348-018.

Blatter, Joachim. "Glocalization." *Encyclopedia Brittanica.* https://www.britannica.com/topic/glocalization.

Bool, Cas. "Het museum als instituut staat ter discussie." *Framer Framed.* https://framerframed.nl/dossier/het-museum-als-instituut-staat-ter-discussie/.

ter Borg, Lucette. "Verkrampt door de Nederlandse identiteit." *NRC Handelsblad,* May 31, 2008. https://www.nrc.nl/nieuws/2008/05/31/verkrampt-door-de-nederlandse-identiteit-11547744-a822169.

Bos, Eltje. "Beleid voor cultuur en migranten: Rijksbeleid en uitvoeringspraktijk, 1980–2004." PhD diss., University of Amsterdam, 2011.

Bos, Jesse, and Hester Poppinga. *Wit over Zwart: Beelden van zwarten in de westerse populaire cultuur.* Koninklijk Instituut voor de Tropen, 1989.

Bourriaud, Nicolas. *Relational Aesthetics.* Les Presses du réel, 2002.

van den Braak, Jolanda. "Met andere woorden: straattaal in Amsterdam." In *Taal in stad en land: Amsterdams,* by Jan Berns with Jolanda van den Braak. Sdu Uitgevers, 2002.

Burns, Alison. "'Show Me My Soul!': The Evolution of the Black Museum Movement in Postwar America." PhD diss.. University of Minnesota, 2008.

Byrne, John. "Be(com)ing Dutch: From Autonomy to Caucus & Back Again, International Contexts." *The Visual Artists' News Sheet* (September/October 2008): 24.

Coetzee, Pieter Hendrik, and A.P.J. Roux, eds. *The African Philosophy Reader.* 2nd ed. Routledge, 2003.

van Damme, Wilfried. "Introducing World Art Studies." In *World Art Studies: Exploring Concepts and Approaches,* edited by Kitty Zijlmans and Wilfried van Damme. Valiz, 2008.

Du Bois, W.E.B., and William Monroe Trotter. "The Niagara Movement's 'Declaration of Principles.'" *Black History Bulletin* 68, no. 1 (2005): 21–23.

van Eck, Mieske. "Dutch." *Brabants Dagblad,* May 31, 2008.

Egbers, H. "Kleuren verschieten." In *Zover het oog reikt: transculturele invloeden in het werk van zes Brabantse en zes van oorsprong niet-westerse kunstenaars.* Provincie Noord-Brabant, 1988.

"Els van der Plas." *Nationale Opera en Ballet.* https://www.operaballet.nl/nl/het-instituut/organisatie/directie/els-van-der-plas.

El-Tayeb, Fatima. *European Others: Queering Ethnicity in Postnational Europe.* University of Minnesota Press, 2011.

Esche, Charles, and Remco de Blaaij. "Terugblik Be(com)ing Dutch." July 2009.

Esche, Charles, and Annie Fletcher. "Welkom bij Be(com)ing Dutch." Exhibition guide. Van Abbemuseum, 2008.

Esche, Charles, Annie Fletcher, and Ivet R. Maturano. *Be(com)ing Dutch: Our Dictionary.* Van Abbemuseum, 2008.

Essed, Philomena. *Alledaags racisme.* Feministische Uitgeverij Sara, 1984.

———. *Understanding Everyday Racism: An Interdisciplinary Theory.* SAGE, 1991.

Evenhuis, Arend. "Waar waren we ook al weer gebleven." *Trouw*, May 31, 2008. https://www.trouw.nl/nieuws/waar-waren-we-ook-al-weer-gebleven~b4f84e60/.

Faber, Paul. "25 mei 1991. De opening van de tentoonstelling Double Dutch: Van allochtoon naar kunstnomade." In *Cultuur en migratie in Nederland: Kunsten in beweging 1980–2000*, edited by Rosemarie Buikema R. and Maaike Meijer. Sdu Uitgevers, 2004.

———. "De Goden zijn niet dood: Nigeriaanse Kunst in Zwolle." *Kunstbeeld* 6, no. 5 (1982): 12–13.

———. "Double Dutch: Tilburg en de rest van de wereld." *Kunstbeeld* 15, nos. 7–8 (1991): 22–23.

———. "Kunst uit een andere wereld: Een niet-Westers vierluik." *Kunstbeeld* 12, no. 12 (1988–1989): 26–28.

———. "'Les Magiciens de la Terre': Honderd tovenaars in Parijs." *Kunstbeeld* 13, nos. 7–8 (1989): 12–16.

Feldstein, Ruth. "Nina Simone: The Antidote to the 'We Shall Overcome' Myth of the Civil Rights Movement." *History News Network*, March 3, 2014. http://historynewsnetwork.org/article/154884.

Fransman, Robin. "Het gaat ook heel goed met de integratie in Nederland." *Centraal Bureau voor de Statistiek*, December 22, 2016.

Gates, Henry Louis, Jr. "Harlem on our Minds." In *Rhapsodies in Black: Art of the Harlem Renaissance*. Exhibition catalog University of California Press, 1997.

———. *The Henry Louis Gates Jr. Reader*. Basic Civitas Books, 2012.

Gilroy, Paul. "Foreword: Migrancy, Culture, and a New Map of Europe." In *Blackening Europe: The African American Presence*, edited by Heike Raphael-Hernandez. Routledge, 2004.

Golden, Thelma. *Freestyle*. Studio Museum in Harlem, 2001.

Grantsaan, Gillion. "Redi musu." In *Wakaman: Drawing Lines Connecting Dots*, by Remy Jungerman and Gillion Grantsaan. Wakaman Project, 2009.

Hagenaars, Albert. "Michael Tedja — Hosselen." *Werkgroep Caraïbische Letteren,* April 27, 2010. http://werkgroepcaraibischeletteren.nl/michael-tedja-hosselen/.

Hall, Stuart. "Black Diaspora Artists in Britain: Three 'Moments' in Postwar History." *History Workshop Journal* 61, no. 1 (2006): 1–24.

———. "David Scott by Stuart Hall." *BOMB,* January 1, 2005. https://bombmagazine.org/articles/david-scott/.

———. "New Ethnicities." In *Stuart Hall: Critical Dialogues in Cultural Studies,* edited by David Morley and Kuan-Hsing Chen. Routledge, 1996.

Hantel, Max. "Rhizomes and the Space of Translation: On Edouard Glissant's Spiral Retelling." *Small Axe: A Caribbean Journal of Criticism* 17, no. 3 (2013): 100–112. DOI: 10.1215/07990537-2378955.

den Hartog Jager, Hans. "Worstelen in plaats van sprankelen." *NRC Handelsblad,* December 19, 2001. http://vorige.nrc.nl//dossiers/stedelijk_museum/tentoonstellingen/article1570693.ece.

"Het beeld Ook als het anders is bedoeld: Stereotypering is racistisch." *NRC Handelsblad,* October 19, 2013. http://www.nrc.nl/handelsblad/2013/10/19/het-beeld-ook-als-het-anders-is-bedoeld-stereotypering-1304504.

Hewson, Martin. "Agency." In *Encyclopedia of Case Study Research,* edited by Albert J. Mills, Gabrielle Durepos, and Elden Wiebe. SAGE, 2010.

Huggan, Graham. *Interdisciplinary Measures: Literature and the Future of Postcolonial Studies.* Liverpool University Press, 2008. DOI: 10.5949/UPO9781846313332.

Huysmans, Frank, Olivier van der Vet, and Koen van Eijck. *Het actieplan Cultuurbereik en Cultuurdeelname 1999–2003: Een empirische evaluatie op landelijk niveau.* Sociaal Cultureel Planbureau, 2009. https://www.scp.nl/Publicaties/Alle_publicaties/Publicaties_2005/Het_Actieplan_Cultuurbereik_en_Cultuurdeelname_1999_2003.

"Introduction." *Becoming Dutch.* http://becomingdutch.com/introduction/.

Jamaludin, Rihana. *De Zwarte Lord.* KIT Publishers, 2012.

Johnson, Gaye Theresa. *Spaces of Conflict, Sounds of Solidarity: Music, Race, and Spatial Entitlement in Los Angeles.* University of California Press, 2013.

Jongenelen, Sandra. "Kunstenaars tussen twee culturen." *Kunstbeeld* 24, nos. 7–8, (2000): 12–16.

Jungerman, Remy, and Gillion Grantsaan. *Wakaman: Drawing Lines Connecting Dots.* Wakaman Project, 2009.

Kamphuis, Bart. "Eén echt schilderij had ik in Suriname nog nooit gezien." *Trouw,* December 14, 1996. http://www.trouw.nl/tr/nl/5009/Archief/article/detail/2661295/1996/12/14/Een-echt-schilderij-had-ik-in-Suriname-nog-nooit-gezien.dhtml.

Karenga, Ron. "Ron Karenga and Black Cultural Nationalism." *Black World/Negro Digest* 17, no. 3 (1968): 5–9.

Keaton, Trica Danielle, T. Denean Sharpley-Whiting, and Tyler Stovall, eds. *Black France/France Noire: The History and Politics of Blackness.* Duke University Press, 2012. DOI: 10.1515/9780822395348.

Keijer, Kees. "Kunst is niet aleen decoratie." *Het Parool,* May 27, 2008.

———. "Museum in debat." *Museumtijdschrift* (July/August 2008): 27.

Kleijn, Koen, ed. *Be(com)ing Dutch: Identiteit en nationaliteit in het Van Abbemuseum.* De Groene Amsterdammer, 2008.

Kleijn, Koen, and Stefan Kuiper. "'Musea lopen verschrikkelijk achter': Interview met Charles Esche en Annie Fletcher." In *Be(com)ing Dutch: Identiteit en nationaliteit in het Van Abbemuseum,* edited by Koen Kleijn. De Groene Amsterdammer, 2008.

Koelemeijer, Judith. "Grachtenpand inspireert niet-westerse kunstenaars." *De Volkskrant,* September 10, 1996. https://www.volkskrant.nl/nieuws-achtergrond/grachtenpand-inspireert-niet-westerse-kunstenaars~bbc50c6d/.

de Kom, Cornelis Gerard Anton. *Wij Slaven van Suriname.* Contact, 1972.

Lafour, Lucien. "Fuchs (1)." *NRC Handelsblad,* November 9, 1996. http://www.nrc.nl/handelsblad/1996/11/09/fuchs-1-7331354.

Landvreugd, Charl. "Notes on a Dictionary: A Polemic Approach." In *Deviant Practice: Research Programme 2016–2017,* edited by Nick Aikens. Van Abbemuseum, 2018. https://vanabbemuseum.nl/fileadmin/files/Onderzoek/ Deviant_Practice/4788VAM_Deviant_Practice_def_HR_ spreads_2.pdf.

———. "Notes on Afro-European Aesthetics and Sensibilities #1: North and Western Europe." *ARC Magazine* 7 (2013): 60–67.

———. "Notes on Black Dutch Aesthetics." In *Conversations on Paramaribo Perspectives,* edited by Mariette Dölle and Malka Jonas. TENT, 2010.

———. "Notes on Imagining Afropea." *Open Arts Journal* 5 (2016): 41–52. DOI: 10.5456/issn.2050-3679/2016s04.

———. "Public-Platform-Open-Letter." In *Blessing and Transgressing: A Live Institute (2012–2017),* by Wendelien van Oldenborgh. Edited by Defne Ayas. Witte de With Center for Contemporary Art, 2018.

———. "Waka Waka Waka #1." In *Wakaman: Drawing Lines Connecting Dots,* by Remy Jungerman and Gillion Grantsaan. Wakaman Project, 2009.

van Leeuwen, Lizzy. *Ons Indisch erfgoed: Zestig jaar strijd om cultuur en identiteit.* Uitgeverij Bert Bakker, 2008.

Lerman, Antony, ed. *Do I Belong? Reflections from Europe.* Pluto Press, 2017.

Levesque, Dawn. "Artists of the Civil Rights Movement: A Retrospective." *Guardian Liberty Voice,* March 2, 2014. http://guardianlv.com/2014/03/artists-of-the-civil-rights-movement-a-retrospective/.

van der Linden, Frénk. "Museumdirecteur Fuchs: 'Het ergste van vreemdgaan is de ontrouw aan jezelf.'" *NRC Handelsblad,* November 2, 1996. http://www.nrc.nl/ handelsblad/1996/11/02/museumdirecteur-rudi-fuchs-het-ergste-van-vreemdgaan-7330346.

Locke, Alain. "Enter the New Negro." *Survey Graphic*, March 1925. http://nationalhumanitiescenter.org/pds/maai3/migrations/text8/lockenewnegro.pdf.

Lockward, Alanna. "Call and Response: Conversations with Three Women Artists on Afropean Decoloniality." In *A Companion to Feminist Art*, edited by Hilary Robinson and Maria Elena Buszek. Wiley, 2019.

Martis, Adi. "Wakaman Goes Caribbean." In *Wakaman: Drawing Lines Connecting Dots*, by Remy Jungerman and Gillion Grantsaan. Wakaman Project, 2009.

Matory, J. Lorand. *Black Atlantic Religion: Tradition, Transnationalism, and Matriarchy in the Afro-Brazilian Candomblé*. Princeton University Press, 2005.

McCarren, Felicia. "Monsieur Hip-Hop." In *Blackening Europe; The African American Presence*, edited by Heike Raphael-Hernandez. Routledge, 2003.

McNiff, Jean, and Jack Whitehead. *Action Research: Principles and Practice*. 2nd ed. RoutledgeFalmer, 2002.

Medendorp, Clazien. *Gerrit Schouten (1779–1839): Botanische tekeningen en diorama's uit Suriname*. Koninklijk Instituut voor de Tropen, 1999.

Meghelli, Samir. "Between New York and Paris: Hip Hop and the Transnational Politics of Race, Culture, and Citizenship." Ph.D. diss., Columbia University, 2012.

Meijer, Emile. *Farawé: Acht kunstenaars van Surinaamse oorsprong*. Aldus Uitgevers, 1985.

Mensink, J. "Double Dutch." In *Double Dutch*. Stichting Kunst Mondiaal, 1991.

———. "Steunfunctie-instellingen en kunst." In *Zover het oog reikt: trans-culturele invloeden in het werk van zes Brabantse en zes van oorsprong niet-westerse kunstenaars*. Provincie Noord-Brabant, 1988.

Mes, Ulco. "Golf van veranderingen." In *Double Dutch*. Stichting Kunst Mondiaal, 1991.

Mignolo Walter D., and Catherine E. Walsh. *On Decoloniality: Concepts, Analytics, Praxis*. Duke University Press, 2018.

Miklódy, Éva. "A.R.T., Klikk, K.A.O.S, and the Rest: Hungarian Youth Rapping." In *Blackening Europe: The African American Presence,* edited by Heike Raphael-Hernandez. Routledge, 2003.

Modest, Wayne. "On the Self-Evidence of Blackness: An Interview with Charl Landvreugd." *Small Axe: A Caribbean Journal of Criticism* 18, no. 3 (2014): 123–36. DOI: 10.1215/07990537-2826497.

Monshouwer, Saskia. "Een kinderdroom: Tijdloze beelden en existentiële inzichten." *Kunstbeeld* 24, no. 9 (2000): 16–17.

———. "Iris Kensmil." *Kunstbeeld* 25, no. 11 (2001): 44–45.

———. "Speels anarchistische installaties van Meschac Gaba: Het musuem als kunstwerk." *Kunstbeeld* 25, no. 3 (2001): 18.

Morris, Aldon D. *Origins of the Civil Rights Movement.* The Free Press, 1986.

Neal, Larry. "The Black Arts Movement." *The Drama Review: TDR* 12, no. 4 (1968): 28–39. DOI: 10.2307/1144377.

Nederveen Pieterse, Jan. *Wit over zwart: Beelden van Afrika en zwarten in de westerse populaire cultuur.* Koninklijk Instituut voor de Tropen, 1990.

Nuis, Aad. *Pantser of ruggengraat: Cultuurnota 1997–2000.* Ministerie van Onderwijs, Cultuur en Wetenschap, 1997. http://catalogus.boekman.nl/pub/96-550A.pdf.

O'Sullivan, Simon. "Notes Towards a Minor Art Practice." *Drain: Journal of Contemporary Art and Culture* 2, no. 2 (2005).

Perrée, Rob. "Brooklyn Museum toont Hip-Hop Nation: Kunst van de straat." *Kunstbeeld* 24, no. 11 (2000): 28–29.

———. "Directeur Okwui Enwezor geeft visie op zijn Documenta: 'Ik dans niet voor geld.'" *Kunstbeeld* 26, no. 5 (2002): 6–9.

———. "Een trip door de hoofdstad van de hedendaagse kunst: New York, A Nuthouse." *Kunstbeeld* 24, nos. 7–8 (2000): 56–59.

———. "Emoties die schuilgaan." *Kunstbeeld* 25, no. 3 (2001): 12–15.

———. "Michael Tedja, Hosselen." *Kunstbeeld*, 2009. http://robperree.com/articles/702/michael-tedja-hosselen.

———. "Latijnsamerikaanse kunstenaars in Nederland 2: De dialoog van Fredy Flores." *Kunstbeeld* 12, no. 7 (1988): 54–55.

———. "Nieuwe stroming in de Afrikaans-Amerikaanse kunst: Vertegenwoordigers van Post-Black." *Kunstbeeld* 25, no. 11 (2001): 16–19.

———. "Suriname and the USA: Black Artists in Various Stages of Obamazation?" In *Wakaman: Drawing Lines Connecting Dots,* by Remy Jungerman and Gillion Grantsaan. Wakaman Project, 2009.

van der Ploeg, Rick. *Cultuur als confrontatie.* Ministerie van Onderwijs, Cultuur en Wetenschap, 1999.

Pontzen, Rutger. "Alles en iedereen in debat." *De Volkskrant,* Achtergrond, November 15, 2007.

Powell, Richard J. "Re/Birth of a Nation." In *Rhapsodies in Black: Art of the Harlem Renaissance.* Exhibition catalog University of California Press, 1997.

Price, Richard, and Sally Price. *Afro-American Arts of the Suriname Rainforest.* University of California Press, 1980.

Rahan, Stuart. "Wakamanproject: Surinaamse kunstwereld is twee naslagwerken rijker." *De Ware Tijd,* Cultuur, July 11, 2009.

Ramaer, Joost. "Prijs voor culturele diversiteit musea." *De Volkskrant,* October 27, 2005. https://www.volkskrant.nl/cultuur-media/prijs-voor-culturele-diversiteit-musea~bf660f77/.

Ransby, Barbara. *Ella Baker and the Black Freedom Movement.* University of North Carolina Press, 2003.

van Rijn, Ilse. "Be(com)ing Dutch." *Metropolis M* 29, no. 4 (2008): 85–86.

Roos, Robbert. "Documenta van Enwezor overtuigt." *Kunstbeeld* 26, nos. 7–8 (2002): 22–26.

van Rosmalen, Ad. "Een wederkerige droom." In *Double Dutch.* Stichting Kunst Mondiaal, 1991.

Ruyters, Domeniek. "Harteloos Nederland." *De Volkskrant,* May 29, 2008.

Rutgers, Wim. "The Netherlands and Its Colonies: Edgar Cairo," In *A Historical Companion to Postcolonial Literatures: Continental Europe and Its Empires,* edited by Prem Poddar, Rajeev S. Patke, and Lars Jensen. Edinburgh University Press, 2008.

ya Salaam, Kalamu. "The Black Arts Movement." In *The Oxford Companion to African American Literature,* edited by William L. Andrews, Frances Smith Foster, and Trudier Harris. Oxford University Press, 1997.

Schama, Simon. *The Embarrassment of Riches: An Interpretation of Dutch Culture in the Golden Age.* University of California Press, 1988.

Scheffer, Paul. "Het multiculturele drama." *NRC Handelsblad,* January 29, 2000. http://retro.nrc.nl/W2/Lab/ Multicultureel/scheffer.html.

Schoonen, Rob. "Cultuur zoekt een weg in veelkleurige wereld." *Eindhovens Dagblad,* Cultuur, January 27, 2007.

Scott, David. *Conscripts of Modernity: The Tragedy of Colonial Enlightenment.* Duke University Press, 2004.

Segers, Mathieu, and Yoeri Albrecht, eds. *Re: Thinking Europe: Thoughts on Europe: Past, Present and Future.* Amsterdam University Press, 2016. DOI: 10.2307/j.ctt1d8hb2q.

Sizoo, Hans. "De vrijheid van Nassar." *Kunstbeeld* 26, no. 2 (2002): 22–23.

Smallenburg, Sandra. "De bevrijder van de schilderkunst." *NRC Handelsblad,* October 31, 1998. http://www. nrc.nl/handelsblad/1998/10/31/de-bevrijder-van-de-schilderkunst-7420825.

Spanjaard, Helena. "Ahmad Sadali een religieuze abstract." *Kunstbeeld* 9, no. 4 (1985): 43–45.

Stoffelen, Anneke. "Wij kunnen juist wat meer experimenteren." *De Volkskrant,* November 8, 2007. https:// www.volkskrant.nl/beeldende-kunst/-wij-kunnen-juist-wat-meer-experimenteren~a862442/.

Sullivan, Patricia. "Civil Rights Movement." In *Africana: The Encyclopedia of the African and African American*

Experience, edited by Anthony Appiah and Henry Louis Gates, Jr. Running Press, 2003.

Szwed, John F. *Space Is the Place: The Lives and Times of Sun Ra.* Perseus Books Group, 1998.

TBA21 Thyssen-Bornemisza Art Contemporary. "EPHEMEROPTERÆ V - Nira Yuval-Davis." *YouTube,* November 18, 2016. https://www.youtube.com/watch?v=fL8rvvCipFM.

Tedja, Michael. *Eat the Frame! A Polymorphic Essay as the Catalogue of an International Art Exhibition in the Netherlands Anno 2009.* KIT Publishers, 2009.

———. *Hosselen: Een diachronische roman in achtenevijftig gifzwarte facetten over beeldende kunst in identiteitsdenkend Nederland anno 2009.* KIT Publishers, 2009.

———. "Narrow Escape." *Kunstbeeld* 26, nos. 7–8 (2002): 10–13.

Tibi, Bassam. *Europa ohne Identität: Die Krise der multikulturellen Gesellschaft.* Bertelsmann, 1998.

Tweede Kamer der Staten-Generaal. *Aanhangsel van de handelingen* 627, November 27, 2008. https://zoek.officielebekendmakingen.nl/ah-tk-20082009-627.html.

Van Abbemuseum. "Who We Are." Archived at https://web.archive.org/web/20190327135114/https://vanabbemuseum.nl/en/about-the-museum/organisation/who-we-are/.

Van Deburg, William L. *New Day in Babylon: The Black Power Movement and American Culture, 1965–1975.* University of Chicago Press, 1992.

"Vanwaar je dacht te vertrekken sta je geplant." *Kunstbeeld* 20, no. 2 (1996): 34–35.

van de Velde, Paola. "Kunstenaars over Nederlandse identiteit." *De Telegraaf,* May 23, 2008.

Vermeulen, Maarten. "Onbegrijpelijke nationaliteit." *Nederlands Dagblad,* May 30, 2008.

Waegner, Cathy Covell. "Rap, Rebounds and Rocawear: The 'Darkening' of German Youth Culture." In *Blackening Europe: The African American Presence,* edited by Heike Raphael-Hernandez. Routledge, 2003.

"Wakaman Walks." *Intendant Culturele Diversiteit.* Archived at https://web.archive.org/web/20160802083053/http://www.intendant.nl/intendant/english/projecten/02/project.php.

Washington, Booker T. "The Cotton States and International Exposition Speech" [Atlanta Compromise speech 1895]. In *The Booker T. Washington Papers.* Vol. 3: *1889–95,* edited by Louis R. Harlan. University of Illinois Press, 1974.

Watts, Jerry. *Amiri Baraka: The Politics and Art of a Black Intellectual.* NYU Press, 2001.

Wekker, Gloria. "One Finger Does Not Drink Okra Soup: Afro-Surinamese Women and Critical Agency." In *Feminist Genealogies, Colonial Legacies, Democratic Futures,* edited by M. Jacqui Alexander and Chandra Talpade Mohanty. Routledge, 1997.

———. *White Innocence: Paradoxes of Colonialism and Race.* Duke University Press, 2016.

Welling, Dolf. "Vechtlustig museum maakt drukte in Eindhoven." *Pulchri* 36, no. 4 (2008): 15.

Welling, Wouter. "Afrikaanse kunst." *Kunstbeeld* (2005): 44.

———. "Dak'Art 2000: Globalisering van de Afrikaanse kunst." *Kunstbeeld* 24, nos. 7–8 (2000): 28–33.

———. "De postkoloniale puzzel." *Kunstbeeld* 32, nos. 12–1 (2008): 58–61.

———. "De vitale traditie van Benin." *Kunstbeeld* 22, no. 3 (1998): 48–51.

———. "Doorbraak en bloei in de Indonesische kunst." *Kunstbeeld* 22, no. 2 (1988): 46–49.

———. "Het Aboriginal Art Museum: De vitaliteit van een oeroude kunsttraditie." *Kunstbeeld* 27, no. 3 (2003): 20–23.

———. "Op de drempel van twee werelden: Altaarkunst uit Afrika en Afro-Amerika." *Kunstbeeld* 21, no. 5 (1997): 45–46.

Wesseling, Janneke. "'Black USA' laat vragen open over de zwarte identiteit." *NRC Handelsblad,* May 16, 1990. http://www.nrc.nl/handelsblad/1990/05/16/black-usa-laat-vragen-open-over-de-zwarte-identiteit-6930066.

Williams, Ella O. *Harlem Renaissance: A Handbook.* Authorhouse, 2010.

Witteveen, Frans J. *Double Dutch Educatief Project: Inleiding bij het didactisch werkboek.* Stichting Kunst Mondiaal, 1991.

Zeqo, Arnisa. "Dare to Imagine: A Conversation with Annie Fletcher on the Be(com)ing Dutch Project." *Simulacrum* 16, no. 2 (2008): 7–9.

van der Zijl, Annejet. *Sonny Boy.* Nijgh & van Ditmar, 2005.

Zijlmans, Kitty, and Wilfried Van Damme. "World Art Studies." In *Art History and Visual Studies in Europe: Transnational Discourses and National Frameworks,* edited by Mathew Rampley, Thierry Lenain, Hubert Locher, Andrea Pinotti, Charlotte Schoell-Glass, and Kitty Zijlmans. Brill, 2012,

———. *World Art Studies: Exploring Concepts and Approaches.* Valiz, 2008.

"Zimbabwe op de berg." *Kunstbeeld* 13, nos. 7–8 (1989): 17–20.

"Zwarte schrijfster: Prinses Irene is een echte bondgenote." *Het Vrije Volk,* September 19, 1984.